# Museum Origins

# Museum Origins

Readings in Early Museum History and Philosophy

Edited by

## Hugh H. Genoways and Mary Anne Andrei

Routledge
Taylor & Francis Group

LONDON AND NEW YORK

First published 2008 by Left Coast Press, Inc.

Published 2016 by Routledge
2 Park Square, Milton Park, Abingdon, Oxon OX14 4RN
711 Third Avenue, New York, NY 10017, USA

*Routledge is an imprint of the Taylor & Francis Group, an informa business*

Library of Congress Cataloging-in-Publication Data

Museum origins : readings in early museum history and philosophy / edited by Hugh H. Genoways and Mary Anne Andrei.
    p. cm.
Includes bibliographical references and index.
ISBN 978-1-59874-196-4 (hardback : alk. paper) -- ISBN 978-1-59874-197-1 (pbk. : alk. paper)
   1. Museums--History.  2. Museums--Philosophy.  I. Genoways, Hugh H.
  II. Andrei, Mary Anne.
AM7.M8726 2008
069.09--dc22
2008005848


Paperback ISBN 978-1-59874-197-1
Hardback ISBN 978-1-59874-196-4

Cover: Interior view of the "Old Ashmolean" from a wood engraving by Orlando Jewitt based on a drawing by W. A. Delamotte. This image first appeared on the title page of the publication *A Catalogue of the Ashmolean Museum: Descriptive of the Zoological Specimens, Antiquities, Coins, and Miscellaneous Curiosities* compiled by Philip B. Duncan in 1836. Published with permission of The Ashmolean Museum of Art and Archaeology, Oxford University, Oxford, UK (Antiquities Negative M1540). Cover design by Ted Genoways.

# CONTENTS

# PREFACE

The purpose of this book is to provide historians and museologists with a broad selection of significant historical writings about museums—their origins, philosophies, and theories on education and exhibition—that may be used as a resource for classroom instruction and as a source of inspiration for scholars interested in the rich history of museums.

No discussion of museum history is complete without acknowledging Edward P. Alexander's contribution to the field. His two biographical studies, *Museum Masters: Their Museums and Their Influence* (1983) and *The Museum in America: Innovators and Pioneers* (1997), are standard resources for teaching museum history and philosophy. Yet, while both works are foundational in scope, the history of great "museum masters" limits our understanding of the role of museums in society and in turn society's influence on the development of museums. By considering the writings of these early "innovators and pioneers" historians and museologists will have a broader understanding of the role of museums in preserving our artistic, cultural, and scientific heritage.

We include essays from fifty-one authors. These authors are for the most part from the United States, but we have attempted to include individuals from other countries: ten from England, one from Australia, and another from Canada. However, some authors included as U.S. writers hail from other countries, including Franz Boas from Germany, Luigi di Cesnola from Italy, Edwin Godkin from Ireland, and Hermann Hagen from East Prussia. We have also chosen as many women authors as possible—seven in all. With the exception of the two articles from antiquity, all articles were originally written in English.

The fifty articles included in this compendium are gathered from books, journals, pamphlets, and newspapers, ranging in time from antiquity to 1925 with an emphasis on the period from 1850 to 1925, which coincides with the rapid increase in the number of museums, particularly in the United States, and a resulting proliferation in museology. Digital databases proved immensely useful in identifying potential articles, especially JSTOR and Project Muse.

In our initial search, we found that individuals associated with natural history museums had undertaken the majority of museum scholarship from 1850 to 1925. (We could easily have filled this book with only these authors.) Although we found a significant number of articles from the disciplinary areas of art and ethnology, we found almost no authors with a primary emphasis on history museums—only Reuben Gold Thwaites falls into this category. This imbalance likely represents the fact that administrators from natural history museums were the first to organize the profession, creating the Museums Association in the United Kingdom in 1889 and the American Association of Museums in 1906. This is not to say that administrators from art and history museums were slow to professionalize; rather, there were simply more natural history museums than any other type of museum during this period, and the scientists in their employ came from a tradition of publishing that gave them a distinct advantage in disseminating their ideas about museums to a wider audience. Readers will find that this selection of readings emphasizes the history and philosophy of museums and includes no discussion of practical or "how-to" techniques, because most museum practices have been supplanted by modern methods, and any historical interest would be too narrow for the scope of this compendium.

An editorial note: Most of the articles are truncated in the interest of economy and scope, but in no way have we changed the meaning of these articles; we removed only sections that emphasized the time period in which the articles were written, as well as occasional repetitious material. We have added ellipses to indicate those points at which material has been deleted.

Researchers interested in further study will find useful the additional sections included in the back of the book: References and About the Authors.

Our work in obtaining and organizing material for this book was facilitated by the Interlibrary Loan Services of Love Library, University of Nebraska-Lincoln; Angie Fox, technical artist for the University of Nebraska State Museum, who transformed numerous electronic files into useable text files; and the facilities of the Scholars' Lab in Alderman Library, University of Virginia. To each of these people and groups, we extend our appreciation. We also extend our thanks to Ted Genoways for his editorial expertise in preparing the introductions and headnotes.

*Hugh H. Genoways*
*Lincoln, NE*

*Mary Anne Andrei*
*Charlottesville, VA*

# ABOUT THE EDITORS

**Hugh H. Genoways** is currently a professor emeritus of the University of Nebraska State Museum. He holds a Ph.D. in biology from the University of Kansas. He has worked for the Museum of Texas Tech University, Carnegie Museum of Natural History, and the University of Nebraska State Museum, where he was director for eight years. Dr. Genoways was involved in the founding of the Museum Science Program at Texas Tech University and chaired the Museum Studies Program at the University of Nebraska-Lincoln for fifteen years. He chaired the founding steering committee and was the first president of the Nebraska Museums Association. Dr. Genoways is a coauthor of *Museum Administration: An Introduction* and editor of *Museum Philosophy for the Twenty-First Century*. He is also coeditor of the *Museum History Journal*, published by Left Coast Press, Inc.

**Mary Anne Andrei** is currently a lecturer in the Corcoran Department of History of the University of Virginia. She has an M.S. in museum studies from the University of Nebraska-Lincoln, and a Ph.D. in the history of science and technology from the University of Minnesota. Andrei has worked for the Invertebrate Paleontology Collection of the University of Montana, Papers of George Washington, and Bakken Library and Museum. Her articles have appeared in *Curator: The Museum Journal, Collection Forum, Collections: A Journal for Museum and Archives Professionals*, and *Endeavor*. Andrei's book *Nature's Mirror* is forthcoming from the University of Chicago Press. She is coeditor of the *Museum History Journal*, published by Left Coast Press, Inc.

# SECTION I

## Museum Origins

This group of seven readings on museum origins begins with two writings from the ancient world. The first is a description of the Museum of Alexandria, which was connected to the Great Library of Alexandria and is believed to be the world's first museum. Classical antiquity scholar Andrew Erskine (1995) has argued that the geographer Strabo's description of the museum—although frustratingly brief and 300 years after the museum's founding—is "our earliest informative account." The second, written by the Roman scholar Varro, is a description of an early game park or zoological park. Both readings provide a brief glimpse at the early traditions that led to the development of the modern museum and thus invite comparisons between the ancient museum, garden, and zoological park and their modern counterparts.

The next essay by Oxford historian Anthony Wood describes the founding of Oxford University's Ashmolean Museum—the first public university museum in the English-speaking world. (We have retained the author's original spelling and punctuation.) The Ashmolean Museum had a broad impact on the remainder of the world as the British Empire spread around the globe.

The broadside by Charles Wilson Peale, proprietor of one of America's first museums, explains the purpose of his museum, which opened to the public in Philadelphia in 1794. The essay by Sara Agnes Pryor provides first-hand insight into the founding of the first house museum in the United States, Mount Vernon, and the unique history of Mount Vernon Ladies' Association under the leadership of Ann Pamela Cunningham.

We chose to include the article by Edwin Godkin because it gives insights into his thinking about museums for New York City before the great institutions that we now associate with the city existed. Hermann Hagen concludes this section with a sweeping history of museums primarily in Western Europe from antiquity to 1875.

## Additional Readings

Alexander, Edward P. 1983. *Museum masters.* Nashville, TN: American Association for State and Local History.

———. 1997. *The museum in America: Innovators and pioneers.* Walnut Creek, CA: AltaMira Press.

Brigham, David. 1995. *Public culture in the early republic: Peale's museum and its audience.* Washington, DC: Smithsonian Institution Press.

Coleman, Laurence V. 1939. *The museum in America: A critical study.* Washington, DC: American Association of Museums, 3 vols.

Findlen, Paula. 1994. *Possessing nature: Museums, collecting, and scientific culture in early modern Italy.* Berkeley and Los Angeles: University of California Press.

Impey, Oliver R., and Arthur MacGregor. 1985. *The origins of museums.* Oxford: Clarendon Press.

Kohlstedt, Sally G. 1991. *The origins of natural science in America: The essays of George Brown Goode.* Washington, DC: Smithsonian Institution Press.

Murray, David. 1904. *Museums: Their history and their use, with a bibliography and list of museums in the United Kingdom.* Glasgow: James Machose and Sons, 3 vols. [Reprint edition from Pober Publishing, Staten Island, NY, 2000.]

Orosz, Joel J. 1990. *Curators and culture: The Museum Movement in America, 1740–1870.* Tuscaloosa: The University of Alabama Press.

Ovenell, R. F. 1986. *The Ashmolean Museum 1683–1894.* Oxford: Clarendon Press.

Schwarzer, Marjorie. 2006. *Riches, rivals, radicals: 100 years of museums in America.* Washington, DC: American Association of Museums.

Sellers, Charles C. 1980. *Mr. Peale's museum: Charles Willson Peale and the first popular museum of natural science and art.* New York: W. W. Norton & Company.

Stearn, William T. 1998. *The natural history museum at South Kensington.* London: Natural History Museum.

# 1

# GEOGRAPHY

## Strabo

*[translated into English by H. L. Jones]* Cambridge, MA: Harvard University Press, Loeb Classical Library, volume 8, 1932 [Book 17, Chapter 1, Section 8 of the original text]

---

*The most famous museum of the ancient world was the Museum of Alexandria. Very little is known about this museum and its functions (Erskine 1995). Yet it clearly was a source of inspiration for the development of modern museums at the beginning of the Renaissance (Lee 1997). Greek geographer and historian Strabo of Amaseia briefly described the museum in his* Geography. *Because he does not mention the famous Library of Alexandria, it is not clear whether it was a separate building or part of the museum (Argyle 1974; Erskine 1995). The following brief selection is Strabo's description of the museum.*

---

And the city contains most beautiful public precincts and also the royal palaces, which constitute one-fourth or even one-third of the whole circuit of the city; for just as each of the kings, from love of splendour, was wont to add some adornment to the public monuments, so also he would invest himself at his own expense with a residence, in addition to those already built, so that now, to quote the words of the poet, "there is building upon building." All, however, are connected with one another and the harbour, even those that lie outside the harbour. The Museum is also a part of the royal palaces; it has a public walk, an Exedra with seats, and a large house, in which is the common mess-hall of the men of learning who share the Museum. This group of men not only hold property in common, but also have a priest in charge of the Museum, who formerly was appointed by the kings, but is now appointed by Caesar. The Sema also, as it is called, is a part of the royal palaces. This was the enclosure which contained the burial-places of the kings and that of Alexander.

# 2

# *RERUM RUSTICARUM LIBRI TRES*

## Marcus Terentius Varro

*[translated into English by Lloyd Storr-Best and Fairfax Harrison] Varro on farming. London: G. Bell and Sons, 1912 [Storr-Best]. Roman farm management: The treatises of Cato and Varro. New York: MacMillan Company, 1913 [Harrison].*

*The following excerpt from* Res rustica, *or "Farm topics," written by the Roman scholar Varro, describes an early Roman game park. Zoological parks and menageries were known in the ancient world from at least the time of the Ptolemys in Alexandria (Hubbell 1935), and in Rome they took on a variety of forms from holding areas for use in the Roman "games and imperial vivaria (animal-enclosures)" (Epplett 2001) to the more pastoral game preserves as described here by Varro (Starr 1992).*

Book III, Chapter XIII. Of wild boars and other quadrupeds [Of game preserves]

Then addressing himself again to Axius, Appius continued:

"You know, of course, that wild boars are kept in game parks, and that those which are brought in wild are fattened with as little trouble as the tame ones which are born in the park, for you have doubtless seen at the farm near Tusculum, which Varro here brought from M. Pupius Pison, wild boars and roe bucks assemble at the sound of the trumpet to be fed at regular hours, when from a platform, the keeper scatters mast to the wild boars and vetch or some such forage to the roe bucks."

"I saw this done," put in Axius, "more dramatically when I was a visitor at the villa of Q. Hortensius in the country near Laurentum. He has there a wood of more than fifty jugera [thirty-three acres] in extent, all enclosed, but it might better be called a *theriotrophion* [place for feeding animals] than a *leporarium* [place to hold hares]; there on high ground he caused his dinner table to be spread, and while we supped Hortensius gave orders that Orpheus be summoned: when he came, arrayed in his long robe, with a cithara in his hands, he was desired to sing. At that moment a trumpet was sounded and at once Orpheus was surrounded by a large audience of deer and wild boars and other quadrupeds poured round us, making as fine a show of game, I thought, as when the Aediles give us a hunt without African beasts in the Circus Maximus."

# 3

# THE LIFE AND TIMES OF ANTHONY WOOD, ANTIQUARY, OF OXFORD, 1632–1695, DESCRIBED BY HIMSELF, COLLECTED FROM HIS DIARIES AND OTHER PAPERS

**Andrew Clark, editor**

Oxford, UK: Oxford Historical Society at the Clarendon Press, Vol. 3: 1682–1695, pp. 54–56, 1894

---

*Oxford historian Anthony Wood presents the early history of the Ashmolean Museum at Oxford University, with an emphasis on the building's architectural design and layout. In 1677, Elias Ashmole (Josten 1960) donated his collection, or cabinet of curiosities, which included natural history specimens, antique coins, books, and engravings, to the university.*

---

May 22 *[1683]*
*Musaeum Ashmolianum, Oxon.*
A larg and stately pile of stone squared, built at the charg of the Universitie, who found such a building necessary in order to the promoting and carrying on with greater ease and success severall parts of usefull and curious learning, for which it is so well contrived and designed.—It bordures upon the west end of the Theater, having a very magnificent portall on that side, sustained by pillars of the Corinthian order with several curious frizes and other artificial embellishments. The front (about 60 feet) is to the street northward, where is this inscription over the entrance in gold characters:—

## MUSAEUM ASHMOLIANUM SCHOLA NATURALIS HISTORIAE: OFFICINA CHIMICA.

The first foundation was laid 14 Apr. 1679 and it was happily finished on the 20 March 1682/3, at which time a rich and noble collection of curiosities was presented to the University by that excellent and public-spirited gentleman, Elias Ashmole, esq., a person so well knowne to the world that he needs no farther *elogium* in this short narrative, and the same day there deposited, and afterwards digested and put into a just series and order by the great care and diligence of the learned Robert Plot, LL.D., who at the worthy donor's request is entrusted with the custody of the Musaeum—By the beginning of May following the rarities were all fixed in their distinct cabinets and places and the roome furnished in every part of it: but it was not opend publicly till after 21 day of that month, on which day their royall highnesses the duke and duchess of York and the princess Ann, with a great number of earles and lords and other persons of quality who either accompanied their royall highnesses to Oxon or came to pay their devotions to them and shew the greatness and sincerity of their zeal to the royal family, were first entertain'd in it, and at the entrance were received with a set speech by Dr. Plot; the vicechancellor, bishop of Oxford, the Doctors of all faculties and both the proctors attending in their formalities. Which being ended they proceeded to take a particular view of the chiefest curiosities, and afterwards were pleased to accept of a banquet prepared for them at the charg of the University.

Take this brief description of this building:—It consists of 10 roomes, whereof the three principal and largest are public, being each in length about 56 feet and in breadth 25. The uppermost is properly the *Musaeum Ashmoleanum,* where an inferior officer alwaies attends to show the rarities to strangers.—The middle roome is the *School of Natural Historie,* where the professor of chymistry, who is at present Dr. Robert Plot, reads three times a week, on Mundays, Wednesdayes and Fridayes, during the term of the chymical course (which continues an entire month), concerning all natural bodies relating to and made use of in chymicall preparations, particularly as to the countries and places where they are produced and found, their natures, their qualities and virtues, their effects, by what marks and characticks they are distinguished one from another, natural from artificial, true from sophisticated, with their several mixtures and preparations in trials and experiments, with the entire process of that noble art, verie necessary to the cure of diseases when carefully managed by learned and skilfull persons.—The lower room, a cellar to which there is a descent by a double pair of staires, is the *Laboratory,* perchance one of the most beautiful and useful in the world, furnished with all sorts of furnaces and all other necessary materials in order to use and practice, which part is with very great satisfaction performed by Mr. Christopher White, the skilfull and industrious operator of the University, who, by the direction of the professor, shows all sorts of experiments chiefly relating to that course, according to the limitation established by the order of the vicechancellor.

Neare adjoyning to the laboratory are two fair roomes, whereof one is designed for a *chymical librarie,* to which several books of that argument have been already presented.—The other is made use of as a *store roome for chymical preparations,* where such as stand in need of them are furnished at easie rates, the designe of this building being not onlie to advance the studies of true and real philosophie but also to conduce to the uses of life and the improvement of medicine.—Neare the Musaeum is a handsome roome fitted for a *Library of Natural History and Philosophy.*

The other remaining chambers are the lodging chamber and studies of the keeper of the Musaeum, whereof one which is most convenient is sometimes employed and made use of for private courses of anatomy.

Accessions are continually made to the musaeum by several worthy persons, as Dr. Robert Huntingdon, who hath given hieroglyphicks and other/Egyptian antiquities; Mr. Aaron Goodyear, to whose generous favour they owe there an intire mummy; and the learned Martin Lister [Lyster], Dr. of Phys., who has presented the University with a larg cabinet of natural rarities of his owne collection and of several Romane antiquities, as altars, medalls, lamps, etc. found here in England. So that it is justly believed that, in few yeares, it will be one of the most famous repositories in Europe.

# 4

# MY DESIGN IN FORMING THIS MUSEUM

## Charles Willson Peale

Philadelphia, PA: broadside, 1792 [archived in The American Philosophical Society Library, Philadelphia: Broadside Collection]

---

*Charles Willson Peale's Philadelphia Museum—arguably the first public natural history museum in the United States—was founded in June 1794, when Peale's private collections were moved from his house on Lombard Street to Philosophical Hall, where they were merged with the collections of the American Philosophical Society (APS). Although the museum is often considered only in terms of its natural history collections, Peale, perhaps best known as an American portrait painter, also exhibited his paintings, and subsequently those of his sons. Peale hoped that his museum, in which he emphasized popular education, would serve as a foundation for a national museum, but his dream was never realized. Two years before the museum's founding, Peale gathered a select group of America's prominent political and social leaders, including influential members of the APS, to promote private financial support for his endeavor. It was at this meeting that he distributed the following broadside.*

---

GENTLEMEN,

I thank you for the honor you do me in the favor of this visit; and I will endeavour to explain to you in as few words as possible, my design in forming this Museum, and the motive which induced me to request you, gentlemen, to take on yourselves the trouble of becoming Visitors and Directors of it.

To collect and preserve all the variety of animals and fossils that could be acquired, and exhibit these publicly, was the first general intention of erecting this Museum; and it was not without the hope of rendering it worth the attention of the world, to the degree of enabling me to enlarge and improve it further and yet further, and that in the end it might become the basis of a great national magazine of those subjects in nature. Altho' all that I hoped for has not been obtained, yet it has so increased as to have become too weighty for me alone to arrange and govern it; and my circumstances are too confined to admit of the requisite advances towards enlarging it. If it has produced to me some income, yet this is but partial, and has become disproportioned to the encrease of labour and the calls for rooms requisite for the further extension of the design. These difficulties, together with the desire to have your countenance and assistance as Visitors and Directors, with the hope that it may induce a more public and general notice of it, are the motive for requesting your friendly services.

I am fully sensible that I cannot say any thing which, to you, can be new in natural history: yet for the sake of method in the subjects I am now about to speak of, permit me to follow the order in which that great man, Linnæus, has given, in his classing the objects of natural history.

In the animal kingdom, man is placed in first class and first order, called *primates*. . . .

By good and faithful paintings the likeness of man is perhaps with the greatest precision handed down to posterity; and I think myself highly favored in having the opportunity, and being able to make the progress I have done, in forming a collection of portraits of many of the persons who have been highly distinguished in their exertions, in the late glorious revolution, and which I am desirous further to enlarge with such characters as you, gentlemen, may deem most proper to be placed in this Museum. Hitherto I had confined myself, in my choice, to a certain line, which I had conceived would be as much as I could spare time for, independant of my other necessary labours to support my family. The portraits of the Presidents of Congress, the Presidents of the state of Pennsylvania, the ministers of high departments, officers in high command, and such other persons who had distinguished themselves in a particular manner; I have taken and preserved, and have done as much as I have been able to afford in this line of the design. But I am sorry that my circumstances or opportunities have not permitted me to add to this collection a number of portraits of other gentlemen of known merit.

There are other means to preserve, and hand down to succeeding generations, the relicks of such great men, whose labours have been crowned with success in the most distinguished benefits to mankind. The mode I mean, is the preserving their bodies from corruption and being the food of worms: this is by the use of powerful anticepticks. Altho' perhaps it is not in the power of art, to preserve these bodies in that high perfection of form, which the well executed painting in portrait, and sculpture can produce; yet the *actual remains* of such men as I have just described, must be highly regarded by those, who reverence the memory of such luminaries as but seldom appear.

The means of these preservations I have considered; and at some future meeting, I hope to be able to lay before you, gentlemen, some specimens for your inspection.

Sorry I am, that I did not propose the means of such preservation to that distinguished patriot and worthy philosopher, Doctor Franklin, whose liberality of soul was such, that it is not improbable that by the interest which I might have made with his friends, he could have been prevailed on, to suffer the remains of his body to be now in our view.

I have already collected some other objects belonging to this class, and have in prospect the obtaining of others, either in whole or in parts, that will be a notable part of this Museum, which I might mention: yet that I may not take up too much of your time, I will pass them over, and speak of the next class, that of brutes.

Here the wilds of America will furnish a very considerable variety; of which as yet I have not been able to enrich the Museum with more than a small collection. I have however the fullest confidence that I know the means of preserving them in their almost perfect forms and that I possess the ardour necessary to go through the labour of preserving our largest animals in a manner that they will keep for ages with little trouble to the master of the Museum.

The giving the proper attitudes (as well as the form) in order to shew their manners and dispositions, I consider as essential to give a tolerable knowledge of the animal. Mere stuffed skins are but a poor resemblance, but they may be kept where nothing better can be had.

The sight, alone, of our large animals, collected together in good preservation, surely would be pleasing if not also instructive: the elk, the moose deer, the buffaloe, the white bear, the sea-cow, the tygers, and many others perhaps unknown (at present) to us: as we may reasonably conclude, since we have seen bones of an enormous size, which have been found in divers parts of America, and which no tolerable idea at present can be formed of what kind of beast they were. But if such a number of those bones were collected together, and made into a complete skeleton, it would lead to an illustration of the animal by analogy: a work that I believe may yet be executed—but if not undertaken soon, the remaining bones will be so scattered over the whole globe, as to render it scarcely possible to get them together again.

The collection of quadrupeds, of which I have only slightly mentioned a very small number, is a work of great magnitude, and the room necessary to contain these alone, would be so costly that to think of it makes me (like some small animals I have seen) shrink back into my shell, until much greater encouragement than I have yet experienced shall enable me to build one.

I will pass on to the second class, that of birds, a very beautiful class of animated nature. According to Linnæus, it contains 930 species; and I am very confident that we possess in America, many which have not yet been known in Europe. Of the rapacious, the first that presents itself to my view, is the American called the bald eagle. I have a fine one, which I have kept alive these four years; it is now five years old; and what is remarkable, it did not shew its white head and tail, until the last past summer; before that period it had the appearance of the other grey eagles, that are preserved in the room; not only the colour of the feathers is changed (which is common to many birds annually) but also its bill and eyes, from a grey brown colour to a yellow of some brightness. The grey-coloured and the bald eagle have been often observed to use the same nest; but it has not been generally known that they were the same bird, but of different ages.

We possess a pretty variety of hawks, but the variety of our owls is much greater. In our thick forests I find birds that perhaps are never seen on the cleared fields, and every succeeding year our country furnishes me with some new species which I had not before. I have not yet been able to procure any specimens of the paroquets which are in our western country, and whether they are like those obtained in the southern parts of America, I do not know.

The birds which inhabit the southern coasts of America, have of late years been found to come in flights more and more northerly: I have a pelican which was shot from a flock of those birds at the entrance of Chester river, in the Chesapeake bay; one other of the same kind of birds, I have heard, was taken at Albany, on the Hudson. Many of our birds are found to change the places of their abode in the different seasons of their visits to us, by reason of the failure of their accustomed food. . . .

The increasing my number of glass cases will, for some time to come, be an increasing expence, although made in the cheapest manner, and which, from experience, I find is the best mode to keep all the small birds. But the birds of the largest size, such as the ostrich, the cassawar, the albatross, and some other very large birds, may, in the method which I must use for preserving large animals, be kept without glass covers, their strength and form being superior to slight injuries.

I will not take up more of your time, Gentlemen, with this beautiful class, than only to mention that I mean to be attentive to preserve not only each specie I can procure, but all its varieties, which in proportion to my success therein, much entertainment will be given to the inquisitive mind.

In the third class, amphibious, Linnaeus has placed many subjects, which strickly speaking, cannot live in either air or water, but principally from their power of suspending or performing the function of respiration in a more arbitrary manner than other animals. Therefore he has placed in this class the sharks, lampreys, sturgeons, and several other kinds of fishes.

The greatest variety in this class is in the second order *serpents,* the greater number of which may be kept in spirits, but the largest kinds, such as inhabit South America, must be skinned and stuffed.

The fourth class, fishes, have in their class a variety on our coasts, which have not, I believe, been yet collected in any Museum: and the mode of preserving those which are not very large, may be done in this manner— take one side of the fish, and preparing a form in wood, then placing the fish on it with the fins extended, and fix the whole on a board, and cover them with glass to keep them clean. This manner would form a pleasing exhibition of this kind at a moderate expence.

I will now, Gentlemen, descend into the inferior parts of the animal kingdom: the fifth class *insects,* a very numerous class, and not destitute of beauty in the eyes of many.

I have made some progress in the collection and preservation of those which America affords, and have found but little difficulty, except in the seventh order of this class, *spiders,* where those beautiful colours which I have seen in the living, are totally lost when they become dried. The progress of the worm into its chrysalis form, some left hanging in the open air, others covering themselves in various substances, and som others buried in the earth, and even passing thro' stagnated waters, to wait the return of another summer's sun to bring them forth flies, in their beauteous feathered wings, those stages of the different kind shewn would be proper.

The sixth class, *worms,* is also a very numerous class, when the corals and carollines are included in it, which, in the latest discoveries, are proved to be composite animals, and opportunities of seeing those various tribes alive and in motion, must be a high feast to the admirer of the wonderful works of creation.

The keeping of many subjects of this class, must be in spirits; but the corals, sea-fans, and feathers, &c. require only care to prevent them from being broke by violence.

Gentlemen, having thus slightly touched on each of the classes of animated nature, and the means to exhibit them in a collected view, I presume a tolerable display of them would have its value, in the pleasure and instruction in natural history, which it would effect, and for the accomplishment whereof no powers of mine shall be wanted.

The further to illustrate the construction of the various bodies contained in these classes, I wish to prepare such a number of skeletons as may shew a due variety of their forms, the smallest of which, of either birds or beasts, must be put into glass cases.

I crave your patience, Gentlemen, while I mention a few other subjects belonging to my undertaking in the designing of this Museum. Of the fossil kingdom, comprehending the earths, minerals, and other fossil matters, which include also petrefactions, it is my wish to make such a display of the various appearances of them, with the results of essays, as shall be generally entertaining and instructive.

The vegetable kingdom also claims our attention in forming a Museum; but it contains such a variety, that I have been fearful to engage in it, as it would add too greatly to my labor and cost. However, some well chosen collections of neatly preserved plants would be highly valued; and the Museum is not totally deficient in this branch.

The articles of *lulus natura* claim a place in the Museum; but as such subjects are not always agreeable to the sight, they will necessarily be received with caution, and the subjects will be but few, until a room can be obtained for that use.

A collection of the arms, dresses, tools and utensils of the aborigines of divers countries, may also fill a considerable space.

Gentlemen, I have now the same sentiments I had when I addressed the public two years past. "That at all events I intend to prosecute the design with such means as are in my power. Should it happily receive the smiles of the public, the progress will be proportionably great, whereas, if it is to depend only upon my solitary efforts, the progress must be so slow, that the whole may fall through."

It is my ardent wish to bring this Museum into such consideration, as to make it worthy the public protection; and at the same time, that my family may not lose the benefits of my assiduous labors of years past, and to enable my children to contribute their future aid to this my favorite undertaking, I am teaching them the methods I use to preserve subjects, and when they are a little better prepared and matured in years, it is my intention to send one of them to collect articles for the Museum from that wonderful store, South America.

I cannot conclude, Gentlemen, without again returning you my very hearty thanks for your goodness, in countenancing the Museum with your approbation of it, and for the aid you are so cheerfully disposed to give to the design, by your consenting to become its visitors, and friends to the further improvement of it—in which your advice and directions will be always thankfully received, and with gratitude ever remembered.

# 5

# THE MOUNT VERNON ASSOCIATION

## Sara Agnes [Rice] Pryor [published as Mrs. Roger A. Pryor]

The American Historical Register and Monthly Gazette of the Historic, Military and Patriotic-Hereditary Societies of the United States of America, 14 pp., January 1895

*Mount Vernon, the historic home of President George Washington, became the first historic house museum in the United States after the ambitious and patriotic Southern matron Ann Pamela Cunningham organized the Mount Vernon Ladies' Association of the Union. Under her leadership the association acquired the house, which was in terrible disrepair, and land in 1860 and pledged to preserve it for future generations in perpetuity. Mount Vernon was designated a National Historic Landmark on December 19, 1960. Sara Agnes Rice Pryor, an active founding member of the association, gives a first hand account of Cunningham's efforts to organize women in the State of Virginia and the subsequent acquisition of the house.*

. . . I should weary the readers of THE HISTORICAL RECORD if I recapitulated the history of "Mount Vernon." Everybody knows it. I believe that Washington's own first mention of it, in characteristic words of moderation, was in a letter written a few months after his marriage: "I am now, I believe, fixed in this seat with an agreeable partner for life, and I hope to find more happiness in retirement than I ever experienced in the wide and bustling world."

The "Mount Vernon Ladies' Association of the Union" was the first patriotic organization of women in the United States. How strange that this fact should be forgotten! We constantly read a repetition of the assertion that the Colonial Dames of America was the first woman's patriotic society. In reality it is the third. The Association for the Preservation of Virginia Antiquities was the second. The first two associations are interesting from the fact that they owe nothing to the contagion of enthusiasm. They were in existence before the great wave of patriotic fervor swept over the country; also before the women's suffrage movement, or women's political movements; before there had ever been societies of women other than societies for reading, study or benevolence.

I remember the first meeting of the Mount Vernon Association in my own town. The most beautiful and dignified member of the family was missing at the noon-day dinner. "Where have you been?" was the chorus that greeted her when she appeared with flushed checks and kindling eyes. "'Where have I been?' To the Town Hall! And more, to a meeting of ladies–yes, *ladies*! Making speeches and passing resolutions like men!"

If a vote had been taken from the younger members of the family, the verdict would have been that surely the world was coming to an end! I well remember my own subdued feeling–that I must be very good in the presence of such a state of things, ladies voting and all that, and my own conservative Aunt Mary entering no protest.

I think this happened in 1853. It was later, I know—in 1854— when the matter was recalled to me by hearing that Miss Pamela Cunningham, of South Carolina, had come to Richmond, Va., to organize the "Mount Vernon Association of the Ladies of the Union, for the Purchase and Preservation of the Home of Washington." A number of my personal friends were enthusiastically enlisted in the cause, and became Miss Cunningham's staunchest supporters. The leading newspaper of Virginia was then the *Richmond Enquirer*, edited and owned at that time by William F. Ritchie, now dead, and Roger A. Pryor. This paper gave its columns unstintedly to Miss Cunningham's, and thus very many of its patriotic articles were written in my own home. The honor of being the first vice-president of the Association was awarded to Mrs. William F. Ritchie, wife of the senior editor. This accomplished lady, who had been, before her marriage with Mr. Ritchie, the Anna Cora Mowatt of the dramatic world, entered upon her duties as vice-president with enthusiasm, ably sustained by her remarkable genius. She lived in a simple little cottage surrounded by a rose-garden, and there the first entertainments were given for the Mount Vernon fund. A patriotic daughter of a patriotic race–she was a Miss Ogden of New York—she led in the noble work of the noble women associated with her. Among these I remember Mrs. G. F. Semmes, Mrs. B. B. Minor, Mrs. W. D. Blair, Mrs. William H. Macfarland, all of Richmond, and all vice-presidents. Other vice-presidents were Mrs. John Tyler (wife of the ex-President), Mrs. John B. Floyd, of Virginia; Mrs. Henningham Harrison, of Baltimore; the accomplished Mrs. William C. Rives, of

"Castle Hill," Virginia; Mrs. Walton, of Missouri. Honorary members were appointed: Mrs. R. Cunningham, of South Carolina; Mrs. Dickinson, of North Carolina; Mrs. William J. Eve, of Georgia; Mrs. Milyard, of Pennsylvania.

This was the first Board of Managers, ninny of them, perhaps all, now dead, and who knows? perhaps keeping their silent bivouac around the spot they loved and honored in their lives!

The Virginia Legislature of 1856 granted a charter to the Association, mentioning five years as the time allowed for the purchase of the tomb and residence at Mount Vernon.

The next step was a difficult one: to obtain the consent of Colonel John Augustine Washington to the sale of his homestead. There was a long correspondence before he consented to part with this sacred home, so rich in inheritance and so dear to him personally. In reviewing this correspondence we are impressed with the fact that Mr. Washington yielded at last purely from a patriotic sense of duty to his country. Finally terms were agreed upon. For $200,000, we would surrender the house and mausoleum and 200 acres of land to the Mount Vernon Association. In a letter written to the Governor of Virginia, he speaks sorrowfully of the waning fortunes of the family, and their inability to keep the property in repair, and his wish that the matter might be speedily settled in order that before his death he might be sure Mount Vernon was in faithful hands. His letters betray a sensitive "mortification at receiving these offerings of patriotism." Doubtless he would have been more than proud to give and not sell the coveted treasure.[1]

To raise, as Miss Cunningham expressed it in her appeal to the patriots of America, the "paltry sum of $200,000," was now the task of the

---

[1] *In 1857 Miss Cunningham laid all the correspondence in this matter before Gov. Wise, of Virginia, and it was in his term of office that Mr. Washington again gave Virginia the refusal of the estate, and final action was taken.*

*Prior to this appeal, negotiations with Mr. John A. Washington for the purchase of two hundred acres of the estate, including the house, tomb, garden, etc., had been made and his consent to sell upon certain conditions obtained. It appears that the Virginia Assembly chartered the Association in 1855, but Mr. Washington, not deeming this charter in full accord with his conditions for sale, withdrew the estate, and in January, 1857, he writes Mr. William F. Ritchie, in reply to his, requesting that the place be offered the State again, heartily expressing his willingness to place the property under the care of Virginia, but only upon the terms stated in his letter of June 16, 1855, to Gov. Joseph Johnson. He further expresses his anxiety for the matter to be settled at the next regular session of the General Assembly of Virginia, and his earnest desire was that before his death he might see the place in the safekeeping of reliable hands, since he fully realized that the waning fortunes of the family were in no wise competent to such a task, dearly as he and they all would have loved to retain possession of it.*

Association. To this end the cultured leader gave all her energies. To this end she enlisted all the talent she could command, visited in person the offices of the *Richmond Enquirer*, inspired the young junior editor to warm, frequent and ardent appeals, and, wisest of all, secured two of the silver-tongued orators of her country to do her bidding. William L. Yancey, of Alabama, gave his impassioned eloquence, and the polished, classic Edward Everett, of Massachusetts, clasped hands, in a common cause, with the fiery Southerner. Money from their lectures literally poured into her treasury.

Well do I remember the first of these lectures of Mr. Everett in Richmond! Miss Cunningham's zeal carried everything before it. To prepare for this lecture, to advertise it, to hold it up as an example to the young orators of Richmond, to fill the platform with representative men and women, all was under her supervision and subject to her orders.

When the evening finally came, a regretful whisper ran through the community. All the tickets were sold and the orator arrived, but Miss Cunningham was ill and could not be present.

At the last moment a small sofa—*a chaise longue*—was pushed on the platform, and upon this the devoted woman was laid, and forgot all her weakness in listening to words which once heard have never been forgotten.

It was not long before the purchase money was all realized, Mount Vernon now belongs to the State of Virginia, and is under the charge of regents appointed, one for each State in the Union. These are all under one president, at this time Mrs. Howard Townsend, of New York. Once every year these regents meet at Mount Vernon. The rooms have been assigned to different States, and are filled with relics which formerly made part of the furnishing of the mansion. These, when so claimed, are genuine. It has been said that Washington snuff-boxes are as numerous as Napoleon china, but there is at Mount Vernon no danger of accepting the spurious article.

The place is lovely. There are the trees planted by the hand of the father of our country. There is the tomb in which his ashes rest. There is the river he loved, which murmurs a gentle requiem as it flows on to lose itself in the great ocean. And there, too, from time to time, comes the devoted band of American women, whose ever-watchful care preserves to us this hallowed spot in freshness and beauty.

# 6

# A WORD ABOUT MUSEUMS

### Edwin Lawrence Godkin

*The Nation,* 1: 113–114, July 27, 1865

---

*Edwin Godkin, associate editor of the* New York Evening Post, *celebrates in this editorial the destruction by fire of P. T. Barnum's American Museum. Godkin denounces Barnum's public museum as a center of disorganization, profoundly unscientific, and a source of amusement only for the lower classes and hails the museum's destruction as an opportunity for the city of New York to endow a new "American Museum"—an American scientific institution that would rival the best of Europe's museums, specifically, the British Museum. It is interesting to note that Godkin makes no mention of the Smithsonian Institution.*

---

Barnum's Museum is gone at last. It has fallen before that conflagration with which it has often been threatened, and which it has more than once barely escaped. The children will miss an accustomed place of amusement for their Saturday vacations. The occasional visitors to the city from the "rural districts" will no longer yield to its irresistible attractions. The worst and most corrupt classes of our people must seek some new place of resort, and other opportunities of meeting one another. A most dangerous man-trap is removed, and without loss of human life. These four considerations make the sober citizen of New York hesitate whether to regret this burning and destruction or not.

But there is another consideration. Were the lovers of curiosities—whether of natural history or of human ingenuity or of historical association—the more pleased by the existence of the collections which are now destroyed, or more insulted by their insufficiency, disorder, neglected condition, and obviously secondary importance? It is one thing to love shells and minerals, and to enjoy collections of them, but quite another to enjoy *every* collection of them. The more truly one loves a good collection well arranged, the more he will be offended by a chaotic, dusty, dishonored collection. The more one loves the order and system of scientific enquiry, the more he will feel personally injured by disorder and lack of system among the materials of scientific enquiry. The more one aspires to neatness, exactness, and care in his own private "cabinet," the more he will revolt at slovenliness in a larger and more public museum. And it is probable that no class of the community was less satisfied with the museum of Mr. Barnum than that class for which it would seem to have been originally intended.

This class is not an unimportant or even a small one. The host of readers whose favorite reading is natural science, the armies of listeners to lectures on geology, that large proportion of our boys and young men who collect and study "specimens" of minerals, all belong to it. The profoundly scientific are not those who care for public museums, unless containing this or that unique treasure. The frequenters of museums are those who cannot themselves give much time or means to the collection, classification, and study of specimens, but who read in the evenings, and would gladly see by day a larger number and a greater variety of helps to understand than their own limited time has sufficed to discover—than their own limited means have sufficed to procure. There are thousands of these earnest amateur students whose amateur studies are not to be despised even by the profounder scholar. These would visit the lost museum rarely, early in the morning when no disreputable crowd was thronging it, looking along the crammed and disordered shelves in the hope of lighting on something which they wished to see, finding it or not as the blind deities of chance might order. Without scientific arrangement, without a catalogue, without attendants, without even labels, in very many instances, the heterogeneous heap of "curiosities," valuable and worthless well mixed together, could not attract our students very often or detain them long.

This class of visitors was never wholly ignored in the advertisements which announced to the world the charms of Barnum's Museum. The "million of curiosities" were mentioned, and their scientific value hinted at; These curiosities were never, so far as we are aware, turned out of the building to make room for fat women, giants, dwarfs, glassblowers, mermaids, learned seals, and dog-shows. The aquaria had a certain attraction for the intelligent, and, in almost any other place, would have been worth frequent visits. Dog-shows in themselves are harmless and not without interest. We desire to give the late "American Museum" all the credit it deserves. For it needs it all. Its memory is not pleasant. It pandered to the most foolish curiosity and to the most morbid appetite for the marvelous. The most gross deceptions were shamelessly resorted to cause a week's wonder and to swell the week's receipts. The "Lecture Room"—once a sort of "lyceum" hall, latterly a minor theatre in look and character—furnished for the entertainment of its patrons the most vulgar sensation dramas of the day. Its patrons were suitably entertained. It has been many years since a citizen could take his wife or daughter to see a play on that stage.

That respectable people never went to this so-called museum we do not assert. There were hours in the day when the halls were nearly empty; and, where certain shells, stuffed birds, and Indian relics are, there is always something to see. But we hold that the class of students of whom we have spoken deserve better mental fare than this dreary refectory could afford.

It is in behalf of this class that we ask for a real museum. It is in behalf of all classes of the community, except that vicious and degraded one by which the late "American Museum" was largely monopolized, that we ask the community for a building and for collections that shall be worthy of the name so sadly misapplied. *Μουσειον, museum, musée;* the word seems full of honorable meaning in every language but our own, and with reason. Home of the Muses, it means, and is akin to "music" and "musing," and to "amusement," too, which is a good word with a good meaning. Collections of animals belong to it, indeed, both living and prepared, collections of minerals and shells, of historical and personal relics, and not only these, but collections representative of all the arts, both industrial and decorative, fine art and artisanship. All those valuable things which men do not consume but keep (money, of course, as it has no value except to represent value, is not in itself a valuable thing, and is not included in our statement) have a home in a museum. And "American," "The American Museum!" when that name is again written across the front of a building, let it be a building worthy in itself and in its contents of the honorable and responsible rank which, by taking that name, it assumes.

The British Museum is a national institution, founded and supported by the revenues and the government of an empire. The American Museum of the future will be such another, and even more worthily lodged. It would be good taste if all local institutions, whether belonging to individuals, to companies, to cities, or to States, would adopt names less inappropriate to their natures. But as long as we have American institutes of various kinds, and American companies of many sorts, all incorporated under State laws and limited in their spheres of action by State boundaries, such observance of fitness as we might desire we certainly cannot hope for. Let New York City, then, create for itself an "American Museum." And let the thing itself be not unworthy of the name it rashly assumes.

By the perseverance and the intelligence of some, aided by a series of happy accidents, New York obtained a park, which was put into the hands of good managers and ingenious and conscientious artists, and was carried on by them to such a point of *quasi* completion that it can hardly be spoiled now, and is likely to remain for ever, to cause posterity to doubt the truth of the future historian's account of misgovernment and corruption in New York in the nineteenth century. Let us try to make our descendants still more incredulous on this point. Let us have a place of public instruction as well as of public enjoyment. Perhaps in the neighborhood of the Central Park itself would be the best place for it; let us establish it there, and try to draw encouragement and a stimulus to exertion from our beautiful neighbor.

Nearly every one who has traveled in Europe remembers something of European museums, even though it be but a shadowy image of them that his mind retains. Something of the wonders contained in that sombre temple in Great Russell Street, and something of the artistic treasures "put out of sight under the shadowy vaults of Kensington;" something of the Louvre and the Garden of Plants; something of the Green Vaults of Dresden, of the half-score museums of Berlin, and of the various *Sammlungen* of Munich—remains to help furnish forth everybody's pleasant reminiscences of his European trip. But perhaps there are few who have thought of this, that a museum should include, to be perfect—that a museum *may* include—all the different collections of all the different kinds. As a good example, more apt to be known to our readers than another, let us take the national collections in London.

The British Museum contains the following collections: 1st, the collection of manuscripts, to guard which the "Trustees of the British Museum" were first incorporated in 1753, and which was first exhibited in 1759; 2d, the library, at first small, increased to many times its original size by bequest of George IV, and now the second library in Europe in size, and the first in practical value—open to the public under wise restrictions, nearly six hundred thousand volumes strong, furnished with the best reading-room in the world, and rich in a world of curiosities and artistic treasures; 3d, the collections of natural history, divided into zoology, fossils, minerals, and botany, magnificent in every department and subdivision, and unequalled in many; 4th, the collection of portraits of sovereigns and famous men, now hung on the walls of the zoological galleries; 5th, the collection of antiquities—Egyptian, Assyrian, Greek, Roman, and British—including in its glorious assembling together of riches the famous Elgin Marbles, the Ninevite and other sculptures of Layard's and Rich's discovery, and the best collection in Europe of the oldest art of all, the art of Egypt; 6th, the ethnographical collection. These are under one roof, not large enough now to cover aright the overgrown and still growing collections. . . .

Such are the national collections. Besides these, there is at Sydenham Crystal Palace a great gallery of casts from sculptors ancient and medieval, and from architectural sculptured ornament, which or the like of which, should belong to Government, and probably will at some future time. The famous collection of living animals in Regent's Park belongs to the Zoological Society, but answers the purposes of a national collection in every respect except in the charge of fee of entrance. To all the others is now to be added the contents of the old India House, a treasury of rarities which a few years ago, with the dissolution of the East India Company, passed into the hands of the Government. So the museum of London is very widely scattered, and lacks as yet worthy buildings to contain it properly. The English, perhaps, are willing to wait until their present labors in search of a good national architecture shall have been crowned with success. Their experiments in public buildings have compared but poorly with the very excellent private architectural work which has been done in Great Britain, and when, not long since, they were on the point of getting a really good building in London, the present venerable Premier put a stop to all that undertaking. Therefore it is cause for rejoicing that so many of the national collections have only temporary homes.

New York may have its choice of departments, and make collections of any kind. A good collection in any department is a work either of much money or of much time; and a *very* good collection requires both. New York can better afford to give money than time for her *good* collections, to begin with, for New York wants her museum at once.

There is talk of a joint stock company which proposes to have a museum and to pay a large profit in money to stockholders. It may be doubted whether a joint stock company can best do such work; whether the sum of three hundred thousand dollars is money enough to do it with; whether this particular enterprise, if successful, will give us what we want, or not rather another undertaking like Mr. Barnum's of yore, which Mr. Barnum himself, also in the field, will delve one yard below and blow to the moon—and then buy out. There is money enough to be had which will not seek pecuniary interest, intellect enough to be had, and experience enough to establish such a museum as we need, if only these three—money, intelligence, and experience—will come together and understand each other. Let New York beware lest Philadelphia and Boston should each step in before her and use the intelligence, the experience, the opportunity, the well stocked markets, and some part of the money which she should secure.

By statute the New York Historical Society is authorized to form a Museum of Antiquities and Science and a Gallery of Art, and is given for this purpose the old arsenal building in the Central Park, with as much ground as the Commissioners of the Central Park will allow. The Society, moreover, has authority either to use the building as it is, to alter it, or to remove it and build anew. The use of this present or future building is given for the use specified for ever, to revert to the Park Commission only on the removal of the collections forming the museum or gallery.

It is well to remember that gift, for it is out of this gift and by the influence and position of the Historical Society that such a museum as we want may perhaps be reared. The Society has already a *good* museum of Egyptian antiquities, a few Assyrian sculptures, historical relics, a library rich in one department, and among its pictures perhaps three or four of a certain value. It is strong in numbers and in the social standing of its members. It surely could not require an unreasonable amount of exertion on the part of such a body to raise what money is wanted and begin the so much needed work.

A society is incorporated, its incorporation dating from 1800, and is granted a portion of land in the Central Park for the formation of botanical and zoological gardens. This society, which has honorable and well-known names in the list of its incorporators, may perhaps be expected to act for us if the Historical Society will not. That more energy is needed in the action of the latter body than it showed in the matter of the Jarves Collection is evident, and that they will show this energy is not certain. We may well look at other companies, and consider what further means may be employed to secure the end we so much desire.

But of one thing let us be certain. No individual or stock company which may undertake to form and manage a museum as a way of making money will be of any great or permanent service to the community. Let those who are disposed to aid any of these movements remember this, that the efforts of an ingenious showman to attract popular attention and make money rapidly are not likely to accrue to popular enlightenment. It would not seem well to such a showman to spend money, time, and thought to make valuable antiquarian and scientific collections, classify and catalogue them accurately, and build a fitting and permanent building to contain them. Perhaps the British Museum, charging twenty-five cents admission fee, would take in less money in a year than did Mr. Barnum's old museum at the same price. Let the would-be stockholder invest his money in a proper enterprise; properly guarded, and take dividends for his reward. Of his abundance let him give to the foundation of a real museum for his own enlightenment, the good of his children, and the honor and benefit of the community.

# 7

# THE HISTORY OF THE ORIGIN AND DEVELOPMENT OF MUSEUMS

## H[ermann] A[ugust] Hagen

*The American Naturalist, 10: 80–89, 1876*

*. . . Hermann Hagen, professor of entomology at the Museum of Comparative Zoology at Harvard University from 1867–1893, provides a whirlwind tour through the early history of museums, especially natural history and science museums. Hagen's discussion spans from early Greek and Roman history to the development of natural history museums in western Europe. One of Hagen's conclusions is that natural history museums need to separate their exhibit and research collections, an idea that was just beginning to take hold in 1876 and would come to shape museums of the post-Victorian era.*

The impossibility of believing that knowledge in natural history would be attained and furthered without collections induced Professor Beckmann to express the opinion in a short but interesting paper on this subject, some ninety years ago, that the origin of such collections was to be found in the old custom of keeping curious and remarkable objects in temples. This opinion gains some ground as the medical sciences are considered to have originated in the written reports of convalescents about their sickness, and the remedies used, which were posted in the temple of Æsculapius for everybody's instruction. There are some interesting facts quoted by the classic authors. The skins of the hairy men from the Gorgades Islands, brought home by Hanno's expedition, were still preserved in the temple of Juno, three hundred years after Carthage was destroyed. The late Professor J. Wyman ingeniously suggested that they might be the skins of the

*Collections = Scientific Perfection* †

gorilla. The horns of the Scythic bulls, exceedingly rare, and alone capable of preserving the water of the Styx, were given by Alexander the Great to the temple of Delphi. The horns of the renowned obnoxious steer from Macedon were presented by King Philip to the temple of Hercules; the abnormal omoplate of Pelops was in the temple at Elis; the horns of the so-called Indian ants, in the temple of Hercules at Erythris; the crocodile brought home by the expedition to the sources of the Nile, in the temple of Isis at Cæsarea. A large number of similar cases are quoted in Professor Beckman's above-mentioned paper. The choice of places devoted to religious service, for such deposits, is very appropriate, every spoliation of them being considered sacrilege. So it happened that such curiosities were preserved many centuries, and the not infrequent additions in such a space of time formed at last a somewhat considerable collection, open at any time and to everybody. The variety of prominent objects was certainly instructive to the observers. . . .

It seems certain that prominent naturalists, such as Aristotle and Apuleius, must have had collections, though there is no direct testimony to that effect given in any of their works still extant. The order of Alexander the Great for hunters, trappers, and fishermen to bring all kinds of natural objects to Aristotle, is well known; Theophrast and Apuleius are also known to have studied and dissected many different kinds of animals, chiefly fishes. Apuleius is the first naturalist known to have found it profitable and necessary to make voyages for the purpose of studying foreign animals, and collecting paleontological objects in the Getulic Alps, but unfortunately all his works on zoology are lost, The Emperor Augustus considered the first prince possessing collections of a scientific nature.

I presume that the certain knowledge of the collections of the great naturalists above quoted was lost, as the collections themselves were quickly destroyed, for lack of means for sufficient preservation. The truth of this explanation is made more apparent since the successive discovery of more convenient and easier means of preservation of objects has made these collections more lasting and permanent through later generations. In a really interesting and obvious way, every new discovery, every improvement in the manner of preservation, has given a newer and stronger impulse to the enlargement of the collections, to the perfection † of science. . . .

The long space of time after Christ's death, nearly twelve centuries, is entirely devoid of interest concerning natural history. Curious enough, and perhaps explaining this lack of interest, is the fact that in the earlier centuries of the Christian era the study of natural history was believed to be in some way a proof of religious infidelity. The reason of this will probably be found in the lack of education and study of the disciples and nearly all the apostles. Discussion would have been impossible, difficult, or of doubtful result. Simple faith covered all. So it happened that the prominent works of Aristotle were nearly lost in Europe. Translations of these into the Arabian language, introduced in the tenth century through Spain, and again translated into Latin, were used, and the original text was perhaps not known until the fifteenth century in the west of Europe. Except a few scanty pages in the works of Saint Isidorus, there was nothing written about natural history before the time of Albert the Great, and of course no collections existed. We are told by Begin, in his work on the natural history of the Middle Ages, that rich abbeys and cloisters possessed indeed some collections of medicinal or poisonous plants, of fossils, minerals, and shells. Even in the time of the Crusaders, such collections were augmented by frequent voyages in foreign countries. Some of these curiosities are still preserved: for instance, in the treasury of St. Denis, in France, the feet of a griffin, sent to Charles the Great by the Persian Shah; some teeth of the hippopotamus, and similar objects. . . .

Science, during the next three centuries, did not advance in a remarkable way; we find nothing but repetition of the statements of Albertus and his disciples, Cantipratanus, Bartholomæus Anglicus, Roger Bacon, Vincentius from Beauvais, and others.

The middle of the fifteenth century, and the time immediately following, is one of the most striking periods in history. The invention of printing, the discovery of America and of the way around Africa to the East Indies, the overwhelming amount of gold and silver gained by trade or war in those new countries and suddenly inundating all Europe, followed by the momentous times of the Reformation, made a change in fashion, in study, and in knowledge, never seen before, and perhaps never to be seen again. Art and science advanced in the same rapid manner, the latter prepared in some way by the large immigration of learned Greeks, after the destruction of the Greek empire by the Ottomans.

The same great time produced some discoveries of the highest importance to the existence and preservation of collections; the most important, now considered by millions as the greatest calamity, being that of alcohol. This fluid was known to alchymists long before, but the use of it as medicine, as drink, and for the preservation of animal substance, certainly not much before 1483. A poem printed in that year, in Augsburg, set forth the excellent qualities of the fluid, and stated decidedly that it had been proved that all meat, fish, and fowl put up in alcohol would be well preserved, and would never decay.

Paper, a very important object for collections, has been known since the beginning of culture in the East, but the use of it became gradually less and less, on account of heavy taxes upon it, from the beginning of the Christian era to the sixth century, and in the twelfth and thirteenth centuries the use of it was nearly forgotten. Cotton paper was carried by

Arabs to North Africa in the tenth century, and two centuries later to Spain. Curiously enough the manufacture of linen paper was discovered through an intentional fraud. People first tried to make cheaper cotton paper by the introduction of linen rags, and very soon observed that the paper was greatly improved by this addition. Of course the manufacture with linen rags alone gave a more perfect paper, and was retained. It is sure that at the end of the fifteenth century linen paper was everywhere used, and cheap enough to displace the costly parchment. It is obvious that the common use of paper was a great advantage to every student. Botanical collections were only possible when the preservation of dried plants could be afforded. Just at this time the name herbarium, with its present meaning, seems to have originated.

Before this time, objects of natural history accompanied only by chance the more valuable objects of trade. Now science seemed suddenly to be awakened, or rather new-born. Every one was in haste to study the new objects, never seen before, and arriving in great numbers from newly-discovered countries. It was a natural consequence that those of the old country should be compared with the new ones, and every student was surprised to find so much around him that lie had never known before. . . .

The desire to possess the largest collections increased in a way easily to be understood, especially as the invention of the printing press had now afforded facilities for making the facts known to the world in a very short space of time. As the trade was in the hands of merchants, of course the collections were in their hands also, or in those of private students. The arrangement and contents of these collections are given in printed lists, the first known of which is that by Samuel Quickelberg, a learned physician of Amsterdam, published in 1565, in Munich. Shortly after, Conrad Gesner published the catalogue of the collection of Johann Kenntmann, a prominent physician in Torgau, Saxony. The whole collection contained in a cabinet with thirteen drawers, each with two partitions, about sixteen hundred objects: minerals, shells, and marine animals; and yet it was thought to be so rich that students made long journeys to see it, and Kenntmann stated that the objects were collected at such an expense as few persons would be able or willing to afford. Similar catalogues are published by Mercati, from Rome, Imperati, from Naples, Palissy, from Paris, and Thurneisser, from Berlin. . . .

It now became the fashion for princes to possess collections. They contained celebrated medicines paid for by their weight in gold. Bezoar, the horn of the unicorn, the Maledivian nut, the Alraun, were perhaps placed side by side with such rarities as the pistol with which Berthold Schwarz tested gunpowder when he had discovered it, with Chinese or Egyptian relics, and what would now be considered bric-a-brac of every kind. The German Emperor Rudolf II., otherwise known for his avaricious and indecent behavior, spent large sums of money for his collections, and paid a thousand gold florins, a very large sum for those times, to his artist Hoefnagel, for drawing the specimens contained in them. The magnificent miniatures on parchment, in four volumes, are still extant. The Princes of Gottorf brought together an admirable collection, called, after the fashion of those times, Kunstkammer (cabinet of art), the remnants of which are still prominent treasures of the collections of Copenhagen and St. Petersburg. . . .

I have enumerated purposely the contents of one collection of this time, and have chosen this particularly because it seemed to be the most interesting, as the description of it was reprinted four times in the years immediately following. A rich and partially classified catalogue of John Tradescant's collections was published in England by his son; but one will not be surprised to find such a heading: "Some kinds of birds and their eggs," and among them "Easter-eggs of the Patriarch of Jerusalem," and "the claw of the roc bird, which, as authors report, is able to truss an elephant."

As numerous other collections of this period were arranged in a similar manner, I prefer to mention only one more, that of the Jesuits in the Collegium Romanuin at Rome, because the catalogue printed in 1678 shows the interior rooms in which the collection was arranged. As Italy was at this time still the leading country of the world in fashion and culture, and the order of the Jesuits influential and powerful, the arrangement of their collection may be considered as a fair example for others in that century, which certainly more or less imitated it, but never surpassed it. We find large, vaulted galleries, connected with vaulted rooms, the floor covered with inlaid marbles, the ceiling with allegorical pictures. The arrangement of the exhibited objects shows a kind of refined taste, and is agreeable to the eye; the taller and more prominent objects being arranged by themselves in the middle, as, for instance, a number of Egyptian obelisks, on the top of each of which were placed emblems of Christianity. Busts and other objects were placed on columns along the wall, the spaces between them being provided with shelves bearing smaller objects. Pictures and astronomical maps fill the upper part of the wall, and heavier things, such as a crocodile, are suspended from the ceiling. Not the least prominent object of the museum is an obelisk, made in the Egyptian fashion, to celebrate the memory of the conversion of the Swedish Queen Christina, the daughter of the most prominent king in the Thirty Years' War, Gustavus Adolphus, the fact of the conversion being expressed on the obelisk in thirty-three different languages.

Just at this time a curious historical essay on the origin and development of museums, and the best arrangement of them, was published, the author of which was probably a certain Major, and this very rare pamphlet, first published in 1674, has been reprinted later in Valentyn's *Museum Museorum*. According to the fashion of the time the author begins with the enumeration of the different names for such exhibitions, and out of forty of these, seventeen are Greek. I think it would be rather hard to remember them all, and even tedious to hear them repeated. . . .

### *The American Naturalist,* 10:135–148, 1876

. . . The old fame of Italy was now declining, and religious fanaticism hindered more and more the development of science. Unfortunately, also, the famous wealth of the Italian merchants was destroyed by the refusal of a number of prominent princes to pay their debts, enormous sums of money advanced by Italian bankers. These circumstances, together with the general change of the old routes of trade, gave an important advantage to the Dutch Protestants. The easily amassed fortune was largely used to advance culture and science, and the small Dutch country became for more than a century the leading nation in fashion, taste, and science, till her French and English neighbors put themselves somewhat roughly in her place. The particular taste of the Dutch people for accurate and correct work in its exaggerated and pedantic character was well adapted for forming and arranging collections so rapidly acquired by a trade with the whole world.

Naturalists seldom equaled, never surpassed, belong to this interesting time, as Swammerdam, Leuwenhoek, Ruysch, Rumphius, Seba, and others. The observations and collections of microscopical objects by Leuwenhoek and Ruysch have till to-day a world-wide or rather a traditional fame, and are still preserved, partly in London, partly in St. Petersburg. Swammerdam himself gives an interesting account of his way of arranging and preserving the collections which were the pride and marvel of the country, seen and admired by prominent princes, who disputed among themselves the honor of acquiring them. This distinguished naturalist invented the mode of preservation of the most difficult objects by inflation, by drying, by injection, and by different chemicals.

The fame of the Dutch cabinets, as the most prominent of the time, induced Peter the Great to visit and study them carefully. A number of the most renowned, bought by him for enormous prices, were transferred to St. Petersburg to arouse an interest in such studies in his country. There are also a large number of more or less similar and expensive collections in France, Denmark, Germany, and England. The celebrated collection of Sir Hans Sloane was later the nucleus of the gigantic one of the British Museum. . . .

The observation of the biology, and the study of the anatomy, of the objects now progressed rapidly with the help of the microscope, and the works of some prominent naturalists of those times are a source of information not yet exhausted. The names of Buffon, Réaumur, Degeer, Roesel, and many others are even now the pride of science in nearly every country. The middle of the last century begins the science of the present time with the immortal works of Linnæus; immense progress was made in the century after, which he foresaw, and it would be almost superfluous to dwell upon the merits of Linnæus.

But it seems to me that one of his innovations in science has a striking value for the advancement of collections, which has been, I believe, somewhat underrated. The invention and use of his binomial nomenclature allowed a scientific labeling of objects.

Formerly all names of objects were designated by the so-called *nomen specificurn* (now called a diagnosis), consisting of a dozen words. Linnæus' use of one name (he calls it a trivial one) for the species and one for the genus facilitated the labeling formerly so tedious and wordy. The advantage is obvious. The clear and logical mind of Linnæus not only purified the system, but also enabled him to purge the collections of a considerable number of fabulous and fictitious objects, sometimes a dangerous task. He was obliged to leave Hamburg suddenly, and by night, because he declared and proved the most expensive and rare object of the collection of the mayor of that city to be a fraudulent manufacture. It was a so-called hydra with many heads, the cranium having been made of weasels covered with snakes' skins. The mighty owner of this exceedingly costly object grew furious and threatened to imprison Linnæus as an impostor.

The "printed instructions" for the arrangement of a museum published by Linnæus in 1753 is the first really scientific essay, and has been followed by most naturalists. Indeed, even to-day we find the principles and rules of Linnæus more or less unconsciously followed in many museums.

Linnæus himself built at his country-seat, Hammerby, his museum, a small, square, brick building, on the top of a hill, with a beautiful view from his garden. I was fortunate enough, thirty-six years ago, to visit the place, just after the death of his youngest daughter. Everything was nearly in the same order as left by Linnæus. The collection and library, as is well known, were transferred to England. I saw them afterwards, one small cabinet containing the herbarium, and a similar one the insects and shells. This souvenir of the great man fills the heart with awe, when one considers the small number of objects forming the basis of his studies and voluminous works.

Among the numerous museums which were arranged according to his system, and described by himself and his disciples, none gratified his pride more than the collection in the Jardin du Roi, in Paris, by order of the king, and against the wishes of Linnæus' celebrated antagonist, Buffon, the director of this institution. . . .

The preëminent value of collections was first recognized when Sweden did not shrink from sending a man-of-war to recover the collections which had been sold in a legal manner to another country. The great advance made by Linnæus was followed by unusual exertions and struggles in nearly every part of the civilized world. Every country had disciples of Linnæus as leading naturalists. Everywhere collections suddenly arose, and only a score of years was needed to recognize that, with the excessive vigor of this time, science had bequeathed a new law of the highest importance for collections: the most careful preservation of described objects, nowadays called types. This new law, seemingly of very small importance, soon gained the most powerful influence over all museums, changing even their interior management and leading in a natural way to more appropriate arrangements. . . .

The aim to preserve everything contained in collections soon demanded a new and most important officer, called conservator. His duty is manifold and burdensome, especially in a rapidly growing museum; the most varied kinds of work belong to him, but all centring in the effort to preserve the treasures of science. In fact, the business of this officer is an art in which there are various degrees of excellence, but in which, as in other arts, no degree of excellence is to be attained without training.

There are a number of scientific matters in which nearly everybody feels himself able to have and to express an opinion, as, for instance, scientific education, local geology, primeval history, management of libraries, and evolution. The arrangement of a museum belongs to the same category, to the detriment of science, which has lost often and heavily by such volunteer efforts. The importance of thorough training for this business is shown by a large and abundant literature. The development of the art of managing collections in the manner above stated was followed, curiously enough, in a natural way by the exclusion of the nonscientific public from them. The inevitable and perhaps irreparable loss of important specimens by persons not accustomed to handle such objects and ignorant of their value, together with the impossibility of securing all objects without impeding their exhibition, was the reason for excluding everybody except naturalists. If we consider that every kind of exhibition necessitates large expenses for large rooms, and for arrangements convenient if not showy, and that just this time of progress demanded immense sums of money, the expedient resorted to will be easily understood.

With few exceptions, perhaps, for a quarter of a century most museums became so exclusive that public admission was considered a hindrance or a nuisance. Even after attempts were made to give up this exclusiveness, something of it remained, and a natural consequence of this tendency was a sort of exclusiveness in the naturalists themselves, who stood aloof with their works and collections for some time, till both were ready for the study and use of the public, just as an artist is not accessible till his work is accomplished.

The great impulse given to science by Cuvier was felt through the whole world, and every naturalist realized the necessity of a renewed and earnest study to enable him to follow the rapid progress of the master. The new way led directly to a comparative anatomy as basis for a comparative zoology. The admirable collections for this kind of study made and established in the Jardin des Plantes by Cuvier and his faithful associate, Laurillard, were at the time unrivaled, and show the immense amount of labor performed before the results could be published.

The aim of Cuvier was so expansive that even his masterpiece, the Régne Animal, was considered by him only as a tool necessary to be manufactured before he could work out the principles of natural history according to his ideas.

The result of this kind of revolution soon manifested itself in every museum, and the French ones under the eye of the master were far in advance. The new era developing the rights of man led directly to the necessity that everybody should be enabled to have his share in this advance of science. Museums were again thrown open to the public, and the peculiar taste for exhibition and show made the French museum, for more than a quarter of a century, the leading and most refined in the world; the other countries followed more or less slowly but steadily in their own way. It is a remarkable fact that even in the Jardin des Plantes, where the low, old-fashioned rooms were very soon overcrowded with objects, it was apparent that such a multitude of facts could be neither agreeable nor useful for public instruction. It was deemed advisable to prepare a separate collection, selected and arranged in a manner to be interesting to the public, which, being prepared according to French taste, was superior to all former ones. It is proper to mention here that just at this time, when Paris was the centre of science for the world, one of the most prominent of the army of ardent disciples of Cuvier was a young student from Neufchatel, Switzerland—Louis Agassiz. The time of Cuvier is the date of the beginning of most of the large museums now in existence; some of them, indeed, were started before, but in a different and far inferior manner, so that few of the contents could be retained when the new start began which influenced so powerfully those of London, Vienna, Berlin, Copenhagen, Stockholm, Munich, and St. Petersburg.

It now became impossible for private collections to compete with the larger and steadily advancing museums, and the old custom which rich merchants had kept up for several centuries of accumulating collections began to disappear, and, to the detriment of science, was rarely renewed. Nevertheless, some of the old collections of this kind have lasted even to our times. Of private collections the museum of Sir Ashton Lever, afterwards, if I am not mistaken, united with the British Museum, was one of the most prominent, and some others known now only through printed catalogues were important.

The Ashmolean Museum, in Oxford, before it was transferred to the new rooms in 1861 was perhaps one of the most curious examples of the old style. Even in America, the East India museum in Salem, before the foundation of the Peabody Academy of Science, was a fair specimen of such collections of various objects of natural history, ethnological materials, and curiosities. . . .

The noblest aim to be fulfilled by these scientific collections is to prepare the way and show how museums intended to advance knowledge, namely, collections for public instruction, can be made and arranged so as to be best fitted for their purpose. I believe that this way will not be difficult to discover, if the purpose and the aim are clearly defined. As text-books must be adapted to the degree of knowledge of the student who is to peruse them, so must museums correspond to the average standard of knowledge in the public which visits them; and as in textbooks this standard may be placed somewhat above the average knowledge, so collections should be formed which would necessitate the public to adapt itself to a higher standard—a thing mankind is always inclined to do.

# SECTION II

## Museum Philosophy

Museum philosophy addresses some of the leading issues that concern museums by considering such questions as: Why do we have museums? What do they do? Why do they do it? Museum administrators over time have responded quite differently to these questions. In reading the following selected articles, one clearly sees that social issues of the day have influenced the ways in which museum administrators develop—and alter—the missions of their institutions.

The articles are grouped into three subcategories. The first category addresses general issues of philosophy: Luigi Palma di Cesnola writes about the power and the value of objects; Frederic A. Lucas explains why we have museums; and Paul M. Rea explains the value of the public museum. The second group concerns philosophies developed for more specialized and regional museums: Herbert Bolton discusses war memorial museums; Erwin H. Barbour examines the value of state museums, as does Reuben Gold Thwaites; and Oliver C. Farrington focuses on the relationship between municipal museums and the communities they serve. The third group includes two articles that examine various aspects of art museum philosophy: Mariana Van Rensselaer makes a case for art museums to consider instituting educational programs to create a more public museum; and Sir John Charles Robinson discusses art connoisseurship.

## Additional Readings

Bennett, Tony. 1995. *The birth of the museum: History, theory, politics.* London: Routledge.

Genoways, Hugh H. (ed.). 2006. *Museum philosophy for the twenty-first century.* Lanham, MD: AltaMira Press.

Hooper-Greenhill, Eilean. 1992. *Museums and the shaping of knowledge.* New York: Routledge.

Pearce, Susan M. 1993. *Museums, objects, and collections.* Washington, DC: Smithsonian Institution Press.

———. 1995. *On collecting: An investigation into collecting in the European tradition.* New York: Routledge.

Preziosi, Donald, and Claire J. Farago (eds.). 2004. *Grasping the world: The idea of the museum.* Burlington, VT: Ashgate Publishing Company.

Sola, Tomislav. 1997. *Essays on museums and their theory: Towards a cybernetic museum.* Helsinki, Finland: Finnish Museums Association.

# 8

# AN ADDRESS ON THE PRACTICAL VALUE OF THE AMERICAN MUSEUM

**Luigi Palma di Cesnola**

Troy, NY: The Stowell Printing House, 22 pp., 1887

---

*The following is the excerpted address given by Luigi Palma di Cesnola, the first director of the Metropolitan Museum of Art, at the dedication of the George West Museum of Art and Archaeology in Round Lake, New York, on July 12, 1887. Cesnola describes museums as object "libraries," praising in turn the value of objects for use in popular instruction. He also commends American museums for earning international prominence but cautions directors against expansion at the expense of fiscal security.*

---

. . . The Museum in general, whether it be one to display the products of art and industry, the relics of human antiquity, the remnants of palaeozoic life, the crystallized beauties of the mineral kingdom, or the gathered specimens from the realm of organized nature, is no mere toy. It is not to be regarded as an index of the money-spending power of this or that individual or association.

The Museum of old was the habitation sacred to the Muses, who were the daughters of Memory; those handmaids of the best thoughts and works of men; who preserved, in systematized and attractive form, all that was worth preserving and transmitting to generations.

Amusement, pure and simple, was the pastime of the *Amousos,* the unlettered or uncultured; who might, indeed—and happily—stray into the abode of better entertainment and higher pleasure, and perchance himself become a child of the Muses, a man of gentler manners and of noble arts; or, in any event, a recipient of blessings, if not a benefactor to his race.

51

It is with this purpose in general that Museums are established today; though the sciences and the arts—the knowledge of the works of the Creator and its reflection in the works of men—have long ago become so extended and multiplied that the temple of the Muses is a mere portal—an antiquated portal, as some think—to the vast ideal palace of many mansions now needed for the light of the nations. The Nine Muses are now crowded out into the colleges, the seminaries, and the libraries; while their unnamed progeny, though ever of social disposition, and flourishing best in each other's company, are obliged, by their very wealth and number, to sit in separate houses, each dispensing her peculiar treasures to her special votaries. But in the light of to-day, when it is recognized that teaching is better done by object than by word, that the thing becomes better known by studying itself than by reading or mastering a description, the Museum, in some degree, is indispensable. No botanist would expect to educate a pupil on the dry descriptions of a floral manual; he would send him to the lily of the field, and to the hyssop that springeth out of the wall. A day among the rocks with the hammer and chisel is worth more to the mineralogist or the geologist than months of book study. A course of *bona fide* inscriptions, or of actual ancient manuscripts, will teach more to the palaeographer than many dry tomes of description, besides shaking his pedantry thoroughly out of him.

A genuine wine-skin and an ancient terracotta lamp will teach the student more in a moment than he can learn from pages of the dictionary of antiquities or the treatise on archaeology.

So the Museum, in any of its branches, is a magnificent, an unsurpassed, library and school of object-teaching; making the casual visitor learn something, whether he be so inclined or not; giving innumerable hints to the book student, and filling countless gaps in his knowledge; a perpetual fountain of riches to the teacher and the lecturer, a source of untold improvement to the special student, a mine of gold for the author and the pictorial illustrator, both popular and learned, and last though by no means least, a resource whence artizanship and handicraft of all sorts may better and beautify our dwellings, our ornaments, our garments, our implements of daily life.

If this be true—and the abundant facts that daily come to my official knowledge surely confirm it—the Museum needs but to be spread, to be multiplied, and to be known, whether on a humble scale or a grand one, in order to be one of the most powerful mean—I will not say of civilization and material wealth, but of the riper fruits of civilization, of increase in all the better sorts of wealth, even those which bring blessing wholly, and add little sorrow therewith. Indeed, instinct long ago taught our schools and colleges the same. It was not this generation, nor the one before it, which saw every college begin to gather its cabinets, and every theological school its biblical or missionary collection; while both were antedated by the medical school. And these same cabinets and collections have played no small part in popular instruction; while again and again they have fired the heart of the youth inclined to special science, and raised a brood of eminent instructors and investigators, who have made America as famous for their achievements as she is for possessing the most prosperous, happy, and enlightened people that the world ever saw.

The purpose, then, of the Museum, is to furnish such an object-library and lecture room as can be had in no other way. It is to be the silent but sure instructor of the casual visitor, while it entertains and delights him. It is to provide food of easy digestion to the man of culture, who would not use his leisure ignobly. It is to furnish the earnest student with the most perfect means for reaching perfection in his special branch of study or art, and for attaining that end by the shortest and most unerring path. It is intended that those who visit this place with no more earnest purpose than curiosity or pastime, shall carry away with them some items of knowledge worth having, whether they will or no. It is intended that those who flock to this place shall find what the books do not and cannot supply, and shall go away with definite and well-shaped ideas—to sprout and blossom in advantageous fruit; that they shall no longer be left to the haziness and impracticability that too often cling to mere book learning, making the vain and the useless loom up larger than the true and the valuable, as the mirage lures on the thirsty traveler with its phantom water. It is intended moreover, that the soul that longs for perfect knowledge, and to pursue as his life-work some one of the lines (for they are necessarily many) indicated in the Museum, shall at least find that degree of nutriment and stimulus in his chosen direction, which will enable him to go out in the great world fully equipped and trained to gather, to its last discoverable item, the harvest of his specialty.

To speak of the scope of this or that particular Museum is in one sense easy; but in another sense it requires no less than a prophet's ken.

It is easy to say what should be the main objects to illustrate Greek or Roman antiquity, or the customs of Palestine, or Biblical archaeology; though the scope of either would be almost limitless.

It might easily be seen, too, that a Museum of either sort would have its own peculiar class of frequenters, and diffuse its own peculiar lessons among the artists, the manufacturers, and the students of its deeper lore. You will pardon me for speaking of what I know best–but it was a matter of course, as the event has shown, that the master jewelers and potters should go to the Metropolitan Museum in New York, and supply the market with reproductions of the beautiful forms left by the Greek and Phoenician workmen of thousands of years ago; but it could not be foreseen that the sculptures, with the engraved gems and vases, would disclose the connecting link of Greek art with the earlier products of Phoenicia, Egypt, and Babylonia. It could be foreseen that the inscribed monuments would be studied by experts in history and the origin of writing; but it could not have been foretold that a tablet-fragment in New York should prove the counterpart of another fragment in the British Museum, and the two together disclose the Babylonian law of inheritance. Nor could it have been foretold that the name of an unknown proconsul of Cyprus should come to light, bearing added testimony to the correctness of the title given to Sergius Paulus in the Acts of the Apostles. Nor could it be foretold that two pairs of stone feet with their bases—the rest of the statue gone—should tell of the migration to Cyprus of an ancient and supposed local Asiatic religion, and furnish a key to the whole settlement of a region hitherto shrouded in mystery. Nor could it have been foretold that a clay barrel of Nebuchadnezzar with its archaic writing should depose from his seat a fictitious Nebuchadnezzar the First, of dim half-mythologic age, and set on his throne the familiar Nebuchadnezzar of the Bible. No; as Blackstone said a century ago, "the sciences are of a sociable disposition, and flourish best in one another's company"; and in entertaining one guest of lofty character, we often entertain many other angels unawares. As the poet Schiller says:

"Never, believe me.

Never alone

Appear the immortals."

I will not, then, attempt to speak to you particularly of the scope of this Museum to-day opened. Its general connection with the schools marks well enough its field of easy definition; and beyond that, unless it belies all precedent, its results will demonstrate, before even one generation has passed away, that its founders have, in more ways than they can now imagine, "builded better than they knew". . . .

The Museum proprietorship can never expect it to be self-supporting, much less of direct pecuniary profit. The establishment is one of those blessings which benefits the community at large; and, like the college, the seminary, the hospital, and the asylum, properly belongs among those institutions which are viewed by the eye of the law as charitable.

A prudent husbandry of its extension funds is on no account to be neglected. "Bricks and Brains," as the homely proverb says, are necessary for every great and good enterprise. Debt is to be avoided as the King of terrors.

This King of terrors, against which even Christian churches afford no sure defense, whose gilded court, especially in our chief cities, is thronged with suitors, who hope to found great enterprises in bubbles and esteem his tinsel promises as pure gold–this remorseless tyrant I have been fighting for the last nine years in behalf of our Museum, and thus far with success, in his very stronghold, New York City. I know how powerful he is with the best of men; how he has force for the weak, and snares for the strong. But I know how much better it is to resist him; how much better to begin on a humble scale and grow by solid accretions, till strength and wealth are at hand, as they will be in due time. It is not a blessing to run in debt; it is a Nemesis, perhaps of slow approach, but with ever suspended sword, and sooner or later sure to strike with ruin. . . .

But there is no room for complaint. The true Museum is a blessing like the air we breathe. No individual could furnish himself with it. It refreshes and vivifies the whole population; and its benefits cannot be estimated in money. The Museum sits higher than on a mercenary seat. I will not say that like Diana it enriches those who make and sell her silver shrines; but it is a source of profit to the merchants and manufacturers, as it is of refinement and instruction to the multitude.

It was truthfully remarked some years ago, by one of our distinguished orators, that the Venus of Melos had brought more wealth to Paris than the Queen of Sheba brought to Solomon. Therein lies the pecuniary profit of the Museum: it is the people's vested fund. The founders know the secret blessing of their labor and benevolence, as it is more blessed to give than to receive; but the patent fact that they can themselves receive no pecuniary reward, is one that challenges high honor from those who receive the benefit, and calls aloud for the co-operation and contributions of all noble-spirited citizens. . . .

Already the influence of the Museum in America is world-wide, already pilgrims come from the Old World to glean necessities from the Museums of the New. Already American collections hold an indelible place in the literature of England, France, Italy, Germany, and there contribute to uphold truth, grace, culture, and excellence; while at home their influence on art and the arts, the manners and the virtue, the comfort and the wealth, of our own beloved people, has progressed beyond the possibility of record or of estimate.

The place of the Museums in the home literature, permanent and periodical, popular and erudite, is already vast and ineradicable. They are visited with delight and profit by every class, from the tired toilers in the kitchens and workshops, the shipyards and mines, to the merchant princes and the devotees of fashion; from the aborigines of the far West to the scions of royalty and the representatives of the nobility of Europe from China and the Isles of the sea to Egypt and Turkey.

To throngs innumerable, both those that have seen and those that have not seen, their lessons speak in many tongues, in many grades and kinds of instruction. The globe alone prescribes the limit of their power and influence to spread the richer blessings of civilization, to advance the reign of happiness, prosperity, gentleness, and virtue. With no ordinary pleasure, then, do I take a kindly proffered part at the opening of this Museum; aid, with highest wishes, I join most heartily in thankful honor to those who have founded it in honest, wise benevolence, and dedicated it to the undying cause of light and truth.

# 9

# PURPOSES AND AIMS
# OF MODERN MUSEUMS

## Frederic A. Lucas

*Proceedings of the Staten Island Association of Arts and Sciences,* 2: 119–124, 1908

*Frederic Lucas, speaking as director of the Brooklyn Museum, presented the address excerpted below in 1907 at a meeting of the Staten Island Association of Arts and Sciences, in celebration of the organization's move to Richmond Borough Hall and in anticipation of its transformation into a general museum of arts and sciences. Lucas credits John Edward Gray and George Brown Goode as the first museologists to enumerate the purpose of museums—to collect, preserve, research, exhibit, and educate—recognized today by the American Association of Museums as the basic function of museums. For Lucas, education stands out as the museum institution's most significant and lasting contribution to society.*

Why do we have museums at all; what are they for; why in this very practical age are millions expended in establishing them, what does the public receive in return for the money it has invested?

All these are perfectly fair questions, the kind that any business man or city official might well ask if called upon to aid in founding or sustaining a museum, and yet they are by no means easy to answer off hand. Merely to answer the question why we have museums would take much time, for like most things, museums did not spring into existence all at once but are the product of long years of growth and evolution, and they are still growing and changing.

The purposes of museums have been well defined by some of the men best acquainted and most intimately connected with them and I cannot do better than give you two of these definitions. According to John Edward Gray, museums are for "the diffusion of instruction and rational amusement among the masses of the people and to afford the scientific student every means of examining and studying the specimens which the museum contains." And thirty years later our own Dr. Goode wrote that "A museum is an institution for the preservation of those objects which best illustrate the phenomena of nature and the works of man and the utilization of these for the increase of knowledge and for culture and enlightenment of the people."

Now, if a museum fulfills its purposes as defined by Dr. Goode, it seems to me that the question whether the public gets the interest on its investment would be answered in the affirmative. Even if it merely preserved a record of the life that with the rapid march of civilization is being ruthlessly swept out of existence, would not the museum serve a good purpose and justify its being? For nowadays the entire face of Nature is being altered by the energy of man, and natural conditions are changing so rapidly that in many places the present generation has little or no knowledge of what was there even fifty years ago.

It is only three centuries since Henry Hudson sailed up New York Bay—there are many edifices in Europe older than that, and yet little remains of what was here then. The inhabitants—the forests, to a considerable extent the very rocks themselves—have disappeared, and the life that then abounded has disappeared with them. And it is one of the purposes of a museum, one of the purposes of this museum, to carefully gather and preserve all objects that may aid in giving an idea of the life that was here three centuries ago and to provide for the information of those who will be here three centuries hence.

But this museum of today is a great deal more than a place where objects are merely preserved, it is an educational institution on a large scale, whose language may be understood by all, an ever open book whose pages appeal not only to the scholar but even to the man who cannot read.

Its mission or one of its missions is to give the visitor a hint of the many interesting things that are to be found close at hand, to show their hidden meaning, in short to teach him to observe and to think.

Now the idea that the museum is an important educational factor in the community is comparatively new, and it is only recently that steps have been taken to put this idea into execution. The early museums were primarily for the student, secondarily for the public, and when a century and a half ago the British Museum was opened to the public, the attendance was limited to thirty a day and admission was by ticket and carefully arranged for in advance. Nowadays when the visitors at our larger museums average from 500 to 1,000 or more a day, this strikes us as amusing, but this was really the germ from which the modern educational museum has developed. And if your attendance should seem small in comparison with that of older and richer museums, it may encourage you to recall that there was a time when what is now the greatest museum in the world had but 1,000 a year.

We are so familiar with public museums that we are prone to forget how very recent they really are and how their aims and objects have changed even within the past twenty-five years. The great Museum of Natural History impresses one as having existed for long years and yet not only this, but every museum in Manhattan has practically come into existence, certainly into active being, in my own day. And yet while museums themselves are far from ancient the idea that they might be utilized on a great scale for the benefit of the public at large is still more recent.

I hesitate to repeat what I have said so often of late that one of the great differences between the old museum and the new is that the one displayed objects while the other aims to illustrate ideas. And yet this is one of the important characteristics of the modern museum. The old museum was merely a storehouse whence students drew the material for their work and into which the public was permitted to gaze. The new museum seeks to interest the visitor in the field of work, illustrates its methods and purposes and displays some of the results. For example, in place of an hundred birds intended only to show just so many species and meaning little to the average visitor, we have a single group showing one of these birds at home, the purpose of which is to show the conditions under which birds live and to interest the beholder in the study of bird life.

The idea that the visitor must be interested, though not particularly new, is again one that has gained general acceptance only recently. Nowadays it is definitely recognized that while a museum is an eminently serious proposition it will not be taken too seriously by visitors, that in fact only a small proportion of them seek it with a definite purpose to be instructed, and so a distinct effort is made to arouse the interest of the average visitor. A museum should take itself seriously but none the less should it provide "rational amusement" for the many by whose funds it is largely supported. And this it does by ever keeping in mind what Dr. Goode used to call the human interest endeavoring to show some object or make clear some idea that will appeal directly to the observer and arouse his personal interest in the museum. To do these things and do them well calls for knowledge and training and I often wonder if the public appreciates the fact that museums do not run themselves; that it takes a trained force to get proper results out of a museum!. . . .

That a museum should be a place for study and research carried on by the few who are directly interested in what seems abstruse science, is really a phase of its relation to the public. We know very well that what is a matter of purely scientific interest today is a matter of vital importance tomorrow, that the farmer, the fruit grower, the physician, for example, depend more and more upon the trained man of science for help in what were once considered matters with which he was not at all concerned. Here and elsewhere, the museum takes the knowledge gained by years of study, puts it into visible shape, and makes it available for all. And, after all, something is due the student for without him there would have been no museum for natural history.

I have said nothing of the field of a museum of art and would only remind you that the Staten Island Association is an Association of Arts as well as Sciences, and suggest that if the domain of Nature has been sadly encroached upon by the labors of man the province of art has been correspondingly widened. Neither have I said anything of what one may call the civilizing influence that a museum exerts upon a community, though this is one of the results, if not among the professed objects of the existence of a museum.

To inculcate the spirit of law and order, to foster a love of the beautiful, to teach the visitor to observe and think, to supply "rational amusement" to the masses, are among the things that a museum does for the public in return for its cash investment. Sidney Smith is credited with having preached the shortest and most effective charity sermon on record. He said, "he who giveth to the poor lendeth to the Lord. If you like the security, come down with the dust," so if you like your museum, support it.

But over and beyond these things are the educational opportunities offered to everyone and, after all, love of knowledge is the supreme test of civilization. Man stands pre-eminent among all living creatures in his desire for knowledge, his wish to know the reasons for all that goes on about him, and according to the extent of this desire does he stand in the intellectual scale. The savage merely wishes to know where he can find something to eat and wherewith he may be clothed, the astronomer casts his eye across millions of miles of space seeking for knowledge of other worlds.

# 10

# THE FUNCTIONS OF MUSEUMS

## Paul M. Rea

*Proceedings of the American Association of Museums*, 6: 51–55, 1912

*Paul Rea, Director of the Charleston Museum in South Carolina, delivered a lecture, excerpted below, before the American Association of Museums in 1911, in which he presents both his philosophical and practical ideas regarding the appropriate functions of museums, using the Charleston Museum—the oldest continuously operating museum in the United States—to illustrate his points. His statement "museums exist for the people" best summarizes Rea's philosophy.*

As we come from our institutions of art or history or science, institutions of various sizes and situated in various parts of the country, and visit the great museums of New York, we are sure to be impressed with the magnitude of their work, the amount of money spent and the results obtained and contemplated. To those of us who come from smaller museums this experience is both stimulating and overwhelming, but if we bear clearly in mind that the fundamental principles of museum administration differ only in degree in large and small communities, we shall go home with renewed enthusiasm and added knowledge and suggestions with which to carry on our own work.

A survey of the museums of the country, however, leaves a very strong impression that the proportion of these which are growing in size and usefulness is far smaller than it should be. It is the purpose of this paper to consider the scope and opportunities of these museums irrespective of size, for the measure of success is the ratio of results to resources.

The scope of a museum is properly determined by the nature of its financial support, viz., whether private; endowed; school, college, university, or society; municipal or national. For the purpose of this discussion the nature of the material, whether of art, history, science, etc., is largely immaterial.

The scope of a private museum may be whatever the wishes of the owner dictate. There can be no other obligation. In the same way the use of endowment funds is usually specified by the donor.

Schools, colleges, universities, and societies are essentially more complicated individuals. When they maintain museums it should be the object of the authorities to conserve the collections and so to administer them as to serve most efficiently the purposes of the supporting institution. Where these purposes are chiefly as an adjunct of class instruction it is generally considered at present that carefully selected collections of limited extent are more useful than extensive general collections. For this reason many institutions neglect museums of considerable size which grew up in a time when different ideas of teaching prevailed or which were created by the enthusiastic devotion of a professor. Under these circumstances there seem to be but two proper courses of procedure, viz.—to develop new uses for these museums which will warrant their proper support, or to transfer the greater part of the collections to institutions which can preserve and utilize them. Unfortunately, the usual course is one of neglect, which results in the destruction or deterioration of material that is sometimes of great value. When this material is unique or of unusual value, its neglect violates an obligation to art or history or science, as the case may be, which institutions of learning above all others ought to respect.

Municipal museums derive their support primarily from tax funds and as such owe their obligation to the people who pay the taxes. These are truly popular institutions in the sense that they exist for the people. National museums are of a similar nature. Until very recent times the municipal museum, as we conceive it today, did not exist in this country. It is significant that the great expansion of museums has come with the realization of an obligation to the people—an obligation which has been met most conspicuously hitherto by cooperation with the public schools. It has been said at every meeting of this Association, as far back as I can remember, that school work is the one topic that always arouses enthusiastic discussion. I believe heartily in this line of work, but I believe there are other fields in which equal success awaits us.

Industrial and economic exhibits are attracting increasing attention. Movements for bird and tree protection have been inspired and guided by museums. Tuberculosis and child welfare exhibits are suggestive in the extreme. Museums exist for the people. Museums are ideal agents of intelligent publicity, appealing to the eye in times of recreation, when the mind is open to impressions. They reach people of all classes through the children. Shall we not make them, then, a clearing house of municipal progress, an expression point of community activity? Publicity of the right sort is essential to the success of popular movements. Why should not the resources of our museums be turned to this work as occasion arises, and must we not believe that such cooperation will result in more generous support for all museum activities?

In large communities the various phases of museum work are divided among several museums; in small communities one general museum must cope with all alone. When such a museum is in a state of stagnation, is it not reasonable to suppose that it is because it is neglecting to take an active part in the life of the community?

As an indication that these principles are capable of successful practical application a specific instance may be cited.

Eight years ago the College of Charleston Museum was overcrowded, under-lighted, many times larger than necessary for class use as a reference collection, yet without resources for active work either for the public or for students. The only funds available were an appropriation of $250 made by City Council. There was no staff, but the professor of biology might devote some of his time to curatorial work in addition to the full work of a department of instruction.

Reorganization began by submitting to City Council a comparison between the status of the Museum and a factory which was being swept out once a week but was never run and consequently paid no dividends. One thousand dollars was asked to run the institution for one year, with the understanding that if it did not pay dividends in public instruction and recreation it would be discontinued. That thousand dollars was used to give lectures and print bulletins to acquaint the people with the nature and possibilities of museum work. The next appropriation was $1,500. The following year City Council gave a building worth $30,000, with $7,500 for remodelling and $2,500 for maintenance. Now the appropriation for maintenance is $4,000.

The commercial bodies and other organizations were told that the new Museum was a public servant and that when they were ready to undertake any work for the good of the community the Museum stood ready to cooperate. One result has been that the Advertising Club raised $2,500 toward the expense of installing the scientific collections in the new building and beginning industrial exhibits. The Museum cooperated with the Park Board in investigating the condition of the city's shade trees and in arousing public interest in their improvement. It was the headquarters of the tuberculosis exhibit. It has undertaken to maintain for the City Art Commission a municipal catalog of works of art in Charleston. It has done much to educate the community to a greater interest in, and appreciation of wild bird life, with the result that when an island on which a colony of snowy herons breeds had been purchased by popular subscription to avert its destruction, the Museum was asked to take title to the property as the natural agent of the community. In short, every effort is being made to associate each department of the Museum with some line of community activity.

Meanwhile, investigations into the history of the Museum traced its origin back to March, 1773, a quarter of a century before any of our other American museums began, and recovered the original prospectus of its founders, a document remarkable for the breadth of plan and high purpose with which it endowed the infant museum. We have told the story of the nurture and development of the Museum under the auspices successively of the Library Society, the Literary and Philosophical Society, the Medical College, and the College of Charleston, and how the community rallied to its support in times of stress through popular subscriptions and state and city appropriations. Today the people of Charleston recognize in the Museum a precious inheritance and a community enterprise pregnant with good works for the betterment of the city and for science. No longer a department of the College, it is known as the Charleston Museum. It is maintained by the City, and developed by the people through member-ships and popular subscriptions. It is free to the public on every week day.

The College has not lost but rather gained, for the Museum not only provides it with classrooms and laboratories, but with all the facilities of a large and active museum. The Medical College is also affiliated with the Museum. The public schools avail themselves increasingly of its coopera-tion. Thus, all the scientific interests of the city are effectively served by one central institution without reduplication of equipment.

I have recited the story of the rejuvenation of our oldest museum to demonstrate the vital relationship that museums may maintain with the people, and of the readiness of the people to rally to the support of muse-ums that are willing to serve them. . . .

# 11

# WAR MUSEUMS

## H[erbert] Bolton

*The Educational Value of Museums & The Formation of Local War Museums.*
Report of Proceedings at a Conference of the Provincial Museums in Britain to
Discuss the Relation of Museums to Education and the Formation of Local War
Museums, edited by E. Howarth. London: William Wesley & Son, pp. 71–78,
1918

---

*Herbert Bolton, writing as director of the Bristol Museum and Art Gallery,*
*confronts the problem of devising a plan to create war museums to honor*
*and remember those killed, wounded, and affected in World War I. He*
*argues that the challenge for those planning and building these facilities is*
*to create a memorial while at the same time presenting a realistic story. As*
*Bolton correctly notes: "War museums must not seek to exalt war, but rather*
*show what war means in national and personal loss."*

---

. . . I have considered what appeared to me to be an adequate War museum for any city, a museum which would give a very faithful and clear
epitome of all the activities and all the efforts of the nation as a whole during the Great War, and of that particular city in the Great War. Whether
the question of War Museums is practicable or not is one which I have
left untouched. . . .

It is clearly evident that the creation of War Museums is considered to
be advisable.

A little consideration will show that unless a definite plan and purpose
be first decided upon, the acquisition of any and every kind of war material will result in the formation of heterogeneous collections comparable to
the contents of a marine store dealer's shop. The Great War has touched

us all so nearly, it has influenced our national life, and marked its tracks so deeply upon the world as a whole, that anything short of the best possible memorial would be distressing and inadequate.

Great and fateful as the war has been and is, I think it is necessary that War Museums should attach most importance to the exemplification of those principles of unity of purpose, and of unselfish striving to a common end for the benefit and safeguarding of all, which make for a successful and happy life for all peoples of the British Empire.

*Why Needful ?*

It is the least we can do to form, as Sir Alfred Mond so aptly says, "Halls of Memory," in which to show an Empire's tribute to the willing surrender of thousands of young lives, given that freedom and home shall be retained, and it is needful, too, to show some tribute of love and honour to the thousands broken in the wars, to those who laboured, and those who suffered, that the highest ideals of mankind may be preserved and continued.

A War Museum seems the best method of showing what were the greatest stresses and dangers ever experienced by the British Empire, and of illustrating the way in which these were met and overcome.

Such a museum can also show how the Empire found and utilised tremendous reserves of power inherent in its sons and daughters, and how the untouched, unknown values of a nation were brought out under trial.

A War Museum can furnish a constant reminder that a nation can, by taking thought, find new sources of mercantile and national development, when ordinary and well-known supplies cease, for under stress of war, the British Empire has accomplished monuments of industrial, agricultural, mercantile and general progress, which under normal conditions would have taken more than one generation to achieve. This ought to be made clear to all.

A War Museum will be a permanent reminder that the crises of a nation may be overcome by the application of knowledge, resourcefulness and application, and by the breaking down of barriers which have hitherto prevented unified action.

We need War Museums as an evidence to future generations of the character, extent, and intensity of this world war, and of the methods and weapons with which it was fought.

We shall need to show its geographical areas, the ebb and flow of war, the engineering and constructional difficulties met and overcome, the nations engaged, and the lessons to be learnt of international independence and relationships.

The material of war is already colossal. The subservience of the whole world to the demands of war we know, and also the baneful effects upon human life and progress. This we must, if we can, make plain and readable, that those who come after shall not lightly emulate the enemy in fantastic visions or in drawing the sword.

Somewhere in each War Museum should be a hall of sacred memory enshrining the names and deeds of those who made the great sacrifice, and who died that we and the Empire might live. Here, too, would we place a local record of service, of men and regiments raised, of hospitals equipped, of war industries created, of new industries started. Here should be visible tokens of every effort, small or great, including the humblest with the greatest.

We may summarise all I have said by saying that a War Museum is desirable as the most suitable permanent memorial of those who fought, and those who fell, and as a monument of the profound change which has operated in all sections of national life, and lifted untold thousands to higher conceptions of public service and duty.

Yet, since the present war is itself the product of the evils of a deliberate glorification of military and naval aims and the lust for power, War Museums must not seek to exalt war, but rather show what war means in national and personal loss, in devastation, and in reversion to barbaric standards. Above all, War Museums should supply an all-powerful incentive to future generations to emulate the wonderful qualities of mind and heart, of discipline and endurance, which have been manifested so abundantly amongst the young men and young women of our time.

A War Museum should instill pride of country, determination of self-efficiency, a sense of personal responsibility, and a determination to maintain personal and national justice and uprightness. . . .

A War Museum should be a proud record, and should show the stake which the locality holds in the nation and Empire. It should, by its record of deeds done, inculcate the adoption of those qualities which make a nation truly great. It should uplift and stimulate high endeavour, and demonstrate the truest nobility of humanity in suffering and loss for the common weal, and it should show the folly and evil of unbridled power and the disaster which overtakes a nation exalting might above right. If we can erect War Museums, which shall honour and keep green the memory of those who are gone, which shall tell the mighty and sorrowful story to those who come after, and act as a deterrent to ruthless war, let us do so.

# 12

# MUSEUMS AND THE PEOPLE

## Erwin H. Barbour

*Publications of the Nebraska Academy of Sciences*, 8 (4): 1–12, 1912

*Erwin Barbour, who served as director of the University of Nebraska State
Museum from 1891 to 1941, writes about the significant relationship
between museums, particularly state museums, and the public they serve.
He extols the virtue of state museums as educational institutions, asserting
that an increase of good moral and ethical behavior in society is linked to
increase in knowledge. Barbour also argues for the need to increase access
for the working class by keeping the museum's exhibition space open on
Sundays and holidays.*

## Museums and the Public

The purpose of this paper is to set forth as plainly as possible, in the time
allotted, the important relation of museums to the public, and to explain
why one museum at least should be maintained in every state. Just as it
is necessary to have libraries, so surely is it to have museums. Libraries
are storehouses for literary productions of consequence to the people;
while museums are storehouses for material objects of art, history, and
nature. Museums are not, as some may imagine, luxuries and extravagances designed for the few, but are necessities demanded by all, and are
thoroughly practical in their aims and ends.

What could be more practical than collections of insects injurious to
vegetation from which to draw important information; or collections of

birds and beasts helpful to man; or of pathological specimens enabling people to understand certain afflictions of man and beast and their remedies? What could be more practical than a collection of building and ornamental stone, minerals and ores, gems and semi-gems, coarse clay and its products, fine porcelain clay and its products? In a like manner, what could be more practical than industrial exhibits of cotton, silk, wool, cork, and textile fabrics.

The most famous definition of a museum is that it consists of well written labels illustrated by good specimens. Well regulated museums may be viewed as archives from which great educational lessons may be drawn. They are popular training schools, academies, and colleges for those without, as well as for those with, schooling.

## Museums and the State

Because of local sympathies and interests, state museums come closest to the hearts of the people, for in them are displayed the agricultural and natural resources of one's own state, the fauna and flora of the region, relics of historic and intrinsic value, augmented by similar material from every country of the world. It is of the utmost consequence to society at large that knowledge be widely diffused, and this is the first and most important function of every state museum. Oftentimes a glance at a well installed exhibit conveys more vivid impressions in a more lasting way than does the laborious perusal of texts. Furthermore, minds unaccustomed to study find a little time spent in a museum many times as profitable as the same time spent in technical reading. Without mental fag, visitors find themselves learning concrete lessons upon each visit. This is the broadest educational opportunity which many people have.

A museum should be a source of great civic pride as well as an unlimited source of pleasurable information, study and instruction. It is the one place which garners the best and most representative material showing the state's resources. Therein are displayed agricultural collections, building materials, animals, birds, fossils, skeletons, relics, and material of special scientific and historic interest, and objects unique in themselves or in their locality. It should be a source of pride not only because it advertises, without exaggeration, the resources of a state to its best advantage, but because it attractively displays material from our own and every country.

Through the medium of these collections, representing the state's agricultural and mineral resources, many people from other states are attracted, and are led to make it their home. The array of a state's resources cannot but inspire confidence. It serves the purpose of a dignified publicity bureau, and is a more genuine and legitimate form of advertising.

## Moral Effect of Museums

The moral effect of museums on the community is invariably wholesome and good, and tends to high citizenship. Since museum exhibits arouse in people the desire to think and study, one of the most important factors of life is gained. Whenever the objects displayed prompt young people to collect and investigate for themselves along any line whatever, their thoughts are taken from commonplaces to more ennobling themes.

In recognition of this important phase, large museums provide distinct "children's museums" especially designed to interest and instruct the young, in nature, art, and science. On special days as many as forty thousand school children visit the American Museum of Natural History of New York City, receiving valuable impressions, and educational stimulus. In a like manner, it often happens that two or three hundred children visit the Nebraska State Museum during the day, and we, too, must soon provide a well equipped child's museum.

## Accessibility of Museums

Of late there has grown up a wide-spread sentiment for the opening of museums of natural history and art on Sunday afternoons, as offsets to the attractions offered by ball games, theatres, and other forms of amusement, considered harmful by many.

For the special benefit of those having no other opportunity for visiting museums and art galleries, it seems wise to keep them open on holidays.

Agassiz's great dictum, "Study nature, not books," is rendered possible through museums to a mass of people who could not otherwise study nature. Most men can travel but little. Since we are unable to go to nature, the museum endeavors to bring nature to us, and assembles objects of interest from the most remote places.

Museums, like libraries, never cease to grow. Considering the value of the material collected and donated by liberal citizens, which is assembled, classified, displayed, and labeled in museums for the use of everyone, the least the state can do is to furnish the necessary exhibition room. . . .

# 13

# STATE AND LOCAL HISTORICAL SOCIETIES
## Reuben Gold Thwaites

*The Iowa Journal of History and Politics,* 4: 245–266, 1906

*Reuben Gold Thwaites, long-time executive of the State Historical Society of Wisconsin, presented the following report,* The Best Methods of Organization and Work on the Part of State and Local Historical Societies, *at the American Historical Association's annual meeting in 1905 in response to a survey undertaken the previous year. The excerpted portion focuses primarily on recommendations regarding scope, purpose, and public presentation of history by state and local historical societies. Many of these ideas continue to guide American historical organizations.*

### . . .Organization

Each historical society is in large measure the product of local conditions and opportunities. But back of these, moulding conditions and taking advantage of opportunities, are needed individuals imbued with genuine and self-sacrificing enthusiasm in the cause. However, enthusiasm will not alone suffice; for the promoters of such enterprises should by their erudition and technical skill command the attention and respect of scholars, while by display of practical common sense, business ability, energy, and convincing arguments, they are at the same time winning the confidence of hard-headed men of affairs. Very likely this is an unusual combination of qualities, and an ideal seldom if ever realized, for historical societies can not pay large salaries. Certain it is, however, that even when liberally endowed, no society has attained its full measure of usefulness without some such personality dominating its affairs. Institutions dependent upon State aid are peculiarly in need of this vigorous personal management. The lack of it has been the undoing of a goodly share of the wrecked or moribund societies—wherein everybody's business was nobody's concern—that strew the pathway of our recent investigation.

The Massachusetts and Pennsylvania societies are prototypes of the privately-endowed organizations of the Eastern States, which without official patronage have attained strength and a high degree of usefulness; while Wisconsin, Minnesota, Iowa, and Kansas similarly stand for the State-supported institutions of the West.

Of recent years, there has appeared in several commonwealths the "State Department of Archives and History." This is an official bureau of the Commonwealth, obtaining the essential personal touch through maintenance of close relations with the State historical society, whose duties, under such conditions, are chiefly literary and advisory. Alabama and Mississippi are the typical examples; but in Iowa the State society, at the seat of the State University, retains a strong individuality in all lines of activity, despite the existence of a liberally-supported historical department at the capital; in Kansas the society has charge of the department.

As to which method is best for new Commonwealths—that of the Alabama type, that of Wisconsin, that of the Iowa compromise, or that of the Kansas union—your committee will not venture an opinion. Each has certain merits, largely dependent on conditions of environment.

When subsidized as the trustee of the State, the society has the advantage of official connection and support combined with a strong, effective personal interest among its widely distributed membership; but there is always a lurking danger of an outbreak of political jealousy of a quasi-private organization being awarded even the officially-guarded expenditure of public funds, and legislative interference is always possible. While it lacks the inspiration of personal backing, the department stands closer to the machinery of government, and although, under careful laws, removed from liability to partisan control, is not likely in the course of its work to arouse official jealousy. Its greatest danger lies in the possibility that the performance of its work may in time become perfunctory, when the public-spirited founders of the department have retired from service.

After all, the principal desideratum is, as we have indicated, the personality back of the work, rather than the form of organization. It would be unwise, even if possible, to attempt the making over of men or of methods, that in their respective environments either promise or have already attained satisfactory results. What is needed, rather, is the betterment of existing methods, and especially the enlisting in the service of well-trained and vigorous executive officers.

Inspired, doubtless, by the example of the Wisconsin society, which is in close, although not official, connection with the University of Wisconsin, there has recently been a strong tendency on the part of Western and Southern historical agencies to associate themselves with their State universities. At the university town, of all communities in the State, exists a body of scholars who can most profitably utilize the collections of the historical society. The scholars need the inspiration of persistent, intelligent collection and publication; the society managers need the academic atmosphere and academic counsel in and with which to broaden and solidify their work; while the historical library finds its raison d'etre in the largest possible clientele of users. Recognition of these facts has, wherever possible, led to a closer union between society and university; but in several States, as in Missouri and Washington, where union with existing agencies seemed impracticable to the universities, the latter have secured the organization of rival State societies at their own seats. Such an arrangement, while doubtless benefiting the universities, is apt to result in divided interest and appropriations. In several Western States, difficulties of this character present problems that doubtless will be many years in the solution.

## Scope and Purpose

Some historical organizations are founded for a single, well-defined purpose—such as the Society for the History of the Germans in Maryland, the City History Club of New York, and the Germantown Site and Relic Society—these of course find no difficulty in determining their functions. But some of the more general societies, especially in the newer States, appear to be confused in this respect, and queries are frequently raised as to their proper scope.

In the judgment of the committee, an historical society, be it sectional, State, or local, should collect all manner of archaeological, anthropological, historical, and genealogical material bearing upon the particular territory which that society seeks to represent. The problem would be simplified, were the ideal recognized that, wherever practicable, there should in each State be some one place where all manner of historical data relative to the Commonwealth at large should be placed for preservation and consultation; and in each community or county a similar treasure house for its purely local records and relics.

It would be superfluous in the present report—which is not intended as an elementary treatise—to set forth in detail the lines of work along which a local historical society may profitably employ itself. But we venture to make these general suggestions: Such an institution may properly make an accurate survey of the archaeology and ethnology of its district; not only itself acquiring a collection illustrating the same, but entering into fraternal relations with neighboring collectors, private and public, and perhaps publishing a cooperative check-list. The records of the county government (or of the town, the village, or the city), of the courts, the churches, and the schools should at least be listed if they cannot actually be procured. Diaries of original settlers, mercantile account-books, anniversary sermons, private letters describing early life and manners, field-books of surveyors, etc., are valuable manuscripts worthy of systematic collection. Local newspaper files are an important source of information, and should assiduously be collected and preserved. Pioneers should be "interviewed" by persons themselves conversant with the details of local history. All manner of miscellaneous local printed matter should be secured, such as society, church, and club year-books, programmes of local entertainments, catalogues and memorabilia of educational or other public and private institutions within the prescribed field of research—nothing of this sort comes amiss to the historical student.

Collections are naturally classified into libraries, museums, and portrait galleries. Into the library are properly deposited all manner of manuscripts, books, pamphlets, leaflets, broadsides, newspaper files, etc. They should be scientifically catalogued, so far as funds will allow, the manuscripts being if possible calendared, or in any event indexed; the least that can be expected is, that manuscripts be properly listed on standard catalogue cards. In the museum and gallery there should be deposited all portraits or relics bearing on the manners, early life, or personelle of the community or region. Public museums are frequently presented with embarrassing gifts; but tact and diplomacy can usually be depended on for eventual elimination. Perhaps in no department of a society's work are common sense and the trained judgment of the professed historical worker more frequently needed than in the conduct of the museum. This is one of the most valuable features of collection, when properly selected and administered; but unfortunately too many of our American societies are the victims of undiscriminating antiquarianism—collection for collection's sake, without method or definite notion as to the actual scholarly value of the relic. Nothing is more deadly, in historical work, than unmeaning museums of "popular attractions."

In several of our States, the archives of the Commonwealth are, when ceasing to be of immediate value in the administrative offices—"dead documents," they have somewhat inappropriately been termed—committed to the care of the State historical society or department of history. While eminently desirable, this disposition is, for various reasons, not immediately possible of attainment in every State. The State society or department may, however, properly interest itself in seeing that the archives are conveniently located and carefully preserved by public officials; and where practicable, offer expert advice as to their proper administration.

## Methods of Presentation

The gathering of material is of basic importance; but much greater skill is required adequately to disseminate that material. So far as practicable, this should be published, in order to secure the widest possible publicity and consequent usefulness.

The publications of historical societies may contain both the original material, or "sources," and the finished product, in the form of monographs, essays, or addresses. State societies should certainly include in their publications everything of value to students to be found in the archives of the Commonwealth; local organizations may with equal profit search their several county and municipal records for all data of historical importance. Bibliographies and checklists of publications relative to State and local history are also desirable.

These publications should be well and attractively printed, on good paper, and as skillfully edited as possible. So far as the canons of scholarship will allow, they should be capable of popular understanding and appreciation. The mass of publications by our American societies is large, although by no means as extensive as it properly might be. Unfortunately, neither the dictates of typographical taste nor of scholarship have always been followed, so that we have upon our library shelves devoted to State and local annals much that is inaccurate as to matter, mechanically execrable, and in general slipshod. It is high time that those historical societies sinning in this respect bestir themselves, and inaugurates a more scientific treatment of their otherwise useful material. We have come to the stage that competent editors are needed quite as much as indefatigable collectors.

State or local bibliography is an important and much needed work, that may well be undertaken by historical societies, each in its own class. The example of The State Historical Society of Iowa in inaugurating a monographic industrial history of that State, and a reprint of important State papers, is worthy of emulation. Many local societies are, in our opinion, spending far too largely of their substance in genealogical research and publications. With numerous professed genealogical societies in the field, to say nothing of the often useful patriotic hereditary chapters—too few of which, however, are publishing things worth while—the general historical organization may with more appropriateness devote itself chiefly to the abundant task of putting forth documentary material and monographs bearing upon its field. Any enterprising and skillfully conducted society, once entering upon publication, will find the possibilities in this direction practically endless. . . .

The museum is also an important, although necessarily limited, means of presentation of material. With tasteful and carefully phrased labels, changing exhibits of books and manuscripts, loan collections, lectures to teachers and pupils of the public schools, bibliographical references, etc., much may here be done to arouse and maintain public interest.

## Interesting the Public

Indeed, this matter of arousing and maintaining public interest is, of itself, an important function of an historical society; but obviously this should be an intelligent, discriminating interest. Field meetings, popular lectures, work with the schools, some measure of coordination with the pioneer and old settlers' societies of the district, pilgrimages to places of historic interest, the promotion of anniversary celebrations, and the placing of tablets upon historic sites, all of these are within the province of the society.

The enlistment of college and university interests is likewise highly desirable, especially in the matter of research and preparing material for publications; although in becoming academic the society should be careful not to remove life itself too far from the understanding and sympathy of the common people. Popularity and exact scholarship are not incompatible. One of the principal aims of an historical society should be the cultivation among the masses of that civic patriotism which is inevitably the outgrowth of an attractive presentation of local history.

Logically, there is no reason why the work of collecting and disseminating historical material should not be quite as much a public charge as that of the public library or of the public museum. But the fact that historical work appears to be best prosecuted by individual enthusiasm, seems to render essential the society organization; and in many communities it is, as already intimated, difficult to convince legislative assemblies that a semi-private body should receive public aid. This objection is not insuperable, provided there are not, as in some States, likewise constitutional barriers. In the West, arrangements have been entered into whereby the society, in accepting public aid, becomes the trustee of the Commonwealth, as the custodian of State property; yet in no sense does the society surrender its scholastic individuality. In Buffalo, the local society bears much the same relationship to the municipality, in return for the latter's annual stipend. Even under the most favorable political conditions, however, there is small chance for the historical society obtaining official aid unless its work is winning popular appreciation. . . .

# 14

## ON THE IDEAL RELATIONS OF PUBLIC LIBRARIES, MUSEUMS, AND ART GALLERY TO THE CITY

### Oliver C. Farrington

Report of Subcommittee of the City Charter Committee of the Chicago Library Club. Chicago, IL: Chicago Library Club, 4 pp.

*Oliver Farrington, Curator of Geology at the Field Museum of Natural History and President of the American Association of Museums from 1914–1916, was chair of the subcommittee that prepared this brief report for the Chicago Library Club in the early 1900s. Although the report pertains specifically to Chicago institutions, it provides unique insight into the philosophy of governance of nonprofit organizations in the early twentieth century.*

The purpose of this Committee, if I have correctly conceived it, is to determine what relations should ideally exist between the public libraries, museums and art galleries of the City of Chicago and the people of the city, in order that the people of the city may derive the greatest possible benefit from these institutions, their right to this benefit being based upon the financial and other support which they give them. Institutions not indebted in any way to the people for support may be eliminated from this discussion. It should be remembered, too, that institutions supported in part by private endowment are by so much removed from public obligation. That the support and maintenance of such institutions by the people is desirable need not be questioned, nor is it important to enter here into a discussion of how many or how large such institutions should be with relation to the population and valuation of the city. Some such institutions exist, more will be established in the future. How shall they be of the greatest good to the greatest number?

Probably the only practical and hence the ideal way for the people to control the derivation of benefits from such institutions is to entrust their interests to a governing Board, who shall seek to promote through the interests of the institutions those of the people.

Of whom, then, shall the Board be constituted? Of how many persons shall it consist? What compensation, if any, should be paid? What should be the term of office of the members? By whom shall the members be appointed or elected? What shall be the powers of the Board? Shall it be divided into parts, or govern all institutions of the character named as a whole! These are questions which should be thoughtfully and carefully answered.

1. Considering the last of these questions first, it is the opinion of the Committee that all institutions of the character named should in some way be treated as a whole. Their aims and purposes are in a large way the same, and it seems desirable therefore that an intimate co-operation and comity should exist between them. The museum illustrates the objects of which the library tells; the library describes the objects which the museum exhibits. Art and science depend upon literature for their preservation and progress, and literature finds its stimulus in art and science. Any way of facilitating communication and mutual action among institutions representing these aims which shall at the same time preserve the individual purpose of each is worthy an effort at adoption.

2. Of whom shall the Board be constituted? The questions with which it must deal will include finance, public welfare and technical progress. It must be as capable in directing the growth of such institutions as in keeping their expenditures within their resources. It would seem, therefore, that in addition to those upon such a board capable in financial management, there should be those familiar with the people's needs from the lowliest station to the loftiest and in addition those versed in art, science and literature.

3. Of how many persons should the Board consist? Large bodies move slowly, and are expensive. Action would be favored by a small, compact number, deliberation and representation by a large one. It should be possible to find a mean which shall best avoid each extreme.

4. What compensation, if any, should be paid? Unrewarded labor, whether in public or private business, is sure to be of indifferent

value. However good the intentions are and however public the spirit is, without an adequate return in some form for service, interests intended to be served will inevitably lag and lapse. The people should not ask or expect gratuitous service any more than an individual. On the other hand, high compensation, instead of attracting the best talent, as might be expected, seems likely, in public service especially, to make the places such as shall be striven for on account of the compensation alone to the neglect of the service for which the compensation was to be received. Here again then it would seem that a mean should be reached providing fair compensation for service rendered.

5. What should be the term of office of members of a governing Board? Short terms prevent acquiring familiarity with duties and profiting by experience. Long terms suffer from senility and indifference. Reappointment during satisfactory service seems to best answer the needs in this respect.

6. By whom shall the Board be appointed or elected? Appointments made by one official suffer from favoritism and the absolute inability of one individual to become acquainted with the needs along many different lines. Appointments by a board are open to the same objection, but in a lesser degree if a board adequate to the situation exists, but no such board seem as yet to have been constituted. Election by the people multiplies the perplexities of the voter and inclines him to escape the perplexities by accepting the nominations of his party managers, whether good or bad. Thus it seems that a commission constituted somewhat like a civil service commission for the purpose of careful consideration of appointments like this would be eminently desirable. Another method of appointment, and one which would seem to be sufficiently ideal, would be that of one member from each board of trustees or staff of institutions of the character we are considering, together with one member of the School Board, one from the City Council, one from a social settlement and three members at large.

7. What should be the powers of such a Board? It is here that ideals are likely to be most rudely jostled by realities. Existing institutions have their methods, customs, traditions, which it would be neither expedient nor wise suddenly to change. It may be said, therefore, that such a Board would find its own powers; that its efforts might properly be simply advisory at first and gradually it might find ways in which more direct service could be rendered. Nevertheless since your Committee has for its province the consideration of ideals alone, the ideal may be stated that the Board should have power to

receive and expend appropriations for and in other ways promote, as they may best be able, the extension and distribution among the people of the City of Chicago of the privileges of her public libraries, museums and art galleries in proportion to the extent to which these institutions are supported and maintained by the people.

# 15

# THE ART MUSEUM AND THE PUBLIC

**Mariana Alley [Griswold] Van Rensselaer [published as Mrs. Schuyler Van Rensselaer]**

*The North American Review*, 205: 81–92, 1917

*Mariana Griswold Van Rensselaer, artist, architect, and landscape designer, writes about issues regarding interactions between museums and the public—many of which remain of concern today—ranging from questions of how much material should be exhibited in museums to questions of a social nature that considered whether or not art museums should exhibit ethnographic materials and industrial arts. Van Rensselaer's educational philosophy derived from her belief that there existed an "intimate connection that may and should exist between art and life."*

. . . The first to consider is the fact that sensitiveness to the beauty that resides in works of art is not synonymous with knowledge in regard to them. True appreciation of the beauty that appeals at once to eye and mind, to sense and soul, must be based upon something more than historical and critical knowledge, even of the widest and wisest kind. But too commonly in the past we have thought that its foundations could be set upon teachings of a far inferior sort—upon a mixture of scrappy historical and biographical information, studio common-places and paradoxes, vague aesthetic theories, and a superficial acquaintance, usually at second or third hand, with what is 'considered the best' in the art of the present and the past. Such 'knowledge of art' as this cannot be of much use; certainly of none in developing a sensitiveness to the emotional, inspirational influence of beauty.

What, then, can be done in the way of teaching true appreciation? Some will answer, Nothing. A person may be taught to paint, they say— taught up to a certain point and if he has certain gifts; but only from art itself can he learn appreciation. And this last is true. It is true that no one can learn appreciation from the words or the books of others. Every one must teach himself. His own eye must be his preceptor. He must look at the actual things of beauty, and look, and look again until they become their own interpreters, speaking their own messages of spiritual as well as technical import. Without this kind of self-education all other efforts are in vain.

But in this essential work of self-instruction, books and teachers can guide and help. A certain amount of historical and technical knowledge is necessary, in-deed, for the right and full understanding of what the eye shall eventually teach itself to see and to love. Only with this kind of aid can we relate the works that we are looking at to the men who produced them, and contrast them with other developments similarly understood; and only by this process can we learn the reasons for the differences between the various forms and phases of plastic art so that, by clearly seeing them, we may deeply feel the intrinsic individual qualities of each, never duplicated in other places or other times. Moreover, no man's eye can be as sensitive as it might become, his judgments as trust-worthy, even his emotions as susceptible, if they are not stimulated and clarified by a knowledge of what other men have seen and thought and felt.

None the less the main preceptor must always be one's own eye, and the way to cultivate its powers must always be to use them. This means that, as conditions are in our country today, almost all valid training in the appreciation of art must be gained in the public museum or gallery. And it follows that in all possible ways the museum, the gallery, should itself facilitate, stimulate, and guide the self-education of the people.

Not by all those who manage our museums or are personally concerned with their development is this implication accepted. In fact, it is fuel just now for fires of discussion. Should an art museum, it is asked, exist primarily for the benefit of the general public or, as some one once said of a university, 'for the cherishing of gifted persons'? The right answer would seem to be that a museum should exist for the gifted person and also for the public at large, just as a public library must serve all classes of men and every grade of mind. Some will insist that the general public cannot profit by an art museum as even the unintellectual may by a library, and cannot, in any degree worth recognizing and working for, be led so to profit. Nevertheless the conviction spreads that the people in general must be considered, and that if the effort be well made it will prove well worth the making. There could hardly be a different decision in democratic communities. "All men are equal," it has been said, in having "an equal right to spiritual activities," and society needs that the opportunity for such activities should to all men be given.

But granted that the effort be worth making, how shall we make it? Here controversies begin again. For example, if a museum is to serve for the cultivation of the public taste, is it well to confine its exhibits to the products of the 'fine arts' strictly so-called? Or may it better include in addition artistic things of which the value is partly industrial, historical, or ethnographical? Again, whatever its scope, should it harbor only things of the very best according to high critical standards? Or should it be more leniently inclusive, accepting the testimony of almost all lovers of art that they began by liking things that were not the very best and gradually, naturally developed a truer taste?. . . .

We have outlived the needy, tentative, timid period when a museum, afraid to make an enemy or to discourage a possible friend, docilely accepted almost all that was offered it—superfluous things, inappropriate things, inferior things, some-times things that ought to have gone instead to the boarding-house parlor or the junk-heap. Nowadays a museum is rarely afraid to reject what it does not want, and a donor is often modest enough to offer, while alive or after death, merely such a selection from his actual or supposititious treasures as the museum itself may see fit to make. It would be of benefit, though, if intending donors would more often find out in advance how the institution they wish to aid may best be aided; and also if they would remember that one very fine object is more to be desired than several of less distinction.

The larger our museums become the oftener it is asked whether, because of the fatigue of body and confusion of mind which result from seeing too many things at once, a number of smaller buildings in various parts of a city would not be better than a single one of great size housing a great variety of collections. It ought to be obvious that any one needs only a little self-control to divide for his own use the largest museum into as many of as small a size as he may prefer to visit. Perhaps it is not as easy for every one to understand how greatly the cost of establishing and building a museum, and especially the heavy cost of running it, would be increased by a policy of dispersion. But the chief argument for large museums is that the more varied in kind are the collections under a single roof, the better are the opportunities for study, whether of a very serious kind or not. . . .

Difficult indeed in a large museum is the task of arrangement, for arrangement means classification, and classification is a problem which seldom admits of perfect solutions—only of more or less satisfactory approximations. Because of the gradual passing of one historical period into another and the interlocking of the activities of different peoples, even the broad assorting of objects of art according to their origins in time and place is not always plain sailing. Then, when all the material for a department has been brought together, shall it be grouped according to kinds or chronologically? Shall all the sculptures of classic Greece, for example, be kept together, all the vases, all the bronzes? Or shall all the things of the archaic periods of Grecian art be associated and, progressively, all those of each later period? The first is the old traditional plan, still adhered to in many departments of American museums and beloved by the special student of some one form of art. The other is more modern; for the average visitor its results are more instructive, and are much more interesting and attractive, as, to give an instance, the popularity of the Egyptian rooms in the Metropolitan Museum clearly shows; and it is certain more and more to prevail or to be combined with the older method of grouping.

Again: Whichever method of arrangement is chosen, should it be guided by a policy of generous inclusiveness or of fastidious selection? If the department is rich in material, should all of this be shown in the main galleries or only the finest objects while the others are kept in reserve where the seriously interested may find them by seeking or be shown them for the asking? This may seem merely a question of degree, but in reality it marks two quite different theories as to how the eye and the mind of the visitor may best be served and as to what kind of visitor is best worth serving. If the public could express its opinion I am sure that it would favor the plentiful display, the opportunity to see, without special seeking, as much as is available of each form and phase of art. We know that experts can decide, much better than we could ourselves, what things are worthy of a place in a museum; but we are not so willing to have them say which among these good things are the best for us to look at. We want, and if we are to enlarge our powers of appreciation we need, to see as much as can be shown us. We want to see for ourselves why some good things are more admirable than others, and to decide which to our own eyes and our own spirit are the most eloquent of beauty and charm. "The world," writes Emerson, meaning that general verdict which in the long run establishes the value of human products, "selects for us the best and we select from that best, our best." Until we can do this we have no true titles of ownership in the domains of beauty.

Moreover, a number of objects of the same kind have a power to interest, to impress, that one or two such objects in isolation may not possess. To say this is, I know, to run counter to certain current ideas—to the idea, for instance, that we ought to imitate the Japanese in their love of the sparse appeal to the eye, of the isolated work of art. But we are not Japanese nor of the same mental and emotional stock. . . .

With the great resources now at their disposal our museums are working out schemes of various kinds for the definite instruction of the public—not all of them as yet but an ever-growing number of the large and the small. Study-rooms devoted to one branch of art or another, hand-books and special treatises, illustrated lectures delivered in the museum or elsewhere to children and to divers classes of adults, tours of the galleries under guidance, loan collections sent to various parts of the city—these are some of the methods that they adopt, always with the conviction that true teaching means advising the eye how to educate itself and there-fore always with the aid of the museum collections. Often they work in collaboration with the college or the school. Sometimes their aim is to inspire workers in the industrial arts, or to increase the knowledge and develop the taste of manufacturers or salespeople, or to aid the teacher of drawing or of history, and some-times simply to cultivate the love of art and beauty. The paths thus opened are wide, and it is not easy to know just how they should be pursued with regard either to ultimate aims or to immediate methods. Little help can be got from precedents, for even in Europe, outside of Italy, the museum of art is a relatively new institution; still more modern, distinctively of our own day, is the desire to utilize it for the cultivation of the people at large; and many of our needs and difficulties are proper to our own land as well as our own time. It is our museums themselves that have started this novel work. It has already been heartily endorsed and facilitated by schools and colleges and by national, State, and municipal authorities concerned with education, but to make it really effective it must also win the support of all others who care for education and who care for art. "What is now needed is a nation-wide appreciation of the value of visual instruction as afforded by museums."

"Visual instruction"—this, it cannot be too often reiterated, is the only valid kind, and for the most part the instructor must be the learner's own eye. Therefore we must think with satisfaction that, whatever else the teaching given in our museums may or may not effect, it can hardly fail to do good by laying in many cases a foundation for what has been called the "museum habit." To look at works of art only, so to say, by accident, to "find time" for them only in an occasional hour when nothing in par-ticular beckons elsewhere, can profit no one much. We must take time for looking at them. We must make time to form a habit which will become, like reading books or going to concerts, a part of the routine of our lives. The difficulty of forming a new habit in busy adult years is a strong argu-ment for opening a museum freely to children whether they come for definite instruction or not. And to cultivate it in children and in adults. The museum should do more than offer instruction, more than get fine things and arrange them well. It should make the looking at them as easy and attractive as possible. . . .

Really, the trouble in most of our American cities is that the people do not feel enough at home in their palaces of art. They enter them too much as though they were the palaces of kings, condescendingly opened for their timid inspection. Many are awed by the space, the silence, and what seems to them the grandeur of their unaccustomed surroundings. They do not need to be discouraged from staying too long. They need to be made to feel that they are very welcome, that the place exists for them. Many other people even among the professedly cultivated—the vogue of loan collections makes it plain—visit galleries of art as a certain kind of woman goes about among the shops, "just to see what they have got," and having superficially seen this, do not come again until the stock has been replenished with novelties. But in some of our public galleries it is largely the fault of the management that visitors do not more often buy with periods of quiet contemplation, and take away in their memories as their own possession for ever, the treasures of beauty that are displayed before them. . . .

Here we find the answer to a question left unanswered on an earlier page: In our large museums of art should the lines be drawn to embrace "fine art" only? Evidently not. Indeed, when we think what art really meant to any really creative people, we must mourn that the term "fine art" has been incorporated in the name and that its implications have been respected in the policy of any large American museum. Evidently the public is right when it takes a special interest in a broadly inclusive collection of the work of a people like the Egyptians, who never made a useful object without striving to please the eye, and seem scarcely ever to have made a beautiful object which did not serve some definite purpose. To show the artistic products of each land and period as inclusively as possible, and with their aid to explain as clearly as possible the intimate interweaving of art with every phase of the life of the people that produced it, surely, in the America of today, which lacks the vivid object-lessons bequeathed by the past to older countries, this is the proper aim of a museum—not to set art aside from life by trying to segregate its higher "purer" forms.

One way to emphasize the intimate connection that may and should exist between art and life is to show the affinities of the art with the history and the literature of any given period. Writing recently in the Yale Review of the study of Greek in our schools and colleges, Professor Goodell explained that, while the study of the language has been falling off, interest in Greek art has greatly increased, so that "museums are now the chief agencies for cultivating a popular interest in old Greece." Should not their contents, he asks, incarnating the same spirit that speaks in the history and the literature of Greece, "claim a large place in the college"? Should not this possibility of high service, I may add, be remembered in collecting and displaying them? And must not any attempt to isolate certain classes of things, even though they be the highest, from their natural relationships in time and place, and to exhibit them simply as specimens of an abstract thing called "fine art," impair even their own esthetic value?

Finally, let us be serious about all these matters but not too serious. Art, after all, is for the pleasuring of man's eye. It must begin with this if it is to do more by touching his imagination, by cultivating that thing called taste which has its spiritual as well as its physical side; and if it stops with the beginning, even so there is something gained. There is a great deal gained in the case of the many who, under our conditions of life, are almost wholly disinherited of harmless forms of enjoyment. . . .

Today we offer our urban populations one beautiful and beneficent thing that medieval people did not have, the public park. But apart from this, what? Little excepting the museum of art. If they find pleasure there, even unaccompanied by such profit as we hope that many of them will also reap, surely the benefit will react upon us all; for to be starved for pleasure is as bad for a man as to be starved for bread and is even more provocative of evil thoughts and deeds.

So a first and foremost duty of a museum room is *not to look dreary*. Yet I remember some that do—some that are cold and colorless, inhospitable, even empty-looking although in fact they contain very beautiful and precious things. It is not enough to show such things. Each room as a whole, the museum as a whole, must at least be pleasing to the sight. If it can be sumptuous, a veritable expression of "the riches of art," so much the better. And why should not a museum dedicated to plastic art be used to further other kinds of esthetic enjoyment which will be beneficial in themselves and will attract people who might not otherwise seek its collections? What most surely and widely attracts our people today is music. Is there any good reason—that is, any unsurmountable reason—why at certain times music should not be provided for them in our art museums as it is in our parks, but of a higher quality than is there appropriate?

# 16

# ENGLISH ART CONNOISSEURSHIP AND COLLECTING

## Sir J[ohn] C[harles] Robinson

*Nineteenth Century*, 35: 523–537, 1894

*Sir John Robinson, Surveyor of the Queen's Pictures, in the Royal Collection Department of the Royal Household of the Sovereign of the United Kingdom, from 1880 to 1901, discusses the decline of art connoisseurship in England at the end of the nineteenth century in the following excerpted article. Robinson indicates that national museums of art were no longer the center of the art world, as a more common class of wealthy "merchants, financiers, and manufacturers," and numerous newly established public museums in England and other countries, now competed for these treasures. The cumulative result, according to Robinson, was a loss of fine art, particularly that of the "old masters," to the uncultured masses.*

A consideration of the present range of art collecting in this country would, as might be expected, display a remarkable reversal of established orders of things and the strangest variations of values and appreciations.

Wealth, it is scarcely necessary to say, is a prime and indispensable factor in these pursuits, and wealth is now so widely and so capriciously distributed that the narrow bounds of former times, when the special predilections of limited classes held undisputed sway, have in our own day been infinitely extended and overpassed.

A century ago the appreciation and acquisition of works of art of all kinds was almost entirely confined to the aristocracy of the land—the nobility, landed gentry, and classically educated few, for whom, in particular, the luxury of foreign travel was within the bounds of possibility. A few rich bankers and merchants, consorting with and blending into the privileged classes, from time to time took up collecting pursuits; but the manufacturer and average trader had not yet thought of adding the graces of art to their homes, and the expenditure of considerable sums on unproductive works of art was not to be thought of by the frugal-minded, middle-class citizen.

If, moreover, such individuals had been solicitous to improve their tastes, and to enter, no matter how humbly and tentatively, into the field of art collecting, there were scarcely any means at their disposal for acquiring knowledge and familiarity with the works and monuments from which their tastes might have been formed.

There were no public art galleries in this country, and only one public museum deserving of the name in the entire length and breadth of the land in which art objects found a place. The scheme of the British Museum only indirectly concerned itself with art, and there was as yet no National Gallery or South Kensington.

Few and hurried visits to the show houses of the richer territorial magnates adorned with their miscellaneous and often in great part apocryphal art treasures, were in short, almost the only opportunities for the inspection and study of works of art in our grandfathers' days.

Art dealers were rare when clients were so few in number, and the shops of the few individuals of that class who were established in the metropolis (for elsewhere no such adventurers could have made a living) were but poorly furnished, and the wares dealt in very limited in kind.

Under this restricted *régime* the public galleries and museums of the Continent of Paris, Rome, and Florence—were the cynosure of all who in any way concerned themselves with art matters; but these were to be visited, if at all, once in a lifetime only. All this is now altered. The rich merchants, financiers, and manufacturers have taken, the places of the cultured and travelled lords and gentlemen of old, and the ancestral mansions and country seats of these latter are now yielding up their accumulated treasures at a far more rapid rate than they were acquired.

Now, however, there is scarcely a town in the land of any importance without its public art gallery and museum, endless special exhibitions take place, and the ubiquitous art dealer is in evidence in every main thoroughfare. Whether this vast increase of opportunity has appreciably improved and refined the national standards of taste in art is a question I have to propound. That it has developed an infinite activity which did not formerly exist is evident, but that it has raised those art standards to a higher level is, perhaps, doubtful.

It need scarcely be said that a taste for collecting may be nothing more than a senseless mania or an elevating and refining pursuit, as the case may be. When there were very few collectors the instances of the former kind were not conspicuous. Now, it cannot be denied that the miscellaneous gatherers of fashionable wares of little artistic value, and the dupes of the ever-increasing race of purveyors of fraudulent art products are as legion in this country, whilst the connoisseurs of real taste and knowledge are perhaps relatively fewer in number. It is indeed a common saying that there are scarcely any of the old race of learned and enthusiastic art amateurs left in England, and almost as few professional purveyors of real acquirements. At the same time there are unquestionable indications that other countries do not follow exactly on the same lines. Certain it is that England is showing a less strong attachment to the highest class of monuments of art than formerly, or than other countries, so that in too many instances our most precious possessions are now being reft from us by the superior appreciation of our continental neighbours.

The field of appreciation of the last-century English art amateur was, it is true, very restricted, but the categories it included were of the highest and most genuine. The terms "high art" and the "fine arts" indicated paintings and drawings of all kinds—prints or engravings, sculpture almost exclusively of the ancient Greek and Roman epochs, engraved gems, and perhaps coins and medals, though these latter formed a class apart, occupying the border-land only, so to speak, of "fine art." In those classes there were ardent and systematic English collectors, for the most part high-born and wealthy—the class to whom high prices and liberal dealing were customary in all relations of life. Doubtless this was a narrow and rather exclusive status in which unreasoning fashion and custom had perhaps as much to do as real understanding of the innate values of things, but the art fashions in those days ran in genuine if too rigidly bounded lines. Nevertheless there were even in the last century one or two notable examples of wider and more sympathetic culture. Horace Walpole and Sir Andrew Fountaine were able to throw off conventional trammels and make excursions in the wider fields of Mediaeval and Renaissance art. The *chefs-d'oeuvre* of goldsmith works and the triumphs of the potters' and enamellers' rafts. Gothic and Renaissance art ornamentation of all kinds, severely kept down and dominated by the all-pervading and infinitely greater prestige of the antique, were undervalued and neglected categories it is true, but the seeds of the vast and perhaps disproportionate appreciation of the present day were at all events sown in this country by these early pioneers. Needless to say that the weathercock of time has veered completely round, and that an age of *bric-à-brac* has succeeded to that of the old rigid classicism. . . .

It will be interesting and pertinent to my theme—that of illustrating the variations and vagaries of taste in collecting in this country—to dwell rather more at length on this specialty of drawings by the old masters. In no other class of art monuments is the history, or, in other words, the successive ownership of the specimens so readily ascertainable, and this from a custom which for obvious reasons was almost confined to this specialty. From the earliest time it has been the habit of possessors of ancient drawings to set their marks of possession upon them in the form of small impressed stamps, or else to write their initials in minute characters usually in the lower corners of the drawings. Others have signed their names in full, sometimes accompanied by information as to the previous history and "provenance" at the back of the drawing, or with critical information as to the authenticity or subject of the work. Innumerable examples of these certificated specimens exist; some bearing a succession of these marks of ownership forming valuable and instructive pedigrees, and adding greatly to the intrinsic value and interest of the drawings. For obvious reasons this custom was confined almost exclusively to this class, and in a less degree to that of prints and engravings. The well-known marks of successive generations of English collectors, from the age of Charles the First downwards, are greatly in excess of those of all other countries, and as the names and periods of activity of nearly all these individuals are well known, it is easy to note the periods of the greatest development of this pursuit.

At the present day this branch of connoisseurship has greatly declined in England, and it will be interesting to take note of the causes which have contributed to bring about this result. In the first place, unquestionably the public museums, both of our own and other countries, have, in the long run, permanently withdrawn from circulation and locked up a large proportion of the most important specimens in this limited category. Naturally at almost every dispersion of the gatherings of individual collectors toll has been taken in this manner. From the mere fact of the increasing scarcity of specimens, the collectors have become less numerous; but changes of fashion and a general lowering of standards of taste and excellence have, I think, had a greater share in bringing about the comparative neglect in which this branch of art has fallen in this country. The collecting of ancient drawings was very actively carried on in the days following the original impulse under Charles the First. The pursuit greatly developed itself further on in the century, and attained to a high pitch during its latter years and the beginning of the succeeding one, in the splendid gatherings of Sir Peter Lely and the two Richadsons. It is to be noted that professional artists of eminence, as might have been expected, have always been the keenest and most enlightened gatherers of these special treasures. Professional appreciation, in fact, came to a climax in the case of Sir Thomas Lawrence during the first quarter of the present century, when probably the great majority of the rarest and finest ancient drawings extant, other than in the mortmain of national collections, were swept into the net of this indefatigable collector. So extensive indeed was this withdrawal of the materials, that the pursuit was practically almost brought to an end and rendered almost impossible to Lawrence's contemporaries; a decided check was thus given to the formation of collections of ancient drawings in England from which it has never recovered.

Although in its turn the great Lawrence Collection was thrown upon the market, the charm was at an end. An era of apathy and ignorance set in. The unique and world-renowned treasures of that great collection were ultimately sacrificed for a mere fraction of their cost, and far too large a portion of them were carried out of England. . . .

One of the chief reasons for the enduring influence of Italy has, however, been already alluded to. It was in the churches and public museums, and the princely and precious collections of that country, that the most extensive and varied aggregation of art monuments was to be found. To the connoisseur then, Italian travel and residence was indispensable to the acquisition of real knowledge and taste; and as the patrons of art in former times were mainly of this class, artists had of necessity to follow in their wake, and to model themselves more or less on the lines of their employers. Hence, again, a reason for the thraldom of the "old masters," for the deep-toned darkness of age, the *atramentum* of old days and antique authority. Needless to say it, a single visit to the Royal Academy Exhibition would suffice to show what a gulf there is betwixt the dominant ideals and styles in art of a century ago and those of to-day. In this age of positive brightness of crude unmitigated pigment, it is hard indeed to realise the feeling which prompted Sir George Beaumont to formulate his well-known dictum that fine pictures should have the low rich tone of the back of an old fiddle. . . .

# SECTION III

## The New Museum

In July 1893, Sir William Henry Flower, director of the natural history departments of the British Museum in South Kensington, delivered his presidential address before the British Association for the Advancement of Science. He credited John Edward Gray, keeper of zoology at the British Museum, with conceiving of what Flower termed "the new museum idea." This concept emphasized the importance of developing educational programs for public instruction that would include an exhibition space separate from the research collections within natural science museums.

Historian Charles Coleman Sellers (1980b) has since challenged Flower's assertion that Gray was the "first" museum administrator to conceive of this idea. In an article titled "Peale's Museum and the New Museum Idea," Sellers asserted that it was in fact Charles Willson Peale, founder of the first public natural history museum in the United States, who instituted "that broad educational purpose" in the Hall of the American Philosophical Society" in the form of "attractive, entertaining exhibits" and "illustrated lectures and demonstrations" in 1794. Whether Gray or Peale first conceived of this idea, it was certainly Flower who first implemented it successfully. Flower promoted the "new museum idea" at the British Museum in the early 1880s—the new building at South Kensington was designed with a public exhibition space separate from the research collections. Assistant

Director of the U. S. National Museum, George Brown Goode, started a simultaneous movement in the United States. The new National Museum building opened in 1881 with prominent space devoted to public exhibition galleries.

The first four articles in this section were written in the late nineteenth century and concern the public side of the "new museum." William Stanley Jevons and George Brown Goode develop a "general theory of administration," and Benjamin Ives Gilman and John Cotton Dana form an interesting contrast as Gilman takes issue with many of Goode's ideas while Dana supports them. The final two essays—Grinnell and Rowe—are some of the earliest discussions of what we now call museum ethics. The emerging interest and "need" for ethics were a direct result of the new museum movement: as museums became more responsive to outside forces there was a developing museum profession that needed to set its standards.

### Additional Reading

Andrei, Mary Anne, and Hugh H. Genoways. 1997. Museum ethics. *Curator: The Museum Journal* 40: 6–12.

Bloom, Joel N., and Earl A. Powell. 1984. *Museums for a new century: A report of the Commission on Museums for a New Century.* Washington, DC: American Association of Museums.

Edson, Gary. 1997. *Museum ethics.* New York: Routledge.

Weil, Stephen E. 1990. *Rethinking the museum and other meditations.* Washington, DC: Smithsonian Institution Press.

———. 1995. *A cabinet of curiosities.* Washington, DC: Smithsonian Institution Press.

———. 2002. *Making museums matter.* Washington, DC: Smithsonian Institution Press.

# 17

# THE USE AND ABUSE OF MUSEUMS

## W. Stanley Jevons

*Methods of Social Reform and Other Papers*. London: Macmillan Co., pp. 53–81, 1883

*William Stanley Jevons, renowned economist and logician, reviews the state of museums in England in the early 1880s in the following condensed article. He argues that the primary use of museums should be for public education but laments that Europe's museums were failing this mission. He cites as the primary agent of this failure the systematic or synoptic exhibits that crowded exhibit galleries with objects—these ideas were foundational in establishing the "new museum" movement. Jevons concludes by calling for professionalization of the field, which later occurred with the founding of the Museums Association in England in 1889 and the American Association of Museums in the United States in 1906.*

It is a remarkable fact that, although public Museums have existed in this country for more than a century and a quarter, and there are now a very great number of Museums of one sort or another, hardly anything has been written about their general principles of management and economy. In the English language, at least, there is apparently not a single treatise analysing the purposes and kinds of Museums, or describing systematically the modes of arrangement. In the course of this article I shall have occasion to refer to a certain number of lectures, addresses, or papers which have touched more or less expressly upon this subject; but these are all of a slight and brief character. The only work at all pretending to a systematic form with which I am acquainted is that upon "The Administrative Economy of the Fine Arts in England," by Mr. Edward Edwards, of the

British Museum. But this book was printed as long ago as 1840, and has long been forgotten, if indeed it could ever have been said to be known. Moreover it is mostly concerned with the principles of management of art galleries, schools of art, and the like. Many of the ideas put forward by Edwards have since been successfully fathered by better-known men, and some of his suggestions, such as that of multiplying facsimiles of the best works of art, are only now approaching realisation.

It is true, indeed, that a great deal of inquiry has taken place from time to time about the British Museum, which forms the Alpha, if not the Omega, of this subject. Whatever has been written about Museums centres upon the great national institution in Bloomsbury. . . .

Depending chiefly upon my own memory of many museums and exhibitions which I have visited from time to time, to endeavour to arrive at some conception of the purposes, or rather the many purposes, which should be set before us in creating public collections of the kind, and the means by which those purposes may be most readily attained. Although the subject has hardly received any attention as yet, I believe it is possible to show on psychological or other scientific grounds that much which has been done in the formation of Museums is fundamentally mistaken. In other cases it is more by good luck than good management that a favourable result has been attained. In any case a comparison of the purposes and achievements of Museums must be instructive.

According to its etymology the name Museum means a temple or haunt of the Muses, and any place appropriated to the cultivation of learning, music, pictorial art, or science might be appropriately called a Museum. On the Continent they still use Musée in a rather wider sense than we in England use Museum; but it is remarkable that, although the art of delighting by sound has long been called emphatically Music, we never apply the name Museum to a Concert Hall. In this country we have specialised the word so much that we usually distinguish Museums from libraries, picture galleries and music halls, reserving the name for collections and displays of scientific specimens, or concrete artistic objects and curiosities of various kinds. As a library contains books which speak from the printed page, or the ancient inscribed parchment, so the Museum contains the books of Nature, and the sermons which are in stones. About the use and abuse of printed books there cannot arise much question. It may be assumed as a general rule that when a person reads a book, he understands it and draws some good from it. The labour of reading is a kind of labour test, and gives statistics to the effect that certain classes of books are used so many times in the year on the average; there is little need to go behind these facts. But it is somewhat otherwise with public Museums, because the advantage which an individual gets from the visit may vary from nil up to something extremely great. The degree of instruction derived is quite incapable of statistical determination. Not only is there great difference in degree, but there is vast difference also in the kind of benefit derived. Many go to a public Museum just as they take a walk, without thought or care as to what they are going to see; others have a vague idea that they will be instructed and civilised by seeing a multitude of novel and beautiful objects; a very small fraction of the total public go because they really understand the things displayed, and have got ideas about them to be verified, corrected, or extended. Unfortunately it is difficult to keep the relative values of these uses of a Museum distinct. There seems to be a prevalent idea that if the populace can only be got to walk about a great building filled with tall glass-cases, full of beautiful objects, especially when illuminated by the electric light, they will become civilised. At the South Kensington Art Museum they make a great point of setting up turnstiles to record the precise numbers of visitors, and they can tell you to a unit the exact amount of civilising effect produced in any day, week, month, or year. But these turnstiles hardly take account of the fact that the neighbouring wealthy residents are in the habit, on a wet day, of packing their children off in a cab to the so-called Brompton Boilers, in order that they may have a good run through the galleries. To the far greater part of the people a large brilliantly lighted Museum is little or nothing more than a promenade, a bright kind of lounge, not nearly so instructive as the shops of Regent Street or Holburn. The well-known fact that the attendance at Museums is greatest on wet days is very instructive.

Not only is a very large collection of various objects ill-suited for educational purposes, but it is apt to create altogether erroneous ideas about the true method of education. The least consideration, indeed, ought to convince any sensible person that to comprehend the purpose, construction, mode of use, and history of a single novel object or machine, would usually require from (say) half-an-hour up to several hours or days of careful study. A good lecturer can always make a lecture of an hour's duration out of anything falling within his range of subject. How then is it possible that persons glancing over some thousands of unfamiliar specimens in the British Museum or the South Kensington Courts, can acquire, in the moment devoted to each, the slightest comprehension of what they witness? To children especially the glancing at a great multitude of diverse things is not only useless but actually pernicious, because it tends to destroy that habit of concentration of attention, which is the first condition of mental acquisition. It is no uncommon thing to see troops of little schoolboys filing through the long galleries of a Museum. No more senseless employment could be imagined. They would be far better employed in flattening their noses for an hour or two against the grocer's shop window where there is a steam mill grinding coffee, or watching the very active bootmaker who professes to sole your boots while you wait.

A great deal has been said and written about the unities of the drama, and "canons" are said to have been laid down on the subject. It does not seem, however, to have occurred to the creators and managers of Museums, that so far as education is aimed at, a certain unity of effect is essential. There may be many specimens exhibited, but they ought to have that degree of relation that they may conduce to the same general mental impression. It is in this way, I believe, that the Thorwaldsen Museum at Copenhagen exercises a peculiarly impressive effect upon the multitudes of all classes of Danes and Swedes who visit it. This Museum contains in a single building almost the whole works of this great sculptor, together with all the engravings and pictures having reference to the same. Very numerous though the statues and bas-reliefs are, there is naturally a unity of style in them, and the visitor as he progresses is gradually educated to an appreciation of the works. The only objects in the building tending towards incongruity of ideas are Thorwaldsen's own collection of antiquities and objects of art; but even these are placed apart, and if visited, they tend to elucidate the tastes and genius of the artist. . . .

I hardly know anything in this kingdom producing a like unity and depth of effect. No doubt the gallery in the British Museum appropriated to the Elgin and other Greek sculptures presents a striking unity of genius well calculated to impress the visitor, provided he can keep clear of the Assyrian bulls which are so close at hand, and the great variety of Egyptian and other antiquities which beset his path. It is in the Crystal Palace, however, that we find the most successful attempt to carry the spectator back to a former stage of art. The Pompeian House is the best possible Museum of Roman life and character. For a few minutes at least the visitor steps from the present; he shuts out the age of iron, and steam, and refreshment contractors, and the like, and learns to realise the past. As to the Alhambra Court, it is a matchless lesson in art and architecture. . . .

In Museums, as a general rule, we see things torn from their natural surroundings and associated with incongruous objects. In a great cathedral church we find indeed architectural fragments of many ages, and monuments of the most diverse styles. But they are in their places nevertheless, and mark and register the course of time. In a modern art Museum, on the contrary, the collection of the articles is accidental, and to realise the true meaning and beauty of an object the spectator must possess a previous knowledge of its historical bearings and a rare power of imagination, enabling him to restore it ideally to its place. The persistent system of self-glorification long maintained by the managers of the South Kensington Museum seems actually to have been successful in persuading people that the mere possession and casual inspection of the contents of the South Kensington courts and galleries has created esthetic and artistic tastes in a previously unaesthetic people. Such a fallacy does not stand a moment's serious examination. It is dispersed, for instance, by the single fact that the fine arts are in a decidedly low state in Italy, although the Italians have had access to the choicest works of art since the time of the Medicis. It might also be easily pointed out that the revival of true aesthetic taste in England, especially in the direction of architecture, began long before South Kensington was heard of. It is to men of genius, such as Pugin, and Barry, and Gilbert Scott, and to no Government officials, that we owe the restoration of true taste in England, only prevented for a short time, as I hope, by the present craze about the bastard Queen Anne style.

The worst possible conception of the mode of arranging Museums is exemplified at South Kensington, especially in those interminable exhibition galleries which the late Captain Fowke erected around the Horticultural Society's unfortunate gardens. When I went, for instance, to see the admirable collection of early printed books, at the Caxton Loan Exhibition, I had to enter at the south-eastern entrance, and after successfully passing the turnstiles found myself in the midst of a perplexing multitude of blackboards, diagrams, abacuses, chairs and tables, models of all sorts of things, forming, I believe, the educational collections of the Science and Art Department. Having overcome tendencies to diverge into a dozen different lines of thought, I passed on only to find myself among certain ancient machines and complicated models which it was impossible not to pause at. Having torn myself away, however, I fell among an extensive series of naval models, with all kinds of diagrams and things relating to them. Here forgetfulness of the Caxton Exhibition seemed to fall upon all the visitors; a good quarter of an hour, and the best, because the freshest, quarter of an hour, was spent, if not wasted. But when at length it occurred to people that it was time to see that which they came to see, the only result was to fall from Scylla into Charybdis in the form of the late Mr. Frank Buckland's admirable Fishery Collection. Now at the Norwich Fisheries Exhibition, and under various other circumstances, nothing can be better and more appropriate and interesting than the collection of fish-culture apparatus, the models of big salmon and the like. But anything less congruous to old Caxton editions cannot be imagined. As a matter of fact, I observed that nearly all the visitors succumbed to these fish, and for a time at least forgot altogether what they were come about. When at length the Loan Exhibition was reached, the already distracted spectator was ill fitted to cope with the very extensive series of objects which he wished seriously to inspect. In returning, moreover, he had again to run the gauntlet of the big fish, the complicated naval machines, and the educational apparatus. An afternoon thus spent leaves no good mental effect. To those who come merely to pass the time, it carries out this purpose; but the mental impression is that of a nightmare of incomprehensible

machines, interminable stairs, suspicious policemen, turnstiles, and staring fish.

But I must go a step further and question altogether the wisdom of
forming vast collections for popular educational purposes. No doubt the
very vastness of the Paris and other International Exhibitions was in itself
impressive and instructive, but speaking from full experience of the Paris
as well as the London exhibitions, I question whether it was possible for
any mind to carry away useful impressions of a multitude of objects so
practically infinite. A few of the larger or more unique objects may be
distinctly remembered, or a few specimens connected with the previous
studies and pursuits of the spectator may have been inspected in a way
to produce real information; but I feel sure the general mental state produced by such vast displays is one of perplexity and vagueness, together
with some impression of sore feet and aching heads.

As regards children, at any rate, there can be no doubt that a few striking objects are far better than any number of more monotonous ones. At
the Zoological Gardens, for instance, the lions, the elephants, the polar
bears and especially the sea lions, are worth all the rest of the splendid
collection put together. After the ordinary visitor, whether young or old,
has become well interested in these, it has an obviously depressing and
confusing effect to proceed through the long series of antelopes. . . .

The evil effect of multiplicity of objects used to be most strikingly
displayed in that immensely long gallery at the British Museum which
held the main part of the zoological collections. The ordinary visitor,
thoroughly well distracted by the room previously passed through, here
almost always collapsed, and sauntered listlessly along the closely-packed
ranks of birds, monkeys, and animals of every possible shape and clime.
If the attention could be stimulated anew, this was done by a few cases containing beautiful birds grouped about nests in the manner of life.
I can positively assert that these few cases were, for popular purposes,
actually superior to the whole of the other vast collections in the room.
The fact of course is that the contents of the British Museum have been
brought together for the highest scientific ends, and it is a merely incidental purpose which they serve in affording a show for young or old people
who have nothing else to do but wander through the store-rooms. The
delectation of loungers and youngsters is no more the purpose of a great
national Museum than the raison, d'être of the Royal Mint is to instruct
visitors in mechanical processes. . . .

I venture to submit that on psychological and educational grounds the
arrangement of diverse collections in a long series of continuous galleries, worst exemplified at South Kensington, but also unfortunately to be
found in the older galleries of the British Museum, is a complete mistake.
Every collection ought to form a definite congruous whole, which can

be visited, studied, and remembered with a certain unity of impression. If a great Museum like the British Museum contains many departments, there ought to be as many distinct buildings, each adapted to its special purpose, so as to exhibit a distinct and appropriate *coup d'oeil.* . . .

After all, the best Museum is that which a person forms for himself. As with the books of a public library, so in the case of public Museums, the utility of each specimen is greatly multiplied with regard to the multitude of persons who may inspect it. But the utility of each inspection is vastly less than that which arises from the private possession of a suitable specimen which can be kept near at hand to be studied at any moment, handled, experimented and reflected upon. A few such specimens probed thoroughly, teach more than thousands glanced at through a glass-case. The whole British Museum accordingly will not teach a youth as much as he will learn by collecting a few fossils or a few minerals, in situ if possible, and taking them home to examine and read and think about. Where there is any aptitude for science, the beginning of such a collection is the beginning of a scientific education. The passion for collection runs into many extravagances and absurdities; but it is difficult to collect without gaining knowledge of more or less value, and with the young especially it is almost better to collect any kind of specimens than nothing. Even the postage-stamp collecting mania is not to be despised or wholly condemned. At any rate a stamp collector who arranges his specimens well and looks out their places of issue in an atlas, will learn more geography than all the dry text-books could teach him. But in the case of the natural sciences the habit of collecting is almost essential, and the private Museum is the key to the great public Museum. The youth who has a drawer full of a few score minerals at home which he has diligently collected, will be entranced with delight and interest when he can first visit the superb collection of the British Museum. He will naturally seek out the kinds of minerals previously known to him, and will be amazed at the variety, beauty, and size of the specimens displayed. His knowledge already having some little depth will be multiplied by the extent of the public collection. The same considerations will of course apply to paleontology, zoology, petrology, and all other branches of the classificatory sciences. . . .

But whatever may be said against particular Museums and collections, there can be no doubt whatever that the increase in the number of Museums of some sort or other must be almost co-extensive with the progress of real popular education. The Museum represents that real instruction, that knowledge of things as they are which is obtained by the glance of the eye, and the touch of the fingers. The time ought to have arrived when the senseless verbal teaching formerly, and perhaps even yet, predominant in schools should be abandoned. A child should hardly be allowed to read about anything unless a specimen or model, or, at any rate, a picture of the thing can be placed before it. Words come thus to be, as they should be, the handles to ideas, instead of being empty sounds. . . .

Another mistake which is made, or is likely to be made, is in forming vast collections of technical objects, the value and interest of which must rapidly pass away. We hear it frequently urged, for instance, that a great industrial country like England ought to have its great industrial Museum, where every phase of commercial and manufacturing processes should be visibly represented. There ought to be specimens of the new materials in all their qualities and kinds; the several stages of manufacture should be shown by corresponding samples; the machines being too large to be got into the Museum should be shown in the form of models or diagrams; the finished products, lastly, should be exhibited and their uses indicated. It is easy enough to sketch out vast collections of this sort, but it is a mere phantasm which, it is to be hoped, it will never be attempted to realise. . . .

It is forgotten that if such a technical exhibition were to be so complete and minute as to afford every information to those engaged in each particular trade, it would be far vaster in aggregate extent than any Great International Exhibition yet held. If it were to be a permanent Museum, ten years would hardly elapse before its contents would become obsolete, owing to the progress of invention. Either, then, the Museum would have to be constantly expanded so as to contain the new alongside of the old, or else the new would have to push out the old. . . .

The same considerations hardly apply to the Parkes Museum of Hygiene now open to the inspection of the public during certain hours at University College, London. This may be regarded as the collection of samples of a most important kind of sanitary Institute. To allow such a Museum to grow to any great bulk, and to preserve all the obsolete forms of syphon traps, sinks and what not, would surely defeat its own purposes. . . .

A good deal has been said about the cellars of the British Museum, where there are supposed to be great quantities of duplicates or other valuable objects stowed away uselessly. I cannot profess to say, from my own knowledge, what there may or may not be in those cellars; but I have no hesitation in asserting that a great national Museum of research like that at Bloomsbury ought to have great cellars or other store-rooms filled with articles which, though unfitted for public exhibition, may be invaluable evidence in putting together the history of the world, both social and physical. If the views advocated above are correct, it distinctly injures the effect, for popular educational purposes, of fine specimens of art and science to crowd them up with an infinite number of inferior or less interesting objects; accordingly a great number of imperfect remains, fragments of statues and monuments, inferior copies, or approximate duplicates, should be stowed away. This both saves expense, prevents weariness and confusion of ideas to the public, and facilitates the studies of the scholar. By far the largest part of the biological collections should be packed in drawers, and only the more distinct and typical specimens exposed to view. But then come a number of zealous, well-meaning men who urge that these drawers and cellars full of expensive articles ought to be offered to the provinces, so that fifty Museums might be filled out of what is unseen in one. Such suggestions, however, proceed upon an entire misapprehension of the purposes of a great collection, and of the way in which the mysteries of the past, the only key to the mysteries of the present, are being unfolded by the patient putting together of link and link.

Of course when two things are real duplicates, like two coins from the same dies, there will not usually be any motive for retaining both in a Museum; a curator will then, as a matter of course, arrange for an exchange of the duplicate with some other duplicate from another Museum. But there may be many things which might seem at first sight to be duplicates, but are not. In many cases the slighter the differences the more instructive these are. The great national herbarium, for instance, ought to contain the floras of all parts of the world, and a certain number of plants will appear to be identical, though coming from opposite sides of the globe. These coincident specimens are, however, the very clues to the former relations of floras, or to the currents, cataclysms, or other causes which can be supposed to explain otherwise inexplicable resemblances. The same is obviously true of all the other biological collections.

It is also true, in a somewhat different manner, of historical objects. If, as the whole course of recent philosophy tends to prove, things grow in the social as in the physical world, then the causes of things can only be safely traced out by obtaining specimens of so many stages in the growth that there can be no doubt as to the relation of continuity. Some of the ancient British coins, for instance, bear designs which to all appearance are entirely inexplicable and meaningless. Careful study, however, consisting in the minute and comparison of many series of specimens of coins, showed that these inexplicable designs were degraded copies of Byzantine or other earlier coinages. The point of the matter, however, is that no one would recognise the resemblance between the first original and the last degraded copy. We must have a series of intermediate copies, as necessary links in the induction. Now it is apparent that if these indispensable links being merely duplicates of each other, are dispersed to the provincial Museums of Manchester, Liverpool, Bristol, Newcastle and the rest, the study of their real import must be indefinitely retarded. Concentration and approximate reduplication of specimens is in fact the great method of biological and historical inquiry. . . .

To distribute the supposed duplicates of the British Museum or of other great scientific collections would be simply to undo the work of a century's research, and to scatter to the points of the compass the groundwork of learning and history. Did we proceed in this country on autocratic principles, the opposite course would be that most beneficial to human progress, namely, to empower the Librarians and Curators of the British Museum to seize whatever books, specimens, or other things they could find in any of the provinces suitable for the completion of the National Collections. . . .

It is naturally a point of the highest importance to ascertain if possible the best constitution for the control of a Museum, and the best mode of organisation of the staff. Without undertaking to argue the matter here as fully as it would deserve, I venture to express the opinion that a Museum ought to be regarded as a place of learning and science, and not as a mere office or shop for the display of so many samples. It ought therefore to be controlled in the manner of a college, by a neutral and mixed board of men of science and of business. Such a council or board will retain in their own hands most questions relating to finance, the structure of the Museum, and what does not touch the professional and scientific work of the curators. They will appoint a chief curator or librarian, and in a case of a large Museum, the chiefs of the separate branches; but will probably leave to the chief curator the minor appointments. If a happy and successful choice is made as regards the curators, especially the chief, it will probably be found that the whole direction of the institution will centre in the latter, who will form the medium of communication between his colleagues the branch curators, and the board. All important matters involving the scientific organisation of the Museum will be discussed among the curators and reported to the board before the latter pass any final decision upon them. The advantages of such a constitution for the purposes in view are manifold. . . .

The British Museum has from its first institution, in 1753, been under the government of a board of trustees including certain family trustees representing the benefactors of the Museum. The inestimable services to many branches of history, learning, and science, which the Museum has rendered throughout its career of little more than a century form a sufficient general justification of its mode of governance. But it may well be allowed at the same time that the repeated complaints as to the conservatism and inactivity of the trustees are not without ground. . . .

I venture to suggest, in conclusion, that the best possible step which could now be taken to improve the Museums of the United Kingdom would be the constitution of a Museum Association on the lines of the well-known Librarians' Association. If the curators of all the public Museums would follow the example of other professional bodies, and put their heads together in a conference, they might evolve out of the existing chaos some unity of ideas and action. At any rate they would take the first important step of asserting their own existence. Let the curators themselves now speak and act, and let them especially adopt as their motto—"Union, not centralisation."

# 18

# THE RELATIONSHIPS AND RESPONSIBILITIES OF MUSEUMS

## G[eorge] Brown Goode

*Science*, 2 (new series): 197–209, 1895

*George Brown Goode, one of the most innovative museum thinkers of the late nineteenth century, presented this paper, excerpted below, at the Museums Association at Newcastle-on-Tyne, England in 1895. It is the summation of Goode's museum philosophy, which he developed during his many years of experience as a museum administrator at the Smithsonian Institution and extensive visits to museums across Europe. Goode credits Jevons (see previous article) with raising similar issues.*

In an article on "The use and abuse of Museums," written nearly fifteen years ago by Professor William Stanley Jevons, attention was directed to the circumstance that there was not, at that time, in the English language a treatise analyzing the purposes and kinds of museums, and discussing the general principles of their management and economy. It is somewhat surprising that the need then made so evident has not since been supplied and that there is not at the present day such a treatise in the English or any other language. Many important papers have in the interval been printed in regard to particular classes of museums and special branches of museum work. Notable among these have been those written by Sir William H. Flower, Professor W. A. Herdman, Dr. J. S. Billings, Dr. H. H. Higgins, Dr. Albert Günther and General Pitt Rivers, and there had previously been printed the well known essay of Dr. J. E. Gray, Edward Forbes' suggestive paper on "Educational Uses of Museums," in 1853, and the still earlier one by Edward Edwards on

"The Maintenance and Management of Public Galleries and Museums," printed in 1840.

No one has as yet attempted, however, even in a preliminary way, to formulate a general theory of administration applicable to museum work in all its branches, except Professor Jevons, who, in the paper already referred to, presented in an exceedingly impressive manner certain ideas which should underlie such a theory. . . .

My ideas are presented, it may be, in a somewhat dogmatic manner, often in the form of aphorisms, and to the experienced museum worker many of them will, perhaps, sound like truisms.

I have had two objects in view:

It has been my desire, in the first place, to begin the codification of the accepted principles of museum administration, hoping that the outline which is here presented may serve as the foundation for a complete statement of those principles, such as can only be prepared through the cooperation of many minds. With this in view, it is hoped that the paper may be the cause of much critical discussion.

My other purpose has been to set forth the aims and ambitions of modern museum practice, in such a manner that they shall be intelligible to the persons who are responsible for the establishment of museums and also to the directors of other public institutions founded for similar purposes, in order to evoke more fully their sympathy and co-operation.

Museums of art and history, as well as those of science, are discussed in this paper, since the same general principles appear to be applicable to all.

The theses proposed are two hundred and fifteen in number and are arranged under the following heads or chapters:

I. The Museum and its Relationships; II. The Responsibilities and Requirements of Museums; III. The Five Cardinal Necessities in Museum Administration; IV. The Classification of Museums; V. The Uses of Specimens and Collections; VI. The Preservation and Preparation of Museum Materials; VII. The Art of Installation; VIII. Records, Catalogues and Specimen Labels; IX. Exhibition Labels and Their Function; X. Guides and Lecturers; Hand Books and Reference-books; XI. The Future of Museum Work.

## The Museum and Its Relationships

### A. The Museum Defined

1. A museum is an institution for the preservation of those objects which best illustrate the phenomena of nature and the works of man, and the utilization of these for the increase of knowledge and for the culture and enlightenment of the people.

## B. The Relation of the Museum to Other Institutions of Learning

1. The Museum in its effort for the increase and diffusion of knowledge aids and is aided by (a) the university and college, (b) the learned society and (c) the public library.

2. The special function of the museum is to preserve and utilize objects of nature and works of art and industry; that of the library to guard the written records of human thought and activity; that of the learned society to discuss facts and theories; that of the school to educate the individual, while all meet together on common ground in the custodianship of learning and in extending the boundaries of existing knowledge.

3. The care and utilization of material objects being the peculiar duty of the museum, it should not enter the field of other institutions of learning, except to such a degree as may be found absolutely necessary in connection with its own work. . . .

## C. The Relation of the Museum to the Exposition

1. The Museum differs from the Exposition both in its aims and in the method of its activity.

2. The Exposition, or Exhibition, and the Fair are primarily for the promotion of industry and commerce; the Museum for the advancement of learning.

3. The principal object of the former is to make known the names of the exhibitors for their own professional or financial advantage; in the latter the name of the exhibitor is incidental, the thing chiefly in mind being the lesson taught by the exhibit.

4. Into the work of the former enters the element of competition, coupled with a system of awards by diplomas or medals; in that of the latter the element of competition does not appear.

5. The educational results of expositions, though undeniably important, are chiefly incidental, and not at all proportionate to the prodigal expenditure of energy and money which are inseparable from any great exposition.

## D. Museum Features Adopted in Expositions

1. Museum methods have been in part adopted by many expositions, in some instances to attract visitors, in others because it has been desired to utilize the occasion to give museum lessons to multitudes to whom museums are not accessible.

2. Those expositions which have been most successful from an educational standpoint have been the ones which have most fully availed themselves of museum methods, notably the London Exhibition of 1851 and the Paris Exposition of 1889.

3. Special or limited exhibitions have a relatively greater educational value, owing to the fact that it is possible in these to apply more fully the methods of the museum. Examples of this principle were afforded by the four expositions held in London from 1883 to 1886—Fisheries, Health, Inventions and Colonial.

4. The animal exhibitions of the academies of art are allied to the exposition rather than to the museum.

5. Many so-called "museums" are really "permanent exhibitions," and many a great collection of pictures can only be suitably described by the name "picture gallery."

### E. Temporary Museums

1. There are many exhibitions which are administered in accordance with museum principles and which are really temporary museums. To this class belong the best of the loan exhibitions, and also special exhibits made by public institutions, like the "Luther Memorial Exhibition" of 1874, the material for which was derived chiefly from the Library of the British Museum, and similar exhibitions subsequently held under the same auspices.

### F. Museum Methods in Other Institutions—"Museum Extension"

1. The zoological park, the botanical garden and the aquarium are essentially museums, and the principles of museum administration are entirely applicable to them.

2. An herbarium in its usual form corresponds to the study series in a museum, and is capable of expansion to the full scope of the general museum.

3. Certain churches and ecclesiastical edifices and classical antiquities in place, when they have been pronounced "monuments," are subject to the principles of museum administration.

4. Many cities, like Rome, Naples, Milan and Florence, by reason of the number of buildings, architectural features, sculpture and other objects in the streets and squares, together with the historical houses duly labeled by tablets, have become practically great museums, and these various objects are administered much in the manner of

museums. Indeed, the number of "Public Monuments" in Italy is so great that the whole country may properly be described as a museum of art and history. A government commission for the preservation of the monuments of history and art regulates the contents of every church, monastery and public edifice, the architectural features of private buildings, and even private collections, to the extent of requiring that nothing shall be removed from the country without governmental sanction. Each Italian town is thus made a museum, and in Rome the site of the Forum and the adjacent ancient structures has been set aside as an outdoor museum under the name of the *Passegiata Archeologica*.

Similar government control of public monuments and works of art exists in Greece and Egypt, and in a lesser degree in the Ottoman Empire, and for half a century there has been a Commission of Historic Monuments in France, which has not only succeeded in protecting the national antiquities, but has published an exceedingly important series of descriptive monographs concerning them.

## The Responsibilities and Requirements of Museums

### A. The Relation of the Museum to the Community

1. The museum meets a need which is felt by every intelligent community and furnishes that which cannot be supplied by any other agency. The museum does not exist except among enlightened peoples, and attains its highest development only in great centres of civilization.

2. The museum is more closely in touch with the masses than the university and learned society, and quite as much so as the public library, while, even more than the last, it is a recent outgrowth of modern tendencies of thought. Therefore,

3. THE PUBLIC MUSEUM IS A NECESSITY IN EVERY HIGHLY CIVILIZED COMMUNITY.

### B. The Mutual Responsibilities of the Community and the Museum

1. The museums in the midst of a community perform certain functions which are essential to its welfare, and hence arise mutual responsibilities between the community and the museum administrator.

2. The museum administrator must conduct his work with the highest possible degree of efficiency, in order to retain the confidence of the community.

3. The community should provide adequate means for the support of the museum.

4. A failure on the part of the one must inevitably lead to a corresponding failure on the part of the other.

## C. The Specific Responsibilities of the Museum

1. The museum should be held responsible for special services, chiefly as follows:

   a. *For the advancement of learning.*—To aid learned men in the work of extending the boundaries of knowledge, by affording them the use of material for investigation, laboratories and appliances.

   To stimulate original research in connection with its own collections, and to promote the publication of the results.

   b. *For record.*—To preserve for future comparative and critical study the material upon which past studies have been made, or which may serve to confirm, correct or modify the results of such studies. Such materials serve to perpetuate the names and identifications used by investigators in their publications and, thus authenticated, to serve as a basis for future investigation in connection with new material. Specimens which thus vouch for the work of investigators are called *Types.* Besides types museums retain for purposes of record many specimens which, though not having served for investigation, are landmarks for past stages in the history of man and nature.

   c. *As an adjunct to the class room and the lecture room.*—To aid the teacher either of elementary, secondary, technological or higher knowledge in expounding to his pupils the principles of art, nature and history, and to be used by advanced or professional students in practical laboratory or studio work.

   To furnish to the advanced or professional student materials and opportunity for laboratory or studio training.

   d. *To impart special information.*—To aid the occasional inquirer, be he a laboring school boy, journalist, public speaker or savant, to obtain, without cost, exact information upon any subject related to the specialities of the institution; serving thus as a "bureau of information."

   e. *For the culture of the public.*—To serve the great general public, through the display of attractive exhibition series, well-planned, complete and thoroughly labeled; and thus to stimulate and broaden the minds of those who are not engaged in scholarly research, and draw them to the public library and the lecture room. In this respect the effect of the museum is somewhat analogous to that of travel in distant lands.

2. A museum to be useful and reputable must be constantly engaged in aggressive work, either in education or investigation, or in both.

3. A museum which is not aggressive in policy and constantly improving cannot retain in its service a competent staff and will surely fall into a decay.

4. A FINISHED MUSEUM IS A DEAD MUSEUM, AND A DEAD MUSEUM IS A USELESS MUSEUM.

5. Many so-called "museums" are little more than storehouses filled with the materials of which museums are made.

## D. The Responsibility of Museums to Each Other

1. There can be no occasion for envious rivalry between museums, even when they are in the same city. Every good museum strengthens its neighbors and the success of the one tends to the popularity and public support of the others.

2. A system of cooperation between museums, by means of which much duplication of work and much expenditure of work may be avoided, is seemingly possible.

3. The first and most important field for mutual understanding is in regard to specialization of plan. If museums in the same town, province or nation would divide the field of work so that each should be recognized as having the first rights in one or more specialities, rivalry would be converted into friendly association and the interests of science and education better served.

4. An important outcome of such a system of cooperation might be the transfer of entire groups of specimens from one museum to another. This would greatly facilitate the work of specialization referred to, and at the same time relieve each museum of the responsibility of maintaining collections which are not germane to its real purpose. Such transfers have occasionally been made in the past, and there are few museums which might not benefit individually, in a large degree, by a sweeping application of this principle. If its effect upon the effectiveness and interest of any local or national group of museums is taken into account, no one can doubt that the result would be exceedingly beneficial.

5. Another field for cooperation is in joint expenditure of effort and money upon labels and catalogues and in the economical purchase of and in supplies and material.

6. Still another would lie in the cooperative employment of expert curators and preparators, it being thus practicable to pay larger salaries and secure better men.

## The Five Cardinal Necessities in Museum Administration

### The Essentials of Success in Museum Work

A museum cannot be established and creditably maintained without adequate provision in five directions:

1. A stable organization and adequate means of support.
2. A definite plan, wisely framed in accordance with the opportunities of the institution and the needs of the community for whose benefit it is to be maintained.
3. Material to work upon—good collections or facilities for creating them.
4. Men to do the work—a staff of competent curators.
5. Appliances to work with—a suitable building, with proper accessories, installation material, tools and mechanical assistants.

### A. Stability of Organization

1. The only absolute assurance of permanence for a museum lies either in governmental protection, in a connection with some endowed institution of learning, or in special organization with ample endowments.
2. The cabinets of unendowed societies, or those gathered and supported by the efforts of individuals, must in time inevitably be dispersed or destroyed.

### B. Definiteness of Plan

1. No two museums can be or ought to be exactly alike. Each should be devoted to one or more special subjects, and should select those subjects not only in reference to opportunity and the needs of the community, but also with regard to the specialties of other museums in the same region, with a view to cooperation.
2. It is the duty of every museum to be preeminent in at least one specialty, be this specialty never so limited.

3. The specialties or departments of any museum may be few or many, but it is important that its plan should be positively defined and limited, since lack of purpose in museum work leads in a most conspicuous way to waste of effort and to failure, partial or complete. . . .

## C. Collections

1. The sources of collections are the following: (a) By gift; (b) by purchase; (c) by exchange; (d) by collection and exploration; (e) by construction; (f) through deposit or temporary loan. . . .

2. Collections which are encumbered by conditions as to manner of disposition and installation are usually sources of serious embarrassment. It is especially undesirable to accept either as a gift or as a loan any unimportant collection with the pledge that it shall be kept intact and installed as a unit. The acceptance of any collection, no matter how important, encumbered by conditions, is a serious matter, since no one can foresee how much these conditions may interfere with the future development of the museum.

3. Gifts, deposits and cooperation of all kinds may be greatly encouraged by liberal acknowledgment upon labels and in public reports. This is but simple justice to the generosity of the benefactor.

   Gifts and deposits are also encouraged by the fact that the buildings are fireproof, the cases so built as to afford perfect protection, and the scheme of installation dignified and attractive. Collections of great value may well be afforded accommodations of a specially sumptuous character and such protection, in the case of priceless objects, as is afforded by special electric attachments.

4. Since the plan and character of a museum is largely determined for all time by the nature of the collections which fall first into its possession, at the time of its organization, the authorities in charge of such an institution at the time of organization should be exceedingly careful in accepting materials which are to serve as a nucleus for its future growth. . . .

## D. Museum Officers

1. A museum without intelligent, progressive and well-trained curators is as in-effective as a school without teachers, a library without librarians, or a learned society without a working membership of learned men.

2. Museum administration has become one of the learned professions, and success in this field can only be attained as the result of years of

study and experience in a well-organized museum. Intelligence, a liberal education, administrative ability, enthusiasm, and that special endowment which may be called "the museum sense" are prerequisite qualifications.

Each member of the museum staff should become an authority in some special field of research, and should have time for investigation and opportunity to publish its results.

3. A museum which employs untrained curators must expect to pay the cost of their education in delays, experimental failures and waste of materials.

4. No investment is more profitable to a museum than that in its salary fund, for only when this is liberal may the services of a permanent staff of men of established reputation be secured.

Around the nucleus of such a staff will naturally grow up a corps of volunteer assistants, whose work properly assisted and directed will be of infinite value.

5. Collaborators, as well as curators, may be placed upon the staff of a large museum, the sole duty of the former being to carry on investigations, to publish, and, if need be, to lecture.

6. Volunteers may be advantageously employed either as curators and custodians, or collaborators.

7. No man is fitted to be a museum officer who is disposed to repel students or inquirers, or to place obstacles in the way of access to the material under his charge.

8. A museum officer or employee should, for obvious reasons, never be the possessor of a private collection.

9. The museum which carries on explorations in the field as a part of its regular work has great advantage over other institutions in holding men of ability upon its staff and in securing the most satisfactory results from their activities. No work is more exhaustive to body and mind than the care of collections, and nowhere are enthusiasm and abundant vitality more essential. Every museum must constantly obtain new material through exploration, and it is better that this exploration should be done by the men who are to study the collections and arrange them in the museum than that this work should be placed in the hands of others.

10. In a large museum staff it is almost essential that certain persons should give their attention chiefly to administrative and financial matters, thus leaving their associates free from occupation of this description. It is desirable, however, that the administrative officers of a museum should be men who comprehend the meaning of museum work and are in

sympathy with its highest aims, and that its business affairs and scientific work should be controlled by the same executive head.

## E. Museum Buildings

1. The museum building should be absolutely fireproof and substantially constructed; the architecture simple, dignified and appropriate—a structure worthy of the treasures to be placed within.

2. Above all things the interior should be well lighted and ventilated, dry and protected from dust.

3. While the museum building should be planned with reference to the character of the collections it is to contain, the fact that unexpected development of rapid growth in some one direction may necessitate the rearrangement and reassignment of halls to different departments should always be kept in mind.

4. Since no two museums can be alike, there can be no general uniformity in their buildings.

## F. Accessories to Museum Work

1. A well-equipped museum requires as accessories to its work:

    a. A reference library for the use of staff, students and visitors.
    b. Laboratories for the classification of material, for the storage of the study-series, and for the use of students and investigators.
    c. Workshops, for preparation, mounting and repair of specimens, and the making and adjustment of mounts and cases, and storage rooms for material not yet available.
    d. An assembly hall, for public lectures, society meetings and special exhibitions.
    e. A bulletin, or other official publication, to preserve the history of its activities, to maintain its standing among similar institutions, to serve as a means of communication with correspondents, and to exchange for specimens and books for the library.

2. In addition to local accessories, the opportunity for exploration and field work are equally essential not only because of considerations connected with the efficiency of the staff, but for the general welfare of the institution. Other things being equal, exploration can be carried on more effectively by the museum than by any other institution of learning, and there is no other field of research which it can pursue to better advantage.

## The Future of Museum Work

### A. The Growth of the Museum Idea

1. There can be no doubt that the importance of the museum as an agency for the increase and diffusion of knowledge will be recognized so long as interest in science and education continues to exist. The prediction of Professor Jevons in 1881, that the increase in the number of museums of some sort or other must be almost coextensive with the progress of real popular education, is already being realized. Numerous local museums have been organized within the past fifteen years in the midst of new communities. Special museums of new kinds are developing in the old centres, and every university, college and school is organizing or extending its cabinet. The success of the Museums' Association in Great Britain is another evidence of the growing popularity of the museum idea, and similar organizations must of necessity soon be formed in every civilized country.

2. With this increase of interest there has been a corresponding improvement in museum administration. More men of ability and originality are engaging in this work, and the results of this are manifest in all its branches.

   The museum recluse, a type which had many representatives in past years, among them not a few eminent specialists, is becoming much less common, and this change is not to be regretted. The general use of specimens in classroom instruction and, still more, the general introduction of laboratory work in the higher institutions, has brought an army of teachers into direct relations with museum administration, and much support and improvement has resulted.

3. Museum administration has become a profession, and the feeling is growing more and more general that it is one in which talents of a high order can be utilized. It is essential to the future development of the museum that the best men should be secured for this kind of work, and to this end it is important that a lofty professional standard should be established.

### B. Public Appreciation of the Material Value of Collections

1. The museum of nature or art is one of the most valuable material possessions of a nation or a city. It is, as has well been said, "the people's vested fund." It brings not only world-wide reputation, but many visitors and consequent commercial advantage. What

Alpine scenery is to Switzerland, museums are to many neighboring nations. Some one declares that the Venus of Melos has attracted more wealth to Paris than the Queen of Sheba brought to King Solomon, and that but for the possession of their collections (which are intrinsically so much treasure) Rome and Florence would be impoverished towns. . . .

Suggestive in this same connection is this remark of Sir William Flower to the effect that the largest museum yet erected, with all its internal fittings, has not cost so much as a single fully equipped line of battleships, which in a few years may be either at the bottom of the sea or so obsolete in construction as to be worth no more than the material of which it is made. . . .

## C. Public Appreciation of the Higher Function of Museums

1. Museums, libraries, reading rooms and parks have been referred to by some wise person as "passionless reformers" and no better term can be employed to describe one of the most important of their uses.

   The appreciation of the utility of museums to the great public lies at the foundation of what is known as "the modern museum idea." No one has written more eloquently of the moral influence of museums than Mr. Ruskin, and whatever may be thought of the manner in which he has carried his ideas into practice in his workingmen's museum, near Sheffield, his influence has undoubtedly done much to stimulate the development of the "people's museum". . . .

   I myself never shall forget the words of the late Sir Philip Cunliffe Owen, of South Kensington, who said to me some years ago:

   "We educate our working people in the public schools, give them a love for refined and beautiful objects, and stimulate in them a desire for information. They leave school, go into the pursuits of town life, and have no means provided for the gratification of the tastes which they have been forced to acquire, and are condemned to a monotonous, depressing life in the midst of smoky chimneys and dingy walls. It is as much the duty of the government to provide them with museums and libraries for higher education as it is to establish schools for their primary instruction."

   The development of the modern museum idea is indeed due to Great Britain in much greater degree than to any other nation, and the movement dates from the period of the great Exhibition of 1851, which marked an epoch in the intellectual progress of English speaking peoples.

2. The future of the museum, as of all similar public institutions, is inseparably associated with the continuance of modern civilization, by means of which those sources of enjoyment which were formerly accessible to the rich only are now, more and more, placed in the possession and ownership of all the people (an adaptation of what Jevons has called "the principle of the multiplication of utility") with the result that objects which were formerly accessible only to the wealthy, and seen by a very small number of people each year, are now held in common ownership and enjoyed by hundreds of thousands.

   In this connection the maintenance of museums should be especially favored, be-cause, as has been shown, these, more than any other public agency, are invitations to the wealthy owners of private treasures, in the form of collections, to give them in perpetuity to the public.

3. If it be possible to sum up in a single sentence the principles which have been discussed in the present paper, that sentence should be phrased in these words:

THE DEGREE OF CIVILIZATION TO WHICH ANY NATION, CITY OR PROVINCE HAS ATTAINED IS WELL INDICATED BY THE CHARACTER OF ITS PUBLIC MUSEUMS AND THE LIBERALITY WITH WHICH THEY ARE SUPPORTED.

# 19

# MODERN MUSEUMS: PRESIDENTIAL ADDRESS TO THE MUSEUMS ASSOCIATION AT THE MEETING IN LONDON, 3RD JULY 1893

## William Henry Flower

*Essays on museums: and other subjects connected with natural history.* London: Macmillan, pp. 37–53, 1898 [seen only in 1972 reprint by Books for Libraries Press, Freeport, NY]

*Sir William Henry Flower, as director of the natural history departments of the British Museum in South Kensington, discusses the ideal architectural design for a natural history museum. Flower advocated creating a space away from public view where the research collections would be kept for study. He believed that a well-defined educational exhibition space would serve to enhance the public's experience, while preserving the "reserve" collections for researchers.*

. . . From what has just been said it will be gathered that in Europe, at least, an ideal natural history museum, perfect in original design as well as in execution, does not exist at present. We have indeed hardly yet come to an agreement as to the principles upon which such a building should be constructed. But as there are countries which have still their national museums in the future, and as those already built are susceptible of modifications, when the right direction has been determined on, I should be glad to take this opportunity of putting on record what appears to me, after long reflection on the subject, the main considerations which should not be lost sight of in such an undertaking.

In the first place, I have endeavoured to work out in detail, in its application to natural history, that most original and theoretically perfect plan for a museum of exhibited objects in which there are two main lines of interest running in different directions and intersecting each other, which we owe to the ingenuity of General Pitt-Rivers. This was explained in his address as President of the Anthropological Section of the British Association at Bath in 1888, and again in a lecture given about two years ago before the Society of Arts. Upon this plan the museum building would consist of a series of galleries in the form of circles, one within the other, and communicating at frequent intervals. Each circle would represent an epoch in the world's history, commencing in the centre and finishing at the outermost, which would be that in which we are now living. The history of each natural group would be traced in radiating lines, and so by passing from the centre to the circumference, its condition of development in each period of the world's history could be studied. If, on the other hand, the subject for investigation should be the general fauna or flora of any particular epoch, it would be found in natural association by confining the attention to the circle representing that period. By such an arrangement, that most desirable object, the union of palaeontology with the zoology and botany of existing forms in one natural scheme, could be perfectly carried out, as both the structural and the geological relations of each would be preserved, and indicated by its position in the museum. Such a building would undoubtedly offer difficulties in practical construction; but even if these could be got over, our extremely imperfect knowledge of the past history of animal and plant life would make its arrangement, with all the gaps and irregularities that would become evident, so unsatisfactory that I can scarcely hope to see it adopted in the near future.

I have therefore brought before you a humbler plan, but one which, I think, will be found to embody the practical principles, necessary in a working museum of almost any description, large or small.

The fundamental idea of this plan is that the whole of the building should be divided by lines intersecting at right angles, like the warp and the woof of a piece of canvas. The lines in one direction divide the different natural sections of which the collection is composed, and which it is convenient to keep apart; the lines crossing these separate the portions of the collection according to the method of treatment or conservation. Thus, the exhibited part of the whole collection will come together in a series of rooms, occupying naturally the front of the building. The reserve collections will occupy another, or the middle, section; and beyond these will be the working rooms, studies, and administrative offices, all in relations to each other, as well as to the particular part of the collection to which they belong. A glance at the plan will show at once the great convenience of such a system, both for the public, and still more for those who work in the museum.

This plan, of course, contemplates a one-storied, top-lighted building, as far as the main rooms are concerned, although the workrooms and studies will be in two or more stories. The main rooms should all have a good substantial gallery running round them, by means of which their wall space is doubled. There is no question whatever that an evenly-diffused top light is far the best for exhibition rooms. Windows not only occupy the valuable wall space, but give all kinds of uncomfortable cross lights, interspersed with dark intervals. On the other hand, for doing any kind of delicate work, a good north light from a window is the most suitable. The convenience of having all the studies in relation with each other, and with the central administrative offices, while each one is also in close contiguity with the section of the collection to which it belongs, will, I am sure be appreciated by all who are acquainted with the capriciously scattered position of such rooms in most large museums, notably in our own. Among other advantages would be the very great one, that when the daily hour of closing the main building arrives, the officers need no longer, as at present, be interrupted in whatever piece of work they may have at hand, and turned out of the building, but, as arrangements could easily be made for a separate exit, they could continue their labours as long and as late as they find it convenient to do so, without any fear for the safety of the general collections.

It will be observed that provision is made for a central hall, which is always a good architectural feature at the entrance of a building, and which in a large museum is certainly useful in providing for the exhibition of objects of general interest not strictly coming under any of the divisions of the subject in the galleries, or possibly for specimens of too great a size to be conveniently exhibited elsewhere. There is also provision in the central part of the building for the refreshment-rooms, as well as for the library and a lecture room, the first being an essential, and the latter a very useful adjunct to any collection intended for popular instruction, even if no strictly systematic teaching should be part of its programme. I may point out, lastly, as a great advantage of this plan, that it can be, if space is reserved or obtainable, indefinitely extended on both sides on exactly the same system without in any way interfering with the existing arrangements; a new section, containing exhibition and reserve galleries and studies, can be added as required at either end, either for the reception of new departments or for the expansion of the old ones. With a view to the latter it is most important that the fittings should be as little as possible of the nature of fixtures but should all be so constructed as to be readily removable and interchangeable. This is a point I would strongly impress upon all who are concerned in fitting up museums, either large or small. The modifications of this plan, to adapt it to the requirements of a municipal, school, or even village museum, will consist mainly in altering the relative proportion of the two sections of the collection. The majority of museums in country localities require little, if anything, beyond the exhibition series. In this the primary arrangement to be aimed at is, first, absolutely to separate the archaeological, historical, and art portions of the collection from the natural history, if, as will generally be the case, both are to be represented in the museum. If possible they should be in distinct rooms. The second point is to divide each branch into two sections: (1) a strictly limited general or type collection, arranged upon a purely educational plan; (2) a local collection, consisting only of objects found within a certain well-defined radius around the museum, which should be as exhaustive as possible. Nothing else should be attempted, and therefore reserve collections are unnecessary. . . . I have elsewhere indicated my views as to the objects most suitable for, and the best arrangement of them in, school museums, so I need say nothing further on the subject now. Indeed, I fear I have exhausted your patience, so I will conclude by expressing an earnest hope that this meeting may prove a stimulus to all of us to continue heartily and thoroughly at our work, which I hardly need say is the only way to ensure that general recognition of it which we all so much desire.

# 20

# MUSEUM IDEALS OF PURPOSE AND METHOD

## Benjamin Ives Gilman

Boston, MA: Boston Museum of Fine Arts, 117 pp., 1918

---

*The following selections are taken from Museum Ideals of Purpose and Method, written by Benjamin Ives Gilman, secretary of the Boston Museum of Art. In "Dr. Goode's Thesis and Its Antithesis," Gilman takes issue with George Brown Goode's definition of "an efficient educational museum," arguing that his thesis cannot be applied to art museums, which he asserts are not inherently educational institutions. In "On the Distinctive Purpose of Museums of Art," Gilman distinguishes between the artistic museum and the didactic museum, or the difference between art and science museums.*

---

### . . . Dr. Goode's Thesis and Its Antithesis

An often quoted sentence from a paper by Dr. George Brown Goode, former Assistant Secretary of the Smithsonian Institution, runs as follows:

An efficient educational museum may be described as a collection of instructive labels each illustrated by a well-selected specimen.

Is this thesis applicable to museums indiscriminately? In a museum of fine art, are the labels really more important than the exhibits; or are the exhibits more important than the labels? Is a museum of fine art at bottom an educational institution or an artistic institution?. . . .

129

Two words in Dr. Goode's formula should warn us against the grievous injustice of condemning as a Philistine a writer so active-minded, acute, and liberal. His thesis is expressly restricted to "educational" museums whose contents are "specimens." Looking further through his exposition, we come upon many plain indications that he grasped, if he did not consistently pursue, the idea of museums non-educational in type, to whose contents the term "specimen" might not apply. He writes of "fine art collections, best to be arranged from an aesthetic standpoint, by artists"; and again, of collections of artistic masterpieces as "shrines" and "heirlooms," and again of "many so-called museums" as in reality "permanent exhibitions." Nor did he offer even his latest ideas on museum administration as finished results, but expressly as material for critical discussion. Yet the criticism he hoped for has hardly taken place. On the contrary, one telling sentence of his has been, as it were, preserved in alcohol, as a final word on the whole subject.

What is a "specimen"? Has the idea any opposite?

We call an object a specimen when we think of certain qualities in which it resembles other things. We call it on the other hand a unicum when we think of qualities in which it differs from any other thing. Now, nothing is absolutely unlike anything else; even a hawk and a handsaw are alike in having teeth. Nor is anything absolutely like anything else; even two peas differ in their strain on the pod. Hence anything we please is always both a specimen and a unicum. It is more or less like other things, and hence a specimen; and it is always also just itself and nothing else, and hence a unicum. But although every object is at once specimen and unicum, it may be that we value it in either way more than we value it in the other; and this is the practical significance of the two words, specimen and unicum. A specimen is a thing we talk of and treat with reference to its resemblances to other timings. Its value, as we say, is illustrative, residing in its abstract bearings. A unicum is a thing we talk of and treat with reference to its differences from any other thing. Its value, as we say, is individual, residing in its concrete self. This is the kind of regard we feel for individuals *par excellence,* or persons. The feeling of Americans for Lincoln is not admiration for a group of qualities—for patience, acuteness, strength of purpose, kindliness, homely wit—but for these and countless other traits as they are embodied in the individual life we recall under that name. Contrariwise, the passion that impels the artist is not a passion for abstract qualities but for a concrete object, limitless source of abstractions, as it grows under his hand. There is but one Venus of Melos, but one Lycidas. There is but one Moonlight Sonata of Beethoven, and but one Three Trees of Rembrandt, many as are the renditions of the one and impressions of the other. Thus we speak quite naturally of the friendship of fine art. The feeling which the artist's other half—the true beholder of his work—feels for his creation is in turn unique, like the regard we entertain toward a human being.

When, therefore, we apply Dr. Goode's formula to collections of fine art we find it talking nonsense, just as a formula of mathematics talks nonsense when applied to facts it does not fit. For a collection of works of art is not a collection of specimens, but a collection of their opposites, namely, unica. More precisely, our primary purpose in showing things concrete in aim is itself concrete and not abstract. In speaking of museums of art Dr. Goode's thesis must be dropped and an antithesis substituted. Their essential nature is not that of collections of abstractions illuminated for us by examples, but that of collections of concrete things introduced to us by ideas. This is the antithesis which is needed and which had been recognized from the beginning at the museum where the controversy started.

The distinction admits of many forms of statement. Museums of science aim first at abstract knowledge, museums of art at concrete satisfaction. A museum of science is a place of pleasant thought; a museum of art a place of thoughtful pleasure. A scientific museum is devoted to observations, an art museum to valuations. A collection of science is gathered primarily in the interest of the real; a collection of art primarily in the interest of the ideal. The former is a panorama of fact, the latter a paradise of fancy. In the former we learn, in the latter we admire. A museum of science is in essence a school; a museum of art in essence a temple. Minerva presides over the one, sacred to the reason; Apollo over the other, sacred to the imagination.

Thesis and antithesis follow deductively. An object of science being specimen, and an object of art unicum, in a museum of science the accompanying information is more important than the objects; in a museum of art, less. For while both are collections exemplifying human creative power, in the museum of science the creation is the general law *repre*sented by the description; in the art museum, it is the particular fact *pre*sented by the object. Thus, as Dr. Goode well said, in a museum of science, the object exists for the description; but as he was not yet ready to say, in a museum of art the relation is reversed—the description exists for the object. A museum of science is in truth a collection of labels *plus* illustrations; but a museum of art a collection of objects *plus* interpretations. . . .

## On the Distinctive Purpose of Museums of Art

Capital stress has in recent years been laid upon the educational functions of public museums, collections of fine art either included without argument or excepted without clearly expressed conviction. The purpose of the following pages is to question the right, thus assumed in fact or in effect, to conceive and manage a public treasury of art as if primarily an agency of popular instruction. According to the Areopagitica, who kills a good book kills reason itself. No less the precious lifeblood of a master spirit, who kills good painting or good sculpture kills imagination itself; and neither truly lives where its designed artistic effect is held permanently subordinate to an adventitious educational end. To preserve and display masterpieces of art, while preferring to the imaginative purpose of the artist an ulterior aim with which the imagination has nothing to do, is to betray the cause of art instead of serving it. There is imposed upon museums of the fine arts by the nature of their contents an obligation paramount to the duty of public instruction incumbent on all museums, the obligation, namely, to promote public appreciation of certain visible and tangible creations through which the fancy of man has bidden his senses follow its flight.

The argument here offered in support of this thesis may thus be summarized. A fundamental distinction is drawn between the esthetic, or intrinsic, and the practical, or borrowed, worth of things; and it is claimed that their artistic quality is a species of the former, and their educational value of the latter. Museums are defined as permanent exhibitions of objects gathered because possessing either artistic quality (museums of fine art) or educational value (museums of science or the useful arts). From these two propositions it follows apodictically that museums of art and museums of other kinds differ radically as institutions of aesthetic, or appreciative, and practical, or instructive aim respectively. Four ways in which fine art, while aiming at appreciation, may result in instruction, are then examined; and in closing, three reasons are given why its educational by-product should in many minds overshadow its proper artistic yield.

It is here sought, in a word, to establish a conception of the essential functions of public museums which shall duly recognize the fundamental distinction between art and science—the purpose to present and the purpose to inform; between concrete and abstract, imagination and reason.

Anything we have to do with may either be to us or bring to us a valuable experience; may have worth either by its nature or its issue. We plant flowers for their own sake; grain for a harvest. In the first case a thing has value in itself; it is an end. In the second case it has value through other things, to which it is the means. In speaking of things perceived by the senses, we may, by interpreting the two words aesthetic and practical according to their etymological meaning *(αισθανομαι,* to perceive by the senses, and *πρασσω,* to bring about) call the former aesthetic, the latter practical value. An aesthetic object, in this sense, is one which needs, to justify its existence, only adequate apprehension; a practical thing is one which approves itself through some valuable outcome.

Of the two fundamental forms of value, a work of fine art may have both; but the one casually, the other essentially. The distinction between fine and useful art rests upon the possession by the former of aesthetic qualities; that is, qualities which give a thing worth simply as an object for our perceptive faculties. The value of a work of fine art as end and not as means, its immediate, underivative worth as mere incorporate vision, pure object of contemplation, is that by which it came to be, that to seize and perpetuate which its maker created it. To be seen in its perfection is the whole of what a work of art as a work of art was made for. It was brought forth to transfer a certain perceptive and emotional content, often more than is consciously apprehended by the maker, to the soul of a beholder through his senses. The constitutive aim of every work of fine art, beyond which as an art-work it has none, is worthily to occupy the powers of apprehension; to bring before other eyes, to transplant into other minds and hearts what was, before the work existed, the passionate secret of the creative faculties of a single man of talent. The ultimate end of every art work is to be beheld and felt as it was wrought, and this end it fulfils whenever any one stands before it and perceives in it the artistic content it was made to convey, enters into the soul of the artist through the gateway of his work. Creation and appreciation, formation in one spirit and reconstruction in another, are the two poles between which lies the whole sphere of art. The whole life history of an art work is summed up in its birth in the imagination of an artist, and its rebirth through the senses of a beholder. Art is of the nature of an open communication, not of abstract notions but of concrete fancies, from the artist to all others whom it may concern. When an art work has said its say, its mission as an art work is accomplished, save as it forever repeats the same message.

Any collection of objects permanently preserved for the observation of spectators forms a museum. Objects may be collected and exhibited either on account of their aesthetic or their practical value. A collection restricted to works of art is one in which the criterion of selection is aesthetic quality, higher or lower. Any object that has none is not a work of art. In a collection of scientific specimens or technical appliances it is a practical quality that is the basis of choice. Unless an object possess some instructive value it has no place in a museum of science or industry. The fundamental distinction between these two principles of selection defines two radically different types of the permanent public exhibitions we call museums: The limiting purpose of the one is aesthetic, and in particular artistic; that of the other practical, and in particular didactic. An art museum is a selection of objects adapted to impress; a scientific or technical museum is a selection of objects adapted to instruct.

By no liberality in the definition of the word education can we reduce these two purposes, the artistic and the didactic, to one. They are mutually exclusive in scope, as they are distinct in value.

They are mutually exclusive in scope; for education, according to received usage, is "the imparting of knowledge or skill"; in other words, the inculcation of habits of thought or action; or, still more briefly, the moulding of personality. The term refers to the spiritual or bodily effect of a course of experience, be its nature what it may. It means that a certain chosen character is impressed upon us; that we are approximated to an ideal of personality, shaped to a model, formed as in a mould. Artistic comprehension, on the other hand, is the pure use of the perceptive faculties upon an object of human creation; it is the seeing of a thing as its maker saw it, in a measure it may be unknown to himself. The term refers to the nature of our experiences, be their effect upon us what it may. It means that the mind rests in its object, simply and fully beholding it, without deserting it for any other interest whatever. The nature of anything and the effect of anything being two wholly different matters, the two aims, that of artistic comprehension and that of instruction, exclude one another. The former seeks to give us experiences of a certain kind; the latter to give us experiences having a certain result. The aesthetic purpose, the aim of art, is to engage the powers; the didactic purpose, the aim of education, is to modify them. Where the sphere of education begins, the sphere of art ends. . . .

Thus neither in scope nor in value is the purpose of an art museum a pedagogic one. An institution devoted to the preservation and exhibition of works of the fine arts is not an educational institution, either in essence or in its claims to consideration. While museums of science or of useful art are a part of our educational system, institutions auxiliary to our schools, our colleges and our universities, aiming at the diffusion of information about the sciences and arts to which they relate, museums of fine art are a part of our artistic life, serving the cause, not of any utility, pedagogic or other, but of art itself. They are institutions auxiliary to that public display of creative genius in the construction and adornment of public buildings and other monuments, which is the first duty of living art to the place of its birth. In their chief function, it is theirs to gather up the art of the past, whose public no longer exists, and offer hospitality to the art of foreign lands, whose public is another than ours. They are instrumentalities by which civilization provides that neither shall antique art be lost, nor exotic art be non-existent to us. The distinctive purpose of an art museum may be precisely defined as the aim to bring about that perfect contemplation of the works of art it preserves which is implied in their production and forms their consummation.

But while this aesthetic office, proper to a collection of works of fine art, is fundamentally different from the didactic function for which other museums exist, there are still three ways in which the former attains or may be applied to pedagogical ends, as well as a fourth in which it can aid its own artistic aims by educational means.

In the first place, the appreciation of art is itself an educational influence. It should be noted that this is not because, like all other experiences of life, those of an aesthetic kind must be supposed to leave the personality in some degree other than they found it. Experience is not on this account didactic. To be didactic it must not simply alter the personality, it must shape it to some model. Apart from the belief that life is all a school, a peasant is not as fully educated as a prince, although the former is subjected to a whole lifetime of trace-leaving experiences, and the latter to no more. For many more ideals, many more shaping purposes, have worked through the experiences of the prince than through those of the peasant. Likewise art is educative only in so far as there exist ideals of personality which work upon us through its creations. But since they are the product of the happier moods of more gifted people, it is fair to assume that in their assimilation we shall tend to be made over in the likeness of what is best in human endowment. In this view of art it is one of the ways in which the good word is passed among the children of men. It is one of the means by which the more fortunate few can permanently impress upon the less fortunate many some of their own excellencies. It is one of the ways in which character teaches by example. Artistic insight is a form of the inter-action of personality to which moral feeling offers the complement; since by appreciation we enter into the joy of another, as by sympathy into his pain. In art, the material of man's experience is re-wrought nearer to his heart's desire. It is a new world, of preferences, satisfactions, and ideals, set beside the old indifferent or sorrowful reality. From its contemplation we come as from a respite, strengthened for that from which it has brought relief; and endowed, moreover, with new patterns in the mind to which to approximate the life. The paradise of artistic creation is not hung in the heavens like an Olympus detached from earth, whose divinities have no thought for human kind. It has its consoling and inspiring outlook also, upon everyday reality. . . .

In the second and third places, works of art have a function both in the promotion of historical learning and the development of technical skill. They are facts and bases of inference in the study of man and his past; and their scrutiny and imitation are means of instruction to those who are seeking command of the like instruments of aesthetic expression. To students both of the humanities and the practice of art, the study of works of art is an indispensable aid.

True. But while it is both possible and desirable to apply the contents of an art museum to educational ends, and while it may often be that a given art work has more instructive than artistic value, it is not its instructive value that makes of an object a work of art. Thus to use art works is again not to use them as they were created to be used, but for another than their native purpose. Not the investigator, not the craftsman, but the beholder—the sight-seer, in the strict and full acceptation of that word—is he for whose benefit art in its totality exists. To be appreciated is its whole end and aim, the fruition of all artistic effort; and neither the moulding of character, the furtherance of historical knowledge, nor the advancement of technical skill. . . .

In the fourth place, an art museum can, and as a matter of fact must, to fulfil its own proper purpose as a treasure-house of the art of bygone times and far-off peoples, perform a special educational work. While it is far from being able to do all that is necessary to enable its visitors to take the point of view of other civilizations, it can still do much to this end, and what it can do it should do. It is true that the capacity to comprehend works of art is in no small degree a matter of native endowment. Yet in its measure it both needs and admits of aid. The right kind of instruction will almost always augment the power of a given person to see what the maker of a given work meant by it; although no amount of training will enable some persons to see what others can see without training at all. Without overestimating the degree in which the information of the public will render it more accessible to an artistic message, the principle is evident that a liberal use of educational means is indispensable to the proper aesthetic purpose of any collection of artistic objects, and is therefore to be included among its duties.

The conclusions of this discussion may be summed up in the statement that while museums of other kinds are at bottom educational institutions, a museum of fine art is not didactic but aesthetic in primary purpose, although formative in its influence, and both admitting of and profiting by a secondary pedagogical use. The true conception of an art museum is not that of an educational institution having art for its teaching material, but that of an artistic institution with educational uses and demands. . . .

# 21

# THE NEW MUSEUM

## John Cotton Dana

The New Museum Series, no. 1. Woodstock Vermont: The Elm Tree Press, 52 pp., 1917

*John Cotton Dana, founder and director of the Newark Museum, outlines his ideas advancing George Brown Goode's concept of the "new museum." For Dana, the educational museum had a duty to serve its community by providing ample opportunities for formal and informal learning. He is highly critical of grand science and art museums whose sheer size and soaring architecture served to isolate them from their communities, thus alienating the audience that most needed them.*

### . . . The Coming of the New Museum Idea

The same open-minded study (did we not believe it was open-minded we would never presume to offer to our colleagues any suggestions whatever) which seemed to us to demonstrate the general futility of conventional museums of whatever character, brought to our attention a movement within the museum field which precisely fell in with the notions we had already acquired concerning museum work.

This movement or activity within certain museums, suggested long ago by Mr. Goode and hinted at broadly by a few students long before his day, has scarcely yet embodied itself in a museum. It is too new, on the one hand, and the old "art gallery" and "collections" ideas of museums are still too powerful, on the other hand, to permit it to express itself fully in an active, complete, and well-rounded institution. There are seeming exceptions to this statement here and there, which will be alluded to later.

This new movement with which we have tried to identify ourselves and in which we have tried to do our part is difficult of description. It is not directed to the erection of Greek or Renaissance facades in parks or corners remote from a city's center. It is not concerned with the construction, behind those facades, of a few grand courts and galleries. Its galleries or work and study rooms are not to be invested with that ancient and ghastly fetish, a top light—something which one may properly hope to escape when he enters a modern building. It is not friendly to that "museum" atmosphere which is depressing and numbing to the sensitive visitor in direct ratio to the self-conscious grandeur and refinement of its architectural container. Nor does this new museum method aim at the acquisition of rare and priceless objects with which to fill rows of cold and costly cases, all peculiarly well fitted, if they do nothing else, to aggravate the foolish pride of the thoughtless citizen; nor at the acquisition of so many objects within any one field as to make a museum distinctly a museum of a certain kind.

## The Value of Mere Collections

Parenthetically it should be said—lest some misunderstand our attitude toward the preservation of rare and beautiful objects, toward the creation of art galleries, toward the making of science collections and collections in any field whatever—that all these things are manifestly useful and have their proper place. We merely hold to the theory that in most cases their immediate utility is vastly over-rated; that their cost is out of proportion to their value; that their managers usually too greatly exalt their acquisitions and forget the entertainment and instructions of those for whom they were professedly acquired; and that their presence, and the dominance of the conventions which go with them, make very difficult the introduction of homelier, more attractive, and more useful objects and methods into the museum world.

Most of us prefer to copy. It is one of the limitations of wealth that it cannot be original in its exercise of one of its prime functions, the practice of conspicuous wastefulness. The rich like to collect what other rich have collected. They add the lust of possession to the practice of patronage of art or science. They think of "grand" public homes of the public's treasures only in terms convention has fixed. Hence remote palaces full of things whose accepted merits in beauty, rarity, age, and cost are excelled only by the paucity of their visitors.

But, as it is well for the public to become possessors of the rich and rare, and as the rich will supply them only under certain architectural and administrative conditions, it is obvious that it would be quite as foolish as it would be unwise to oppose the growth of the conventional museum.

Our attitude of criticism which is, we fully realize, quite negligible as such, is born merely of the belief that a better type of museum, a museum properly so-called, indeed, is possible, is in fact inevitable, and that some of the energy and money which now goes to the old kind of museum store-house may well be diverted to the new kind of museum work-shop. And that belief is expressed in this pamphlet as a partial explanation of the character of the constructive suggestions we make later.

## The General Theory of the New Movement

The general theory of the new movement we are trying to describe seems to be this:

Each community can use to good advantage a certain quantity of material in formal and informal training through the eye. This training, this visual instruction, every member of every community is gaining in some measure every working moment of his life. In each community there is a tendency toward rather special and somewhat limited interests in the visual field, by reason of the special industrial, commercial, and educational activities of that community. We believe that it will pay any community to add to its educational apparatus a group of persons which shall form the staff of a local institution of visual instruction and to put in the hands of these persons modest sums with which they shall acquire, label, describe, arrange for show, and prepare for lending such objects as careful study and experiment shall suggest in the expectation that staff and objects combined will do for the community these things at least, and, one may hope, in time many others:

1. Entertain—and be ready to try to interest and instruct—such as may have the wish and the time to visit casually the institution's headquarters.

2. Entertain and more definitely and generally instruct—in classes and conducted groups, by labels, leaflets, handbooks, talks, and illustrated lectures—such adults as may be induced to come to see special exhibits, also at the institute headquarters.

3. Entertain, interest, and still more definitely instruct children who may be sent to the institute's headquarters from schools on stated occasions and for certain specific observations the objects observed

and the talks and the reading expounding the objects being closely related to school work and to the age and stage of mental development of each group that comes.

4. Prepare for schools single objects and groups of objects with such labels, leaflets, lantern slides, and instructors as the proper use of each may demand, and lend these to schools as the school authorities may designate, all being fitted, of course, to make easier the work of teaching and to make broader and more effective the work of the pupils.

5. Place in schools—as opportunity and fit occasions and the felt need of teachers, supervisors, and the management may indicate—single objects and large and small collections of objects, fully labeled and accompanied by pictures, leaflets, and pamphlets; all being such as may entertain and instruct both teachers and pupils, and particularly such as may be found to give constant and almost daily assistance in adding interest and value to studies and in broadening the experiences of pupils and in awakening new interests in them. These to be changed as use and circumstance suggest.

6. Place in convenient and easily accessible rooms (like store rooms on business streets and in special rooms with separate entrances in school buildings) single objects and small, well-rounded collections in art, science, industry, ethnology, and other fields, such as experience shows will attract a large number of visitors. Manage these branch institutes when possible as veritable independent teaching centers, with leaflets and cards descriptive of the museum's work and its acquisitions for distribution, and with skilled attendants who can describe and instruct as opportunity offers.

7. Discover collectors and specialists and experts in the community and secure their cooperation in adding to the museum's collections; in helping identify, describe, and prepare labels and leaflets; in arousing the interest of young people in the museum's work and in finding such boys and girls as may wish to make collections of objects of any kind for themselves or for the museum.

This development of the collecting habit among the young, with its accompanying education of powers of observation, its training in handwork, its tendency to arouse interests theretofore unsuspected even by those who possess them, its continuous suggestions toward good taste and refinement which lie in the process of installing even the most modest of collections, and its leadings toward sound civic interest through doing for one's community a helpful thing—this work of securing the cooperation of boys and girls, making them useful while they are gaining their own pleasure and carrying on their own education, is one of the coming museum's most promising fields.

8. Lend to individuals, groups, and societies, for any proper use and for any reasonable length of time, any of the museum's objects, whenever it is clear that things thus lent will be of more service to the community than when they are resting, relatively unseen and unused, in the museum's headquarters.

9. Prepare and display, at the headquarters, at branches, and in schools, carefully selected objects which are products of the community's activities in field, factory, and workshop. These will be local industry exhibits. They may be so small as to show in a very easily transported case a few of the major steps in the manufacture of a simple object. They may include merely a group of completed objects, interesting for their beauty or complexity, or for the high technical skill of the craftsman who made them. Or they may be so extensive as to fill every available inch of space the museum controls and to illustrate many aspects of one field of industry, and so general as to give a bird's-eye view of all the industries of the whole community. These may be planned to attract and interest the business man, or to draw to them the women, or to arouse in young people a healthful curiosity in the activities of their community and the results of the daily labor of men and women—their fathers, mothers, brothers, and sisters, in the field, the store, and the factory.

10. Keep the museum and its activities continually before the community in the daily press, and publish and distribute as many leaflets, posters, broadsides, and cards descriptive of the museum's acquisitions as conditions seem to warrant. At the proper time publish leaflets and booklets, based on the museum's material, proper to be used as reading lessons in the schools.

11. Connect the work the museum may do, its objects, and all the activities of its staff, with all the resources of the public library. In doing this, many books and journals will be displayed near objects on view, references to books and journals will be made on labels and in leaflets of all kinds, and the library will be asked to show placards and notes and to distribute things the museum may publish descriptive of its purposes and activities. . . .

# 22

# THE MUSEUM CONSCIENCE

## Joseph Grinnell

*Museum Work*, 4: 62–63, 1921

*Although Joseph Grinnell's article on "The Museum Conscience" specific-
ally addresses issues for scientific collections, his emphasis on order, accuracy, and simplicity in managing collections are universal principles. As
the first director of the Museum of Vertebrate Zoology at the University of
California, Grinnell had first-hand experience in using and teaching these
ethical principles to students.*

The scientific museum, the kind of museum with which my remarks here
have chiefly to do, is a storehouse of facts, arranged accessibly and supported by the written records and labeled specimens to which they per-
tain. The purpose of a scientific museum is realized whenever some group
of its contained facts is drawn upon for studies leading to publication.
The investment of human energy in the formation and maintenance of
a research museum is justified only in proportion to the amount of real
knowledge which is derived from its materials and given to the world.

All this may seem to be innocuous platitude—but it is genuine gospel,
never-the-less, worth pondering from time to time by each and every
museum administrator. It serves now as a background for my further
comments.

For worthy investigation based upon museum materials it is absolutely
essential that such materials have been handled with careful regard for
accuracy and order. To secure accuracy and order must, then, once the
mere safe preservation of the collections of which he is in charge has been
attended to, be the immediate aim of the curator.

*Order* is the key both to the accessibility of materials and to the appreciation of such facts and inferences as these materials afford. An arrangement according to some definite plan of grouping has to do with whole collections, with categories of specimens within each collection, with specimens within each general category, with the card indexes, and even with the placement of the data on the label attached to each specimen. Simplicity and clearness are fundamental to any scheme of arrangement adopted. Nothing can be more disheartening to a research student, except absolute chaos than a complicated "system," in the invidious sense of the word, carried out to the absurd limits recommended by some so-called "efficiency expert." However, error in this direction is rare compared with the opposite extreme, namely, little or no order at all.

To secure a really practicable scheme of arrangement takes the best thought and much experimentation on the part of the keenest museum curator. Once he has selected or devised his scheme, his work is not *done,* moreover, until this scheme is in operation throughout all the materials in his charge. Any fact, specimen, or record left out of order is lost. It had, perhaps, better not exist, for it is taking space somewhere; and space is the chief cost initially and currently in any museum.

The second essential in the care of scientific materials is *accuracy.* Every item on the label of each specimen, every item of the general record in the accession catalog, must be precise as to fact. Many errors in published literature, now practically impossible to "head off," are traceable to mistakes on labels. Label-writing having to do with scientific materials is not a chore to be handed over casually to a "25-cent-an-hour" girl, or even to the ordinary clerk. To do this essential work correctly requires an exceptional genius plus training. The important habit of reading every item back to copy is a thing that has to be acquired through diligent attention to this very point. By no means *any* person that happens to be around is capable of doing such work with reliable results.

Now it happens that there is scarcely an institution in the country bearing the name museum, even though its main purpose be the quite distinct function of exhibition and popular education, that does not lay more or less claim to housing "scientific collections." Yet such a claim is false, *unless* an adequate effort has been expended both to label accurately and to arrange systematically all of the collections housed. Only when this has been done can the collections be called in truth *scientific.*

My appeal is, then, to every museum director and to every curator responsible for the proper use as well as the safe preservation of natural history specimens. Many species of vertebrate animals are disappearing; some are gone already. All that the investigator of the future will have, to indicate the nature of such then extinct species, will be the remains of these species preserved more or less faithfully, along with the data accompanying them, in the museums of the country.

I have definite grounds for presenting this appeal at this time and in this place. My visits to the various larger museums have left me with the unpleasant and very distinct conviction that a large portion of the vertebrate collections in this country, perhaps 90 per cent of them, are in far from satisfactory condition with respect to the matters here emphasized. It is admittedly somewhat difficult for the older museums to modify systems of installation adopted at an early period. But this is no valid argument against necessary modification, which should begin at once with all the means available—the need for which should, indeed, be emphasized above the making of new collections or the undertaking of new expeditions. The older materials are immensely valuable historically, often irreplaceable. Scientific interests at large demand special attention to these materials.

The urgent need, right now, in every museum, is for that special type of curator who has ingrained within him the instinct to devise and put into operation the best arrangement of his materials—who will be alert to see and to hunt out errors and instantly make corrections—who has the *museum conscience.*

# 23

# MUSEUM ETHICS

## L. Earle Rowe

*Proceedings of the American Association of Museums, 11: 137–143, 1917*

*This article is perhaps the earliest American publication to discuss the issue of museum ethics—written eight years before the American Association of Museums's first code of ethics for museum workers (AAM 1925). Earl Rowe, Director of the Rhode Island School of Design, addresses a range of ethical issues—many of which are pertinent today—including the necessity for museum directors to have a willingness to loan collections, to respect other museums and encourage cooperation and collaboration, and to cultivate a positive relationship with dealers, collectors, and staff. He emphasizes that the museum director, as the most influential of all museum personnel, must be held to the highest possible standard. Rowe also cautions all museum workers against accepting fees for services and personal collecting.*

For the past twenty-five years the museum world has been discussing the development of museum policy along two lines, the scholastic and the esthetic. Each has its adherents, and each offers advantages not available in the other. Gradually has developed a type of museum which seeks to adopt the esthetic without losing sight of the value of the scholastic point of view.

We have in our discussions considered as features of museum policy such points as the emphasis on usefulness, the development of every function, the willingness to be of service to everybody, the employment of business methods and system, the use of exhibitions, lectures, and publications, careful attention to cases, backgrounds, installation, labels, etc., and the proper care of the works of art with which we are entrusted.

This discussion of museum policy has been of distinct advantage. It has clarified the ideas of those responsible for the line of action, it has emphasized the need of proving the value of the work, and it has led to a greater interest on the part of an increasing public. On the other hand, there are certain features of the relation of museums to each other, and especially of the museum to dealers, its members, scholars, and to its staff, which come directly under the head of museum ethics. These have not as yet been discussed in detail. Is there not something to be said on this subject, or are we going to let our museums work out their own salvation, irrespective of others' experience? Perhaps there has been a hesitation in discussing the subject as being too intangible and too general for our meetings. This may be true, but if by a presentation of some of the points in question which come under the heading of museum ethics we may be led in our discussion to crystallize into definite form the results of our experiences, they will doubtless prove of distinct value.

The subject of ethics is not before us for discussion in its philosophical sense, but in one much more definite. Ethics in general has been defined as the "Science of conduct or duty" (Bascom). Usually the term is applied to that conduct or duty which is related to moral procedure. The museum profession throughout has been developed on such a high plane that, except in very rare cases, the element of moral procedure has not departed from the most desirable standard. But there are activities of museum and staff which do come before us for discussion, and which, perhaps remotely, do have a moral significance.

Up to the present time the art museums have done little in the direction of cooperation. Each has jealously guarded its possessions; each has developed its store or study rooms which care for material not on general exhibition, and has rarely been willing to consider the loan or gift of this material to less fortunate institutions, In the case of larger museums there has been a decided reluctance to consider requests for loans from other institutions. Also, the larger museums have hesitated to ask the smaller museums for important works of art which are needed for special exhibitions, for fear that by doing so they might in turn be asked to make similar loans. There is much to be said on both sides of this problem. On the one hand, the institution is the custodian of works of art which cannot be duplicated, and there are the risks in transit of damage, fire, or theft. It must frankly be admitted that the more a work of art is handled, the more difficult it is to keep it in condition. But with agreement on this point, is there not a great deal of material quite beyond the reach of many a struggling museum, which is infrequently or never used in the larger museum and only takes valuable space? It does not reduce in any way the independence of the smaller museums to accept such loans, nor need it make them feel that they are feeders for the greater ones. The chief difficulty in the way of such cooperation lies in the fact that gifts are usually given with real or implied conditions, and the museums feel bound by them. This the institutions must overcome by concerted effort.

Other phases of the relations between the museums themselves also come within the limits of our subject. In the open auction room there may always be gentlemanly competition for the highly desirable work of art, but in the outside world there are courtesies which have been found highly desirable for general progress. For instance, there is the question of museums respecting the particular interests of others. If a smaller museum is particularly interested in the acquisition of some of the historical and artistic material created in its own vicinity, is it quite courteous for another to seek to acquire these objects at a time when it is known that the first museum is still interested? Such procedure is always possible when wealthy institutions bring to bear the pressure of their financial resources. This has little application to objects for sale at a distance from the place where they have a particular interest. It might prove of distinct advantage, both financial and otherwise, to advise other museums of opportunities for acquisition.

The chief place of museum ethics in the relations between similar institutions lies in allowing each to work out its own problems, unless assistance is asked; in respecting the fields of special interests; in advising each other of opportunities for purchases which may not be necessary for the larger collections; and especially in placing at the disposal of other institutions the advice of such experts as may be found in the staff. This does not mean constant demand on the experts, but an occasional courtesy of this sort which will be widespread in its influence. We are but at the beginning of such cooperation, and the American Association of Museums can do much to encourage this relation.

In its relation to dealers and the auction room, the museum soon finds that a very definite line of procedure and conduct is most advisable. Unless a dealer is in a fair way to impose on a prospective buyer, the museum should not interfere. The reputable dealers, even if they do act on the principle that a "work of art is worth what you can get for it," rarely give occasion for interference. On the other hand, the relation between dealer and museum should be cordial, considerate, and most business-like. It is customary for the dealer to quote a special price to the museum. There is nothing objectionable in this. There is divided opinion, however, as to the advisability of an institution accepting gifts from dealers. Here it depends on the dealer. If the gift is made from real interest in the work and a desire to help, that is one thing; but if it is made in the Oriental sense, with a view to developing such obligation on the part of the museum as will further particular or general business interests, it is unwise to accept the gift.

There is likely to be a difference of opinion as to whether it is wise for museum officers to give names of prospective buyers to the dealers, or to take buyers to the dealers' galleries. The difficulty is to avoid the impression of a secret understanding between the museum and the dealer. Each case has to be decided on its merits and the circumstances should determine the course to be pursued. Unless closely watched, this procedure might easily work against the welfare of the institution and the confidence of the collector. It certainly is unwise to give the names of prospective buyers to any dealer who may visit the city or seek an introduction.

Let us take the relations between the museum and the connoisseur or collector. Simple museum policy calls for as intimate a friendship as possible, for from such sources come the best support and many of the finest gifts. On the ethical side the museum should always deal fairly with him, by recognizing that he is learning by experience, that his opinion is honest, that it is his money which is to be paid for the object under consideration, and that only by friendly advice can he be influenced or led. There is also the delicate question of whether advice should be offered without its being asked for, but generally-speaking, it should be reserved for such a request from the collector.

As an instance where this relationship is desirable, let us assume that there is a possibility of a gift of certain works of art. The museum is wise which seeks to encourage such gifts without conditions, but is it just for us to accept a whole group of objects merely for the sake of one or two of decided importance? There are museums which never take collectors into their confidence by saying frankly, "So much can we show, the rest must go into our study series and store rooms, with small chance of their ever being shown," Unless this is followed, it is neither fair to the collector, just to his connoisseurship, nor wise in the long run for the museum; for other museums, less fortunate than the one immediately under consideration, would welcome and exhibit much or most of the material. I do not mean that we should ever depart from our ideal principles of a selective museum, but we should be fairer to ourselves, the collector, and other museums by stating the case clearly to the collector and perhaps recommending that his gift would be more acceptable elsewhere.

There is a grave question whether it is good policy to impose or accept fees for services rendered to connoisseurs or collectors. We grant that few institutions are so wealthy that every source of income is not desirable, but the institution can work more independently and honestly, and on a higher plane, when there is no remuneration in sight. This applies especially to advice regarding care and preservation of objects, and their authenticity. There is nothing to criticise in the practice of most museums of charging a small percentage as commission on sales made in its galleries. It is, however, not wise to emphasize the commercial side, and museums should encourage sales from exhibitions to hold the excellent works of art in the city and not for financial return. The more frank and open the museum staff, the greater is the confidence and loyalty of the collector.

In the opinion of many there are certain features of the relations of museums to director and staff which are of very great importance. The museum has presumably engaged the members of its staff because of knowledge or experience, and not for any social reason. If this is the case, then it is of the greatest importance that the museum should recognize this fact, should allow the staff to carry on its most effective work, and should hold that the members of the staff are working for its interests. Unfortunately all museums have not always held this view, with the result that the work of the museum for the time being has been seriously hampered. If there is community of interest, breadth of vision, and confidence in just treatment on both sides, the work will indeed advance most satisfactorily.

The most important person in a museum in many ways is its executive officer, the director. Called to fill a position of great trust, which demands executive ability, business acumen, great knowledge of his special subject, breadth of vision to appreciate all the interests of his museum, and a scholarship which commands respect, he finds that his road is not an easy one. Therefore there are certain features of museum conduct which directly apply to him. For example, under no condition should he personally accept fees for advice given, nor should he accept gifts or commissions for assisting friends or members of the museum. Especially should he avoid accepting favors or gifts from artists, dealers or commercial houses. In this way he is free to exercise independent judgment, and his advice is above reproach. Exception cannot be taken to his accepting remuneration for lectures outside of his museum, as these do not place him under any obligation, and are usually delivered in his free time. But if he is lecturing about the museum and collections under his charge no fee should be accepted. In this respect he should so judge his time and strength that his work for the museum will not suffer.

There is also a great question whether the director or any other staff officer of the museum should be a collector of such objects as the museum is acquiring, Generally speaking, the wisest course is to avoid being a collector. In this way there can be no question about the possibility of personal interest taking precedence over that of the museum. Proof might easily be offered which would show the wisdom of such a course. It might also be noted that if the director is not a collector, there will be less incentive for dealers, artists, or other interested parties to make gifts for ulterior motives.

Opportunity is sometimes presented for an officer of a museum to work for two places at once. While this is within the range of possibility, it may prove somewhat undesirable. No man can work for both institutions and give the same kind of service, for naturally he gives the museum where he is longest employed, or from which he receives the largest fee, the best of his knowledge and strength. If, for example, there comes an opportunity to secure a work of art, there is little question which museum will have first choice. The length of time that a second museum is willing to consider objects already discarded by the first depends upon the size and quality of its collection. The best way seems to be that suggested above, whereby the services of an expert staff are available for other museums, the first one always to be conversant with the arrangement, and no charge to be made to other galleries for the service.

The relations between director and staff also deserve close study. Admitting differences in circumstances, it has been shown that where mutual respect exists, with full appreciation of the organization, and a unity of purpose in the furtherance of the general welfare of the museum, there is no need for the friction which sometimes exists.

Much more might be said, but perhaps enough has been presented in this paper to open up lines of discussion of great interest to every one present. By our differences or agreement of opinion we might so crystallize some of the features of museum ethics that they will assist us in our own work and benefit other institutions or individuals who may meet some of these problems for the first time. Then will we discover that a constant employment of strict museum ethics is also good policy.

# SECTION IV

## Museum Education

This section contains ten articles about popular instruction—known today among museum professionals as "informal education." Many today consider the American Association of Museum's 1969 *Belmont Report* as the impetus for an educational movement in American museums. Although in the decade following the report, there was an enormous increase in educational programming, these articles reveal that, in fact, museum professionals have been thinking and writing about museums as educational institutions for the last 150 to 200 years. It is also important to note that half the articles in this section were authored by women—both an indication of the critical role they played developing educational programming in the early twentieth century and a reflection of the fact that early women in the museum profession were often limited to roles as public educators, rather than researchers.

The writings of Anna Billings Gallup, Carolyn Morse Rea (published as Mrs. Paul M. Rea), and Edward S. Morse will seem most familiar to today's museum educators as they focus on programs for K–12 children. Although Frederick Starr and Frank Collins Baker also address K–12 education, they focus on how universities can use museums to augment instruction. Starr urged for the development of "school museums" and Baker promoted the value of museum exhibits in visual education. Elizabeth Manning (Gardiner) Whitmore explores the role of the art museum "docent."

Henry Scadding, Thomas Greenwood, and Laura Woolsey Lord Scales discuss the use of museums to educate adults, particularly the working class—as Americans increasingly emphasized education as a means of social reform. Finally, Winifred E. Howe's essay is an early example of a museum education mission statement and guidelines.

## Additional Readings

AAM. 1969. *America's museums: The Belmont Report.* Washington, DC: American Association of Museums.

———. 1992. *Excellence and equity: Education and the public dimension of museums.* Washington, DC: American Association of Museums.

Blackmon, Carolyn, Teresa K. LaMaster, Lisa C. Roberts, and Beverly Serrell. 1988. *Open conversations: Strategies for professional development in museums.* Chicago: Field Museum of Natural History.

Diamond, Judy. 1999. *Practical evaluation guide: Tools for museums and other informal educational settings.* Walnut Creek, CA: AltaMira Press.

Falk, John H., and Lynn D. Dierking. 1992. *The museum experience.* Washington, DC: Whalesback Books.

———. 2000. *Learning from museums: Visitor experiences and the making of meaning.* Walnut Creek, CA: AltaMira Press.

Hooper-Greenhill, Eilean. 1994. *Museum and gallery education.* London: Leicester University Press.

———. (ed.). 1994. *The educational role of the museum.* New York: Routledge.

Karp, Ivan, and Steven Lavine (eds.). 1991. *Exhibiting cultures: The poetics and politics of museum display.* Washington, DC: Smithsonian Institution Press.

Leinhardt, Gaea, Kevin Crowley, and Karen Knutson (eds.). 2002. *Learning conversations in museums.* Mahwah, NJ: Lawrence Erlbaum Associates.

Paris, Scott. G. (ed.). 2002. *Perspectives on object-centered learning in museums.* Mahwah, NJ: Lawrence Erlbaum Associates.

Pittman-Gelles, Bonnie. 1981. *Museums' magic & children.* Washington, DC: Association of Science-Technology Centers.

# 24

# THE CHILDREN'S MUSEUM AS AN EDUCATOR

**Anna Billings Gallup**

*Popular Science Monthly*, 72: 371–379, 1908

*Anna Billings Gallup was a pioneer of children's museums in the United States. At the time she wrote this article, excerpted below, she was curator of the first museum designed specifically for children, the Brooklyn Children's Museum, a division of the Brooklyn Institute of Arts and Sciences. Gallup maintains that the object of the children's museum should be to offer educational programs not provided at school or at home; the success of which depended on understanding the tastes and the interests of children. Gallup's educational programs reflected her philosophy that the "keynote of childhood and youth is action."*

The Children's Museum is the only museum of its kind in the world. Although it has not reached its tenth birthday, it has won a permanent place in its own community and has awakened in this and foreign countries an interest in new lines of educational advancement suggestive of greater possibilities.

The origin and early history of this pioneer museum illustrate the power of small beginnings. Its life commenced in the residence of an attractive suburban estate which the city had taken for a public park, the Brooklyn Institute of Arts and Sciences having leased the house as temporary store room for its scientific collections. Upon the opening of the Central Museum of Arts and Sciences and the consequent removal of the most valuable institute property, the utility of the old residence would have been at an end had not its picturesqueness of situation suggested a branch museum for the benefit of children.

In December of that year, 1899, therefore, the Brooklyn Institute trustees opened to the juvenile public two small rooms of the Bedford Park building. Although the original exhibits consisted of little more than a few insects, shells and stuffed birds, the eagerness with which children sought them proved the necessity for enlarging the scope of work.

Some of the aims in establishing this children's branch were: to form an attractive resort for children tending to refine their tastes and elevate their interests; to create an active educational center of daily help in connection with school studies; and to suggest new subjects of thought for pursuit in leisure hours.

The method of procedure involved first, the necessity of collections attractive and stimulating to children and also helpful to the teachers of those children; second, a system of instruction that would lead to profitable results through voluntary endeavor on the part of the child.

The formation of suitable collections and the work of putting instruction on a practicable basis have involved the expenditure of time, as well as labor and money. But that progress has been made is shown in the contrast between the original collections and the twelve exhibition rooms of today furnished with specimens, models and pictures related to nearly every phase of children's intellectual interest.

These collections illustrate zoology, botany, United States history, mineralogy, geography, and art. They are attractive in appearance, simple in arrangement and labeled with descriptions adapted to the needs of children, printed in clear readable type.

Our zoological collections are installed in five rooms whose contents are prepared for children of varying ages. The youngest children seek the room of "animal bones," where common mammals and birds of Long Island are to be found with their nests and young. High school pupils make use of synoptic exhibits and particularly of the insect room with its local insects, life histories of common forms, and living bees, ants and silkworms. Bird exhibits attract and delight visitors of all ages from the two-year-old baby, who can only say "Chicken, chicken" as he points his chubby fingers indiscriminately to the condor, albatross and flamingo, to the white-haired grandparent whose "hunting days" are recalled by the mallard duck and grebe.

That their conceptions of geography may not end with maps, globes and charts, we employ model groups to acquaint children with remote peoples of the earth, especially type races from the various zone belts. One of these scenes depicts the life of the Eskimo, his costume, shelter, implements and industries. The story of his life struggles and the influence of his environment on appearance and conduct are easily understood. From the comparative study of an increasing number of such models, children readily perceive the importance of climate and physical features of localities in determining human settlement, industries and commerce. . . .

A children's museum library occupies two rooms in the museum building, and is a part of the museum work. Its 5,000 volumes comprise the best works on natural history, in its broadest sense, and closely related subjects. The library supplements the work of the museum in providing books useful to its staff in preparing collections, in furnishing additional information to visitors and in offering books on the lines of school work for the benefit of teachers and pupils. Two trained librarians in constant attendance enable visitors to consult books without formality and through an acquaintance with the contents of school curricula, the exhibition materials of the museum, and most important of all, the children themselves, the librarians not only furnish desired information, but guide and direct the tastes of young readers. Further than this, the library shows to parents and teachers the most interesting and helpful nature books, and aids them in selecting those best suited to the needs of their children. . . .

Through the *Museum News*, a joint monthly publication of the Brooklyn Institute Museums, principals and teachers in Brooklyn are informed of the half hour natural science, geography, and history talks, given in the children's museum lecture room. Teachers are invited to bring classes to these lectures (which are illustrated with lantern slides, models and experiments) or to study museum exhibits correlated with school work. Some member of the museum staff is always present to render every assistance to visiting classes. Objects and models are taken from the cases and used in demonstration, living specimens from vivaria and aquaria are shown to the nature study classes, questions are answered, in fact everything that can economize the time of the visitors and increase their enjoyment is done. Another privilege extended to schools is the use of stuffed birds, boxes of insects and other "loan material," distributed for class-room study.

The demand for the privileges of a Children's Museum may be seen from the readiness with which schools and individuals accept them. More than 125 schools, many of them remotely situated, send pupils and teachers to our museums; 561 visits from teachers alone in search of definite information were recorded in the school months of 1906, and for the same period the Children's Museum lectures attracted an attendance of 17,353. The average annual attendance for the past five years has exceeded 94,000 visitors.

It would seem from the statistics that a Children's Museum if not a life necessity, is indeed an unquestioned blessing to a great city like our own, whose population is boxed in apartments or brown stone blocks of such vast extent as to place the country beyond the experience of many children. The advantage of a cheerful, sunny, attractive museum rich in natural objects, artistically displayed, where children are sure to find a sympathetic welcome, where they are safe and happily and profitably occupied, is scarcely appreciated until we pause to consider the influence for good or evil of habits acquired in leisure hours, and of the demoralizing influence of crowded city streets and back alleys. . . .

Two years ago, in response to an expressed demand from the boys, the museum began a course of lectures in elementary physics, and in connection therewith invited those interested to come to the museum on certain afternoons to experiment individually with favorite pieces of apparatus. The boys found the utmost pleasure in the liberty thus granted—they experimented under the guidance of a member of the museum staff, they read library books in connection with their experiments and within a few months had set up a wireless telegraph station. The original work of these boys would be a credit to any institution, for they applied themselves regularly and diligently until they had learned to send and receive wireless messages; meanwhile, the experience of placing the station and keeping it in working order had fitted them to take charge of other stations. Early this summer, when the schools closed, three of these "boys" received offers of remunerative positions with one of the commercial companies to take charge of wireless stations on board of ocean-going steamships to South America, Panama, West Indies, Bermudas, Key West and other places of interest along the Atlantic seaboard. One of the boys, who had learned to collect and mount insects when he came to the museum as a primary lad, made a very creditable collection of tropical insects which he brought to the museum, carefully preserved and labeled with interesting data. . . .

Some have maintained that physics and electricity are subjects not germane to museum work, and that a museum should remain loyal to its old purpose of collecting, preserving, classifying and exhibiting objects of scientific value. While the original object of a museum should be kept in mind, we must not lose sight of the fact that a children's museum calls for such modifications and adaptations of methods as will enable children to use it, and here we must remember that the keynote of childhood and youth is action. Any museum ignoring this principle of activity in children must fail to attract them. The Children's Museum does not attempt to make electricians of its boys, nor is its purpose to do the work of any school. Its object is rather to understand the tastes and interests of its little people and to offer such helps and opportunities as the schools and homes cannot give. With that, its mission ends, and the success or failure of its work will be proportional to its skill in meeting individual needs. . . .

Every September children returning from country outings hasten to tell us of their holiday pleasures, not the least of which is the deeper appreciation of this world of nature of which the museum has given them broader knowledge. Examples of the quickening and stimulating influence of the museum in individual cases could be multiplied indefinitely, and to these could be added the appreciative testimony of parents and teachers, were it necessary to prove by argument its real value to the community. But, happily, the day is passed when its excuse for existence is questioned, or when the Children's Museum is regarded as an extravagant investment yielding small returns. On the contrary, the returns would warrant the increased expenditure, and this seems to be a necessity of the near future.

The present Children's Museum has long since outgrown its quarters. Its exhibition halls, its lecture room and its library are often so over-crowded with eager children as to defeat objects of their visits. The New York legislature, however, has recently passed a bill authorizing the city to erect a new Children's Museum Building at a cost not to exceed $175,000. With the improved equipment thus provided The Children's Museum would not only serve a larger number of children, but would also serve them more efficiently in proportion to expenditure.

Through publications from the German press we learn that certain educators in Berlin are advocating a children's museum for that city. Meanwhile in our own country museums are beginning to feel the importance of giving more attention to the education of children. In large cities the field for smaller museums is always increasing, and one can but hope that the time may soon come when a system of these institutions, each studying and adapting itself to the needs of its particular locality, will be working as branches of a large central museum, with its skilled artists, modelers, taxidermists and preparateurs.

As a small museum in a large city serves a moving population, its service to the individual is necessarily limited by a constant change of clientele. Smaller towns, on the other hand, offer conditions for an almost ideal development. The Fairbanks Museum, in the little town of St. Johnsbury, Vermont, is an excellent example of museum leadership in a small center.

Since the Children's Museum has demonstrated its worth to one community there is reason to expect that it will make its way into others and the variety of problems to be solved in adapting its work to new conditions offers one of the most attractive fields of modern education.

# 25

# THE RELATION OF THE MUSEUM TO THE SCHOOLS

## Carolyn [Morse] Rea [published as Mrs. Paul M. Rea]

*Bulletin of the Charleston Museum*, 3 (3): 21–32, 1907

---

*Carolyn Morse, an early museum educator, was married to Paul M. Rea, Director of the Charleston Museum in South Carolina, at the time she wrote this article, excerpted below. Morse explores the connection between museums, libraries, and public schools in providing educational experiences for school children. Innovative in her approach, she promoted the use of "series of small loan collections in convenient portable cases" that she sent around to the public schools—still a popular strategy today—to augment the one-time visit to the museum.*

---

Perhaps no one thing is more clearly indicative of the new epoch of activity upon which the Museum entered two years ago than the request which has come from your County Teachers' Association to be told "How the Schools can use the Museum". . . .

I believe I am right in saying that no limit to the educational possibilities inherent in the museum idea has yet occurred to the mind of the modern museum worker. The museum is as yet, however, an almost unrecognized factor in our educational system. Only the handful of men engaged in the pioneer work of development realize its tremendous possibilities.

Most of us still cling to our old-fashioned notion of a museum, or, perhaps more correctly, to our notion of an old fashioned museum as a sort of "stuffed animal house". We consider it a very respectable place of amusement for children. They are always interested in the mummy and beg to be shown the skeleton of the man of whom so many hair-raising stories are told. The idea of a museum, however, as an institution co-ordinate with the public library in its sphere of public usefulness, to be as eagerly and frequently visited and used—that idea has probably never occurred to most of us and is, in fact, still dormant in the minds of most communities.

The museums themselves are, for the most part, to blame for this. It is only too easy to understand why people have not felt repaid for their trouble in coming to visit our own Museum, for the collections have scarcely been in a condition to interest, much less instruct, the general public. To the scientist, museums are admittedly of interest and use, but few are yet willing to grant that they have any real, practical everyday value for the rest of us.

The reason for this misapprehension is not far to seek. A museum has been fitly compared to an iceberg, in that it is eight-ninths concealed below the surface. A broad foundation of thorough scientific investigation may not be of immediate interest to the general public, yet it is essential to any museum worthy of the name, and upon it depends the nature and quality of the superstructure which is arranged for the benefit of the public, viz.—the exhibition collections, together with those aids to their enjoyment and understanding, of which I shall later speak. Concerning this portion of the institution, teachers, as leaders and guides of one great class of the community for whose benefit it is especially designed, should be well informed.

The exhibition collections are, first of all, not to be considered as a collection of objects merely, but as a collection of ideas, fully illustrated by objects. These are planned, arranged and labeled wholly with a view to their educational possibilities. Take for illustration, the small group of mounted beavers in our own collections. The mere specimens themselves, with a common and scientific name attached do not convey sufficient interesting or useful information to the ordinary visitor to warrant the investment of public or private money in their accumulation for exhibition purposes. If these animals were mounted amid accessories reproducing their natural surroundings, if they were accompanied by pictures and models illustrating their home life and habits, by maps showing their distribution and notes of local occurrence, and, most important of all, by labels, setting forth in clear, simple language, information such as might be conveyed by a curator at one's elbow, then this group would have a definite educational value which casual visitors would appreciate and student or teacher could ill afford to be without. . . .

The impossibility of an attempt to duplicate such a series of instructive exhibits in all the schools of the city is at once obvious, and yet the disadvantages associated with a single central museum containing illustrations for school lessons have, perhaps, occurred to you. To obviate these in part, a series of small loan collections in convenient portable cases can be made up from duplicate material in the possession of the Museum and sent out to schools desiring them for a period of time, to be replaced by other collections at the request of the teacher. These collections should contain beside the specimens and labels, brief notes giving necessary information and a bibliography of the subject treated for the benefit of the teacher. If possible, a special instructor should be in charge of these collections, visit the schools and direct their management, devise means for making them thoroughly useful and, if necessary, conduct classes for either teachers or children. The territory thus supplied by the central museum, with illustrations and objective material for work in geography or elementary science would be limited only by the funds and resources of the Museum.

In the Museum library and reading room, both teachers and children will find valuable aid along the lines of school work. Books without specimens give imperfect ideas of life and things as many of you can testify from your own experience. But books and pictures *with* specimens make a complete working outfit for scholar or teacher. The Mu-seum library supplements the school text-books in a way that the public library can not do, since it can not properly specialize in any one or two departments. The range of books, beginning at simple nature readers for little children would ascend through the scale of attractive, helpful books, adapted to the varying needs of children of school age to the more technical works which furnish much needed aid to the busy teacher. . . .

Arrangements should be made at the Museum for the comfort and convenience of the classes visiting the building accompanied by their teacher. A lecture room or classroom may be provided on request and the specimens needed arranged therein. If it is desirable, a demonstrator or lecturer from the Museum can be in attendance, or the class and its teacher may be left undisturbed to do their work as they please. Free lecture courses, illustrative of the studies pursued in the schools may be given at the Museum at times suited to the convenience of teachers and pupils. In brief, the Museum should stand ready to carry out any reasonable request from the schools for aid in their work to the extent of that portion of its resources which may justly be employed in this direction.

And, finally, as a means of keeping in touch with the teachers, of spreading information concerning special exhibits, loan collections or work going on at the Museum of particular interest to the schools, and of announcing the dates and subjects for lectures, a Bulletin, published by the Museum should be mailed to the principals for distribution among the teachers and children who apply for it. . . .

# 26

# IF PUBLIC LIBRARIES, WHY NOT PUBLIC MUSEUMS?

**Edward S. Morse**

*Atlantic Monthly,* 72: 112–119, 1893

*Edward Morse wrote the following excerpted article while serving as director of the Peabody Essex Museum, Massachusetts. Written in reaction to the passage of the Public Library Act, Morse urges the passage of similar legislation to establish town museums across the state of Massachusetts. He promotes the public museum as an opportunity to encourage the art of collecting natural objects by educating the public about its local natural environment, flora and fauna, which in turn would inspire in young and old an interest in science and the arts.*

. . . If the public library is established primarily for educational purposes, surely the public museum should come in the same category. The potency of an object in conveying information beyond all pages of description is seen in the fact that in the museum a simple label associated with a veritable object is often sufficient to tell the story at a glance; the eye seizes the essentials at once.

The rapid development of the modern arts of illustration, and the conspicuous use of these methods in books, magazines, dictionaries, and even the daily papers, attest the power of the pictorial art, barbarous as it is in many cases, in imparting information quickly and clearly. If illustrations are so important in the modern publication—and to do without them would seem well-nigh impossible—how far more important it would seem to be to provide an exhibition of the objects themselves in science, art, and history, to which the public might have free access!

A museum adds dignity to a trifle. What seems a worthless object to the minds of the multitude becomes at once endowed with interest when carefully framed or mounted, and clearly labeled. Furthermore, the object is seen to have a definite relation to other equally common objects with which it is associated; a lesson is learned, and sooner or later the observer finds an added interest in his studies, if indeed he is not aware for the first time of regions of thought utterly unknown to him before. The charm that attends the demonstration of the minor factors of natural selection comes from the love of causality.

Charles Kingsley, in an address to workingmen, said: "You must acquire something of that industrious habit of mind which the study of natural science gives, –the art of comparing, of perceiving true likenesses and true differences, and so of classifying and arranging what you see; the art of connecting facts together in your mind in cause and effect."

The public museum fosters the art of collecting; and of all habits to encourage, in the young and old alike, the habit of collecting is one of the best. It has been said that one who does not learn to play whist is laying up a dismal old age; the same might be said of one who has not cultivated the collector's spirit. It induces habits of neatness, order, and skill, says one writer. Young people are kept out of mischief, to middle-aged people it is a rest and relaxation, and old people find in their collections a perennial source of pleasure.

Professor Goode quotes an eminent English lecturer as stating that our nation is deteriorating in regard to culture; that where, twenty years ago, five hundred towns supported, year after year, courses of lectures on scientific and literary subjects, to-day scarcely fifty of these places feel encouraged to continue the effort. If there is no apparent reason for this decadence, then it will be well-nigh useless to hope for the establishment of museums. If, however, it can be shown that with the advent of the lecture bureau the market was flooded with poor or sensational lecturers, comic readers, etc., and as a result the lecture platform, as we formerly knew it, became converted into an amusement stage; if, furthermore, it can be shown that the magazine literature of the country gives far greater space to matters of science and art, thus providing the kinds of intellectual food formerly given from the lecture platform, then we may hope that there is no decadence in the culture of the people, and that an interest in public museums may be easily aroused.

A change has certainly taken place in the last thirty years in the tendency of the community toward collecting objects of natural history. Private collectors of shells, insects, birds, etc., were far more numerous thirty years ago than they are to-day. The same is true of England. An eminent authority laments that "private collections are failing in Liverpool and all around; and teaching is everywhere hard and hardening in its results."

Yet there is surely no dying out of the collector's spirit in certain lines, as witness the thousands interested in postage stamp collecting, with their established societies and periodicals. . . .

First and foremost, then, the town museum should illustrate the natural products of the immediate region. By natural products is meant, of course, the animals, plants, rocks, and minerals found in the county, or possibly in the State; for a county collection would require but a few extra-limital forms to compass the State. Second, a general collection of similar material from elsewhere, to show the relation of the county to the rest of the world. Anatomical, physiological, and morphological series should next find place in such a museum. The minor factors of natural selection, such as protective, alluring, and warning coloration, mimicry, etc., should be illustrated, as far as possible, from collections made in the immediate neighborhood. And finally, a series of forms to show the phylogenetic development of the animal kingdom should in some way be given. Such a series would require large floor space, and the solution of many perplexing problems as to form of cases and methods of display. Yet a scheme of this sort must ultimately be devised. The importance of developmental series is clearly brought out by a comparison between the famous Cluny Museum in Paris and the University Museum at Oxford under the charge of Professor E. B. Tylor. In the former is a homogeneous mass of beautiful and elaborate objects of mediaeval times, each exciting thought so disjointed that fatigue soon ensues from the rich surfeit, and one comes away with the feeling that he has seen a marvelous lot of most exquisite objects in the dim light of an artistic receptacle. Not an emotion has been evoked that will be set vibrating again unless he drops into a choice bric-a-brac shop, and the medley there seen pleases him less in its *ensemble* than that of the Cluny collections; with the advantage, however, that he can buy, if he has the means, and not burn with envy. The Pitt-Rivers collection now displayed in the Oxford Museum arrests the thoughtful attention at every step; inquiry is provoked at every turn; doubt may be engendered, yet ever after one finds fertile subjects to think about, to discuss, or to impart to one's friends. In other words, the collection has stimulated inquiry; and this is what a properly arranged collection should always do.

This, then, is a general idea of what a public museum should be. It has been attained in part by the Peabody Academy of Science in Salem. The collections comprise, first, a remarkable series of the animals and plants, rocks, minerals, and archaeological specimens collected in the county of Essex. These collections are continually increasing as new forms are added. They occupy upright cases to an extent of over three hundred running feet, or a superficial area for their display of nearly three thousand square feet. Besides this there is an epitome collection of the animal kingdom, brought from all parts of the world, requiring an area of sixteen hundred square feet for its proper display; and finally, an ethnological collection, arranged by countries, filling a hall sixty by forty-eight feet with broad galleries and spacious cases. These collections are all fully and clearly labeled. At close intervals throughout the entire collection special colored labels are displayed, calling attention, by title and shelf number, to books in the public library referring to the immediate group; so that a student or pupil from the public schools need only transcribe on a bit of paper a set of numbers, and present it at the delivery window of the public library, to be provided at once with the books on the special subject desired. Great credit is due to Mr. Robinson, in charge of the museum, for the good taste shown in the arrangement of the collection, and to Mr. Jones, the librarian of the public library, for cooperating so heartily in the work of the Academy.

Courses of lectures are given in the Academy Hall every year, which are practically free to the public. The city librarian usually supplements these lectures by printed lists of books treating of the subject matter of the lecture, and these lists are distributed to the auditors. A like service is often done for the free courses of lectures given by the Essex Institute. In this manner, these three institutions cooperate with one another in utilizing the collections in their possession in an educational way, and for the good of the general public. The collections thus made available are the results of years of devoted labor by many ardent students and collectors. . . .

Finally, in the museum of the future the errors of the past should be avoided. Private collections, when given to a museum, must be incorporated with the other collections. Collections should not be accepted with the condition that they are to have separate rooms or cases for their display. There are occasions when an exception can be made; as when, for instance, the collection is far more complete than the one already possessed, though in this case the smaller collection should be merged with the larger. An inconvenience has always arisen from the continual accession of material which necessitates the rearranging of collections for their admission. This difficulty can be overcome by setting apart a special room or a set of cases, in which the donations can be kept for one year, this receptacle to be plainly marked "New Accessions to the Museum!" In this way a rearrangement, and consequent disturbance, takes place only once a year. Furthermore, the exhibition of these accessions separately will stimulate the activity and pride of local collectors and others interested.

Above all, the bane and misery of dubious accumulations should be avoided. A specimen is either of use, or it is not. If worthy of preservation, it should find its place in the collections; if not, it should be transferred to those who will make use of it, or be destroyed. The rubbish which accumulates in many of our museums, and is hoarded from year to year with the hope that it may some time be of use, is paralleled by the collections of junk with which some are inclined to encumber their premises. . . .

# 27

# THE MUSEUM IN EDUCATIONAL WORK

## Frederick Starr

*Educational Review*, 3: 254–259, 1892

---

*Frederick Starr, biologist, ethnologist, and anthropologist, was a firm believer in the educational value of the public museum. He specifically championed the usefulness of "school museums," or teachings collections, to augment science instruction in public schools from primary to higher education.*

---

In discussing the relation of museums to educational work several topics must be considered: (1) the museum in elementary and secondary schools, (2) the museum in the college, (3) the museum in the university, (4) the public museum in education.

1. Whether elementary work in science shall be taught in common schools or not, is a question that is hardly before the public. Such work has been widely introduced, sometimes with, sometimes without, good results. I believe it has come to stay. A child must be led to think for himself, to observe closely, to discriminate, to classify, to express himself simply and clearly. Such results can be obtained in no way so well as by science work. What museum ought an elementary school to possess in order to assist such work? No work in science is of particular value, unless it is practical study of specimens. The best specimens are always those that the children bring in. But such gatherings are usually heterogeneous; some of the objects are of value, many are not. From this mass of material, however, the best things should be saved, suitably prepared, and arranged in safe

cases. The children will very soon come to have delight and pride in the growth of this little school cabinet, and every effort should be made to encourage such feelings. In the George Putnam School in Boston, where excellent work in elementary science is done, there is an Annual Display Day. At that time, in each room of the building, hundreds of pretty and interesting objects gathered by the children are displayed, on great tables, to parents and friends. . . . In one room of the school there is an admirable collection of shells gathered or brought together by the children themselves, and the knowledge of shells and their molluscan occupants that the children had gained would have done credit to many a college student who had "passed" his examinations in zoology. At Pasadena, Cal. science teaching is combined with the work in English and drawing in a most satisfactory way. Some of the prettiest results possible came from children in lower grades, who had made studies upon the commoner wild flowers, which they gathered for themselves. These cases are mentioned, not as models or wonders, but simply to show what can be done when children in common schools are set to work to make their own museum. With children thus at work, what will the school museum contain? First, local material gathered by the children themselves and used as a basis for language lessons or other work: second, considerable material presented to the children by friends; this will be of every sort and coming from all places. To select and keep the best of the specimens of both kinds is no easy task, but it should be done. . . . The museum should always be adapted to the work attempted: and what is the object of science work in the lower grades? Surely it is not the amount of botany, or zoology, or geology learned. . . . His thought should have been stimulated, and his wonder excited, by seeing the great green "worm" weave its silken cocoon about it; by watching its forthcoming in the springtime and the wonderful development of color that rapidly transforms those shapeless flaps into wings of beauty. . . .

A high-school museum is a somewhat different matter. The natural sciences here are taught, in considerable measure, for their subject matter. Here systematic series are more in place, but even here all material of that kind should be reduced to a minimum. It is desirable, it is needed, but it should be no more than necessary. In high-school museums one thing particularly should be the aim to secure a *complete* local series. . . . Of course science should be taught in field work; class excursions should accumulate the material, and class work should prepare it for the cases. The pupils and not the teacher should secure the local series. . . . Many of our city high schools now have apparatus, equipment, and laboratory facilities such as many colleges did not possess a few years since; if such outfit for teaching is used, we should soon have in many schools of academic grade just such collections as we here describe.

2. What, and how much, should the college museum contain? Here the object of scientific study, particularly where subjects are offered as electives, is the material of science itself. While here a local series is desirable, and almost sure to be gathered, there must be a systematic series, one in which there should be few breaks; if possible, none. But the college museum is not necessarily very large; it may be so, but it must be well balanced. Such a series, as I have said, need not be large; there should be in zoology specimens illustrating both morphology and structure of all the more important groups of animals; in botany, an herbarium illustrating the chief points in the coarse structure of plants and the characters of most importance in classification; in physiology, little more than a mounted and unmounted skeleton with the usual series of anatomical models (fresh material for study from lower animals is better than any quantity of poor permanent preparations in jars); in geology, a few hundred typical specimens of minerals, rocks, and fossils carefully selected to illustrate structure and history; besides these, a good lot of microscopic preparations illustrating histology, both animal and vegetable, and rock structure, is desirable.

3. Although we thus draw close limits for the college museum, we do nothing of the sort for that of the university. Here there should be a wealth of material. To the university, with its advanced students and specialists, should go the great special collections in every field. The museum of the university is primarily for study; no doubt, however, some display of specimens is necessary, and even a great display may be pardoned. Such a display is of value to the public and gives ground for local pride in the institution. Much, very much, the major portion even, of the university museum may never be seen by anyone but the special student.

I have striven to make one idea clear. The object of science study varies with each grade of school. What that object is must determine the character of the museum. The proposition is simple and fundamental, but it is very often overlooked. . . . A museum without a teacher behind it, and in it, is the deadest of dead things.

4. And I believe firmly in the educational influence of the public museum. Public museums are new to us in America. Our great museums may be counted on the fingers, and there are not many small ones. Our museums, too, are seldom under governmental control, but are private property of associations or societies, many of them with no

adequate fund, and few, if any, paid officers. Often they depend for success, or even for life, upon interested individuals, whose removal means disaster. But public interest increases, and great museums will be more numerous in the near future. Such museums ought always to be educational centers, and should have a definite relation to every school, of every grade, within their reach. . . .

# 28

# THE MUSEUM, THE ORIGINAL EXPONENT OF VISUAL EDUCATION

**Frank C. Baker**

*School Science and Mathematics*, 22: 651–655, 1922

*Frank Baker, long-time natural history curator at the Chicago Academy of Sciences and the University of Illinois, discusses the difficulties associated with the use of museums "as an efficient aid" in visual education in the following excerpted article. Although he is critical of public museums for not presenting their exhibits in a manner accessible to school-age children, he acknowledges a positive trend toward displaying museum groups, or dioramas, as they enable the student "to visualize the whole realm of nature, history and art." He also writes of the importance of teaching collections for supplementing general science courses at the university level.*

We hear a great deal in these days about the value of visual education, and a society has been organized for the promotion of this method of teaching. This is indeed one of Nature's most effective methods of teaching her children the laws of the universe. It is said that we acquire much more information through the eye than through any other sense organ of the body. One often hears the expression "seein' is believin'," which expresses this truth in a homely way.

The museums of science and art have been for many years pioneers in the field of visual education, bringing to the public, more or less imperfectly in the earlier years, the facts of Science and the beauties of Art. The museum is often called the "people's university," and it is quite true that the great majority of the population of our large cities acquire their only

knowledge of the great world about them by visits to the museums, art galleries, and zoological gardens, where the fowls of the air, the beasts of the
field, and the fishes of the sea, past and present, are gathered together in
such an assemblage as Noah never dreamed of in his day and generation.

The value of the museum as an efficient aid in educational work is
fully realized by but few educators. Even in many of the large cities there
is little real cooperation between the local museum and the educational
system, and this is by no means entirely the fault of the museum administrators. Visual education seems to center about pictures, lantern slides
and moving pictures, and the aid that may be rendered by the museum
exhibits is, in the main, unthought of. Perhaps many of our museums are
to be held responsible for this condition, their exhibits being so often
entirely useless to the teacher because of faulty installation, of value to the
systematic student, but valueless to the general teacher. The cooperative
association of school and museum in New York, Chicago, Milwaukee, and
some other cities, augurs well for the future of the museum in finding its
true place in the educational system of the present age.

In a recent article on the "Contribution of Museums to Public School
education," Mr. Peter A. Mortenson, Superintendent of Public Schools
of Chicago, says: "The value of museum material as a factor in reinforcing
school instruction has, no doubt, been recognized generally enough, but
the difficulty lying in the way of its wider utilization has been the failure
to find the museum material so organized that it would appeal to the
dynamic interests of the children and at the same time portray the life that
it was collected to represent." The larger museums, and even some of the
smaller museums presided over by far-sighted curators, are removing this
unfavorable criticism, and are preparing some of their exhibits to meet the
requirements of the teacher of the grade school.

That the museum is also of value in reinforcing instruction in the universities and other higher institutions of learning seems equally certain,
supplementing by the exhibits the material used in the classroom and
laboratory, the larger value being in the coordination of all the material
which may have been seen in the classroom only as isolated parts of the
whole subject. This value of museum material has been recognized for
many years and almost every college and university has its museum, even
though it be a small one. Of late years some of the universities have drifted
away from the use of the museum, hence the unsatisfactory condition
of much of the material in many university collections and the general
poor opinion of most of such collections among museum men. I wish to
indicate, briefly, some of the ways in which the museum may be useful in
supplementing the general courses given in a university. . . .

And in the natural sciences—geology, zoology, botany—the museum
is indispensable because it visualizes the courses given in the different

branches. The student pursuing a course in systematic zoology may study the synoptic collection, arranged so that the major groups are exhibited to show their development from simple to complex organisms, their relation to each other and to the past history of the earth, the extinct groups being shown with the recent groups. Such an exhibit links together all life, showing it to be interrelated on every hand.

The student of geology may crystallize his course in historical geology or paleontology by consulting the exhibits of fossils, in which he may follow the changes of life from its first definite appearance in the early Cambrian seas to the latest prehistoric period. Here can be shown as nowhere else, the dying out of one type of life and the advent, almost instantaneously as it seems, of another. Such examples as the dying out of the Ammonites in the Cretaceous, the rise and fall of the huge saurians in Mesozoic times, and the advent of the mammals in Cenozoic times indicate the usefulness of such exhibits. The subject of coal can also be made more understandable by an exhibit of the peculiar flora of the Carboniferous. The evolution or descent of an animal and its modification during descent can be shown most effectively by groups arranged with specimens or restorations, supplemented by illustrations, so that the student grasps almost instinctively the significance of the subject. Such lines of descent as the horse, sloth, elephant, and armadillo can be very effectively shown. . . .

The modern group idea has revolutionized museum exhibits. By this medium we are able to visualize the whole realm of nature, history and art. No longer must animals be seen only on shelves arranged in rows, like canned goods in a grocery; they may now be seen in their natural environment, in occupations such as they perform when unmolested by their arch-enemy, Man, the elaborateness and breadth of vision being limited only by the pocket book of the museum. In one museum may be seen the bird life of an island in the distant Pacific; in another, one may hunt the mountain sheep or the grizzly bear in the great mountains of the west; or visit a bird rookery in Florida or the islands of the West Indies. The fast disappearing native races of this and other continents may return and perform their ancient tribal ceremonies in the groups of the museum, which often appear so lifelike that one almost expects the wax effigy to breathe or to throw an upraised spear or stone through the glass of the case. . . .

These examples might be amplified indefinitely, but enough have been given to show that the museum is a potent agency in modern education, a fact that is, perhaps, not fully realized by educators in general. The museum is too often thought of as a storeroom or mausoleum in which musty specimens are stored away to be pored over by spectacled savants who live in a world by themselves. It is sadly true that this conception is not without foundation, for there are many museums in universities, colleges, normal schools, and academies, which are this and nothing else.

But the modern museum is a vastly different thing, filled with objects potentially arranged, awaiting use by all progressive teachers.

In closing, may I use the words of one of England's greatest museum men, Sir William H. Flower, who says, "It is not the objects placed in a museum that constitute its value, so much as the method in which they are displayed and the use made of them for the purpose of instruction."

# 29

# THE FUNCTION OF THE MUSEUM INSTRUCTOR

## Elizabeth M[anning Gardiner] Whitmore

*The Metropolitan Museum of Art Bulletin*, 11 (9): 198–200, 1916

---

*The following article by Elizabeth Whitmore, assistant to the director of the Worcester Museum of Art, appeared in a special issue of the "Educational Work of Art Museums." Whitmore describes the art museum docent (Giltinan 2008) as the individual responsible for placing the museum's collections "as completely as possible within the reach of the public" by both imparting to visitors an aesthetic appreciation for art objects and by placing these objects in an historical or cultural context. She presents two scenarios to illustrate how this might be accomplished.*

---

The present day finds all our public institutions in a state of anxious self-scrutiny and reorganization. When court, hospital, school, and even theatre and department store, are overhauling established traditions and testing them by the modern standard of efficient service to an often indifferent public, it is not surprising to find a similar quickening in the activities of our museums. As Mr. Benjamin Ives Gilman neatly puts it, the museum *gardant* and *monstrant* (the place of safe repository and orderly display) has become the museum *docent,* bent on placing its treasures as completely as possible within the reach of the public—or, more often, on stimulating the public to do a little reaching. Hence the modern development of explanatory labels and popular handbooks; hence, above all, the creation, in some form or other, of the office of museum instructor, with its varied duties of story-telling for children, addresses to schools and clubs, and the more intimate guidance of small groups of individuals.

But if the office is already established, the exact nature of its function is still under dispute. Put in the baldest form, the question is this: "Should the docent (to use a title that is at all events non-committal) aim to impart information about the object, or to develop appreciation of its qualities?" The advocates of the first view plead that love of beauty is an emotion, and cannot be taught; that facts, on the other hand, are something that can be safely imparted, that they at least give the object the added interest that comes from a local habitation and a name, and often put it to use as an illustration of some outside study—say history or geography. They hint that thus the museum collection becomes serviceable even to the multitude who "have no eye for beauty." Per contra, the retort is made that the love of beauty is indeed an emotion, but one which is latent in all normal human beings, and which can, by judicious suggestion, be kindled; that facts regarding the origin and historical relations of a given work of art are, however, quite irrelevant to appreciation, and tend rather to stifle it; and that the docent, therefore, should confine his comments largely to matters of line, hue, and texture. The two sides would demand docents of very different temperament—one the thoughtful student, the other the sensitive artist (in perceptions, if not in actual accomplishment).

Now, some years' actual experience and a good deal of observation of others who are or have been engaged in the same work have led me to believe that these apparently opposing aims are not mutually exclusive; that both are justified, and that, to be successful, each must borrow something from the other. The instructor must rouse emotion, the appreciator must provide a background of fact. In short, the distinction lies rather in method and emphasis than in the materials used, or in qualifications of temperament and training.

Both the common qualities and the distinctions can best be illustrated by a concrete case. The docent, let us say, on his first hour of duty meets a class of high-school pupils sent to the museum for "background" in Greek history. They go together into the collection of Greek vases, and he pours forth to the class at large his facts. "These queer black and red objects, upwards of 2,500 years old, are not curios, they are just dishes. This one the girls used for bringing home the day's supply of water; you can see them doing so in the drawing on its side." Then follows the little description of the village fountain, perhaps illustrated by other vase-paintings, and the comparison with present-day conditions. Again, attention is drawn to a kylix, with the very banquet in which it was used portrayed on its side—a reminder of the dinners in Herodotus or Plato where the guests lay on just such couches, and slaves like these scampered about refilling the cups. And so vase after vase will make vivid the meagre and often half-grasped accounts learned for school recitations, till the youngsters begin to feel that these re-mote Greeks were after all lively flesh and blood like themselves. But even as an illustration of history the talk will not be complete until the docent has gone back, say, to the first vase, and has pointed out its essentially Hellenic traits, the same traits which appear in the temples and the poems and the carefully articulated systems of government which the class has studied. . . . Thus the class as a whole carries back to its books some sort of *mise-en-scene* for the deeds of fifth-century Athenians, and at least a few elect members have caught a glimpse of something in the character of the doers that transforms the tale from disjointed annals to an inevitable development. And this flash of new light, absolutely relevant to the aim of the classroom instructor, came through a true, if incomplete, appreciation of the vase.

The following hour has perhaps been engaged by a woman who wants to see some of the less familiar collections. A little questioning reveals that she is not conscious of any special predilection; so she suggests, "Suppose we take something related to our own daily life; how about dishes?" Back they go to the Greek vase collection, to the very hydria that formed a starting-point for the class; and with the adult visitor, as with the children, the surest way of fixing attention is a word or two of preliminary fact: age, use, something about the original owners. But the piece thus introduced becomes, this time, not a symbol of Greek life and spirit, but a thing with a character of its own. The visitor's experience in lifting a heavy filled pitcher by the side handle and trying to steady it so that the water shall not surge out at the lip will make her quick to detect the perfect fitness to use in number and placing of handles, and in the sharp confining in-curve of the shoulder. It will then be easy, by showing her earlier examples, to lead her to discover how the curve of the body, the meeting of neck and shoulder, the swelling out of the handles at their junction points, have all been studied and developed till they afford to the eye a sense of exquisite adjustment similar to that which the structure gives to the user's muscles. Before long the visitor discovers that the docent, instead of offering her difficult points of connoisseurship, or solemn rhapsodies on Beauty, has given her principles in accordance with which she, too, can observe and analyze and enjoy; and thereafter her own comments and questions will determine what else they shall look at together. . . . The visitor's gain, when the hour ends, should be not only a new sensitiveness of observation that enables her to search for and delight in the significant distinctions of form and spirit, but also the discovery that such observation will be keener and more enjoyable the more deeply it is tinged with the sympathy that comes from historical and technical knowledge.

It is evident that the docent's equipment must be the same, whether he is to meet class or single guest. He must know, first, the objects in the collections with an intimacy sufficient to perceive clearly their characteristic traits, practical and aesthetic; second, the history of their times, at least far enough to sympathize with the circumstances and problems of their creators; and third, the varied museum public, so that he can seize quickly on the appropriate object and facts to kindle the interest of each visitor or group. In the first case he is presenting a lesson, necessarily predetermined, to a class as a whole; he uses museum material; he is an instructor pure and simple.

In the second case, however, he drops the class-room manner, and becomes the host, alert to give his visitors pleasure by presenting to them his familiar friends among the collections. His task is a matter of self-effacing social tact, first in choosing congenial subjects for introduction, second in unobtrusively giving the guest such information as will place him *en rapport* with his new acquaintance, and lastly in so revealing the latter as to lay the foundations of a friendship that may be continued without further intervention from himself.

Both functions, then, belong legitimately to the museum instructor; but while in the one he is cheered by the consciousness that he is offering a serviceable and (under present conditions) otherwise unobtainable supplement to the curricula of the regular schools, into the other he throws himself with the enthusiastic conviction that he is helping fulfill the peculiar purpose of his chosen institution, the museum.

# 30

## MUSEUMS AND OTHER CLASSIFIED COLLECTIONS AS INSTRUMENTS OF EDUCATION IN NATURAL SCIENCE

### Henry Scadding

*The Canadian Journal*, 13: 1–25, 1871

*Inspired by the exhibits at the Exposition Universelle in Paris in 1867, Henry Scadding, president of the Canadian Institute, developed a doctrine to promote museum education. His primary concern was to increase the educational value of systematic collections, which he argued should be arranged with a specific educational objective in mind—a topic of interest to the public—to create a "gallery of illustration." In this way the visitor would see that the objects held more than an aesthetic or entertainment value and would use the exhibits as an "instrument of self-education."*

. . . One desire which I found myself haunted with, on returning home fresh from a brief—too brief—inspection of the marvelously diversified, but beautifully classified contents of the Paris Exhibition, was to impress upon all with whom I held any communication, and especially on young Canadians about to travel, the practical, self-educating use to which they might put their visits to Great Britain and the continent of Europe, where access is so easy to grand and extraordinary assemblages of objects, industrial, scientific and artistic, either temporary, like the successive international expositions, or permanent but constantly augmenting, like the national museums to be found in capital cities and university towns.

For the most part, I fear, such collections are approached by the tourist, from Canada as from elsewhere, in a light and trivial spirit are gazed at simply as displays of so many singular, or beautiful, or very useful objects.

But the doctrine which I longed to impress, and which I of course at the same time knew to be neither novel nor abstruse, was, that in the mind of every one about to enjoy the advantage of access to a great classified collection of objects anywhere, there should be a pre-arranged scheme of examination; a certain intention; a definite aim and object: there should be, if practicable, some especial subject of study, or a particular point in some especial subject of real interest to the observer, on which additions to his store of knowledge were sincerely desired. Then, at once, the great museum or other large classified assemblage of objects—although access to it could be had only for a few days, or even for a few hours—ceases to be a mere show or plaything, and is transformed into a gallery of illustration—a delightful and precious instrument of self-education; a means of mental expansion, intellectual enrichment, and positive increase of personal competency, in whatever sphere of duty the observer may be noting.

And the subject which, amongst a host of others, I thought might conveniently have a large amount of light thrown on it by such extensive collections as those to be met with at the present day in Great Britain and on the continent of Europe, was Natural Science, in some one or other, or all, of its divisions, of Mechanical Philosophy, Chemistry and Physiology.

Natural Science is a subject which is now more or less attended to in all our schools, I believe; but of course only its most elementary principles are expounded there; and the appliances for illustration are, of necessity, circumscribed and meagre.

A few days, or even hours, judiciously spent in some such collection as that which was to be seen in the Universal Exhibition at Paris, by a youth familiarized with and interested in the elementary principles of Natural Science, might be productive to him of results of life-long importance. Not only, in a general way, would his mental view be likely to be widened, but his profession or career might be happily decided by an extra impulse there given to a taste, tendency or talent; and a hint, or idea, caught from things and processes then for the first time seen, might lead in practice afterwards to fame and riches, and to the increase of a country's resources. . . .

Ought not Education to mean this—the indoctrination of each successive crop of youth with at least the elementary principles of all contemporary ascertained human knowledge, with a view to practical purpose in subsequent life? Would not Education, if it signified this, and was this, be the means of saving a great number of human beings from a great deal of blind, aimless action, and from a great number of blunders and mistakes, and so be the means also of economising a great deal of the world's precious time? Should not each generation of our youth be as a colony swarming off from an old, well-constituted and wise state, carrying with it, in germ at least, the knowledge and experience of the parent community, and starting from the point to which that had managed to attain? Especially in respect to the subject to which in this address particular reference has been made—the subjects commonly embraced under the term Natural Science—should not an adequate indoctrination of the young be secured?

It is one of the chief distinctions of the era in which we live, that Nature has been, to an extraordinary extent, interpreted—not interpreted fully: work in that direction remains to be done in the generations that will succeed us—but interpreted in very many respects; and so interpreted as to make clear certain consequent duties on the part of man, as well as certain practical advantages to be enjoyed by man in virtue of and acquaintance with that interpretation. . . .

To come back again then to the particular thesis with which this address has been occupied in the main, the place and function of museums and other classified collections in a system of education, popular or abstruse, are clearly seen. The admirable order which objects, simple and complex, raw and wrought up, are therein made to take, even to the eye, impresses in a powerful manner the reign of law in Nature; and they enable the student of Nature, professional or amateur, to make, with immense convenience and great rapidity, personal examinations advantageous to his own enlightenment and advancement in knowledge and skill, which would otherwise be all but impossible for him to make.

I have offered the advice that our youth, who at school or college have received instruction in the first principles of Natural Science, should make a specific use of the great Collections which in so many quarters they will discover in their tour in Great Britain and on the continent of Europe. I have advised that a scheme or plan should be beforehand decided on, to be closely followed during the days or hours which they are able to devote to such collections.

Visits to Boston, Philadelphia and Washington might in like manner be utilized.

The Geological Museum at Montreal should be deliberately and minutely examined. Laval, at Quebec, also contains scientific treasures.

Our own University Museum at Toronto is of coarse familiar ground already to our young lovers of Natural Science. It will be found a good antepast to the feasts that await them on their visits to larger establishments. It presents some good studies in ornithology and entomology. I wish our own small Museum, connected with the Canadian Institute, were richer in objects, but it is not wholly to be despised. The formation of a "Provincial Museum" was one of the objects to be promoted by the establishment of the Canadian Institute. The first section of our constitution reads as follows:—"The Canadian Institute has been established by

Royal Charter, for the purpose of promoting the Physical Sciences, for encouraging and advancing the Industrial Arts and Manufactures, &c., effecting the formation of a Provincial Museum, and for the purpose of facilitating the acquirement and the dissemination of knowledge connected with the surveying, engineering and architectural professions."

When an institution like the University of Toronto establishes a Scientific Museum on a good scale by the side of an humble collection like that which the Canadian Institute, with only limited resources, has been enabled to make, the latter necessarily becomes somewhat insignificant. Nevertheless there is a field which our Museum might occupy. It might be made a repository of Canadian archaeological and historical objects. The collections in the Normal School buildings, Toronto, exist expressly for educational purposes, and repay a studious examination. Barnett's Museum, at the Falls of Niagara, is by no means a common-place repository of objects. Some very fine genuine Egyptian mummies may be seen there. Our annual Provincial Exhibitions might also be utilized by a student visiting them with definite intention and purpose.

Now, I desire it to be observed, that in all that I have thus far said, I have not supposed for a moment, that Natural Science is to be the sole subject-matter of instruction or study in a system of Education. I have only been insisting that in a system of Education adapted to modern men, Natural Science must have its due place. . . .

But what we inculcate is this, that in addition to all these subjects, at the present time it is expedient, it is reasonable, it is devout, to assign a high place in schools to the knowledge which will help a youth from the very beginning of his career to a true view of the Earth on which he lives, of its constituent parts, of its relations as a member of Universe. It is expedient, it is reasonable, it is devout, to assign a high place in education to the knowledge which from the beginning of his career will help a youth to soundness and suppleness of body and mind; which, throughout life, will render him, consciously, an interested and skilled worker in his place in the great Whole; and as such a happy man, going on his way rejoicing, singing and making melody in his heart.

# 31

# THE PLACE OF MUSEUMS IN EDUCATION

## Thomas Greenwood

*Science*, 22: 246–248, 1893

---

*Thomas Greenwood, considered the leading trade journalist in early
twentieth-century England, was a great promoter of the public library
as an educational resource for enabling the working-class to self-educate.
Greenwood linked increase in knowledge with improved social behavior and
thus saw the museum as another site for promoting social reform. In the
article excerpted below he likens the public museum to a library, filled with
objects instead of books, and contends that museums should be recognized as
occupying a place in the national education system. He suggests how exhibits
might be designed, organized, and labeled to better facilitate informal
learning and to avoid "museum drunkenness," or what is known today as
museum fatigue.*

---

The most casual observer of educational methods could not fail to notice
that the receptive mind of a child or a youth learns from an infinite variety of sources. We all know that we begin at one end of education, but
there is no period in life of the most aged where the other end is reached.
Frequently, again, that information which does not absolutely form part
of the ordinary process of education, but which comes from unexpected
quarters, is of as great a service in the development of the mind as any
set lessons can possibly be. "Whatever becomes suggestive to the mind
is of educational value. That Museums have from their very nature the
very essence of this suggestiveness is patent. It may be true that of themselves alone they are powerless to educate, but they can be instrumental
and useful in aiding the educated to excite a desire for knowledge in

the ignorant. The working man or agricultural laborer who spends his holiday in a walk through any well-arranged Museum cannot fail to come away with a deeply-rooted and reverential sense of the extent of knowledge possessed by his fellow men. It is not the objects themselves that he sees there, and wonders at, that cause this impression, so much as the order and evident science which he cannot but recognize in the manner in which they are grouped and arranged. He learns that there is a meaning and value in every object, however insignificant, and that there is a way of looking at things common and rare, distinct from the regarding them as useless, useful, or merely curious. These three last terms would be found to be the very common classification of all objects in a Museum by the uninformed and uninitiated.

After a holiday spent in a Museum the working man goes home and cons over what he has seen at his leisure, and very probably on the next summer holiday, or a Sunday afternoon's walk with his wife and little ones, he discovers that he has acquired a new interest in the common things he sees around him. He begins to discover that the stones, the flowers, the creatures of all kinds that throng around him are not, after all, so very commonplace as he had previously thought them. He looks at them with a pleasure not before experienced, and talks of them to his children with sundry references to things like them which he saw in the Museum. He has gained a new sense, a craving for natural knowledge, and such a craving may, possibly, in course of time, quench another and lower craving which may at one time have held him in bondage—that for intoxicants or vicious excitement of one description or another. . . .

Vast collections of objects, whether in Museums or Exhibitions for educational purposes, do not always accomplish the object in view. Doubtless the vastness of the collections in some of own Exhibitions in London, and those which have been held in other cities, has been very impressive, but it may be gravely questioned whether any mind has carried away many useful impressions from the infinite multitude upon which he has had an opportunity of looking. The general mental state very frequently produced by such a numerous display is that of distraction. There is such a state of mind as picture drunkenness or Museum drunkenness, and this should be carefully guarded against. There should be in Museums and Art Galleries a more extensive use of folding screens, so that anyone so disposed could shut themselves off from the crowd while they study a case or a picture minutely. A few striking objects well and carefully studied are infinitely better and of greater educational worth than a number of things at which there is only a casual glance. . . .

Charles Kingsley, addressing working men, with reference to their requirements, says: "We must acquire something of that industrious habit of mind which the study of Natural Science gives. The art of seeing, the art of knowing what you see, the art of comparing, of perceiving true like-nesses and true differences, and so of classifying and arranging what you see, the art of connecting facts together in your own mind in chains of cause and effect, and that accurately, patiently, calmly, without prejudice, vanity, or temper."

The late Ralph Waldo Emerson, writing on the same subject, says: "Manual labor is the study of the external world." This kind of manual labor should be taught, in schools. Children's habit of collecting and arranging objects of interest should be encouraged. The study of a single branch of natural science, such as constructive botany, may be made the means of cultivating habits of neatness, order, and skill. The analysis of plant forms would illustrate the application of geometry to ornamental purposes, and open up wide fields for the development of decorative taste and manipulative skill. But cramped by the restrictive rules of our result system, these sources of useful culture are neglected; and, therefore, our children are turned out of the educational mill imperfectly prepared for the further processes necessary to qualify them for taking their part in the struggle for existence.

All this proves the necessity for Museums having the closest possible connection with elementary as well as advanced education. The uses of constructive botany, as referred to in the short quotation from Emerson, are especially helpful as a suggestive study to the mind. For this branch of education Museums are the best text-books which can be provided, but in order that specimens in these branches of natural science "be properly and usefully studied they require to be explained by competent teachers. It is in this respect that practical and efficient curators can be of the greatest service in giving short and informal explanations of some of the specimens in their Museums."

As far back as 1853, there was delivered at the Museum of Economical Geology, in London, a lecture by the late Professor Edward Forbes, on the Educational Uses of Museums. In one part of this lecture he spoke as follows: "In their educational aspect, considered apart from their educational applications, the value of Museums must in a great measure depend on the perfection of their arrangement, and the leading ideas regulating the classification of their contents. The educated youth ought, in a well-arranged Museum, to be able to instruct himself in the studies of which its contents are illustrations, with facility and advantage. On the officers in charge of the institution there consequently falls a heavy responsibility. It is not sufficient that they should be well versed in the department of science, antiquities, or art committed to their charge. They may be prodigies of learning, and yet utterly unfitted for their posts. They must be men mindful of the main end and purpose in view, and of the best way of communicating knowledge according to its kind, not merely to those who are already men of science, historians, or connoisseurs, but equally to those who, as yet ignorant, desire to learn, or in whom it is desirable that a thirst for learning should be incited". . . .

How far are we from yet realizing this ideal, and how slowly we seem to progress in so desirable a direction! Still there are many signs that the conscience of the nation is at last awakened, and if we see to it that all the discussions at present filling the air do not end simply in talk, but that practical good shall be the outcome, then our progress during the coming twenty-five years will not be so discouraging. In no better way can this ideal be realized than by an acute recognition of the place Museums should occupy in our national system of education.

# 32

# THE MUSEUM'S PART IN THE MAKING OF AMERICANS

## Laura W[oolsey] L[ord] Scales

*The Metropolitan Museum of Art Bulletin,* 12 (9): 191–193, 1917

*In the following excerpted article, Laura Scales, instructor at the Museum of Fine Arts, Boston, writes of the museum's social mission to initiate recent immigrants into American culture. Scales's attitude toward immigrants, although racist and stereotypical, affords the twenty-first-century historian and museologist with a unique insight into the perceived social duties of museum professionals at the turn of the twentieth century.*

If there may be a text without a sermon, the text for this paper is found in the remark of a little girl who was visiting the Boston Art Museum. She was in the room of colonial portraits, and while she was looking up at the faces of Washington and Adams, Warren, Hancock, and "Dorothy Q," she was told that these were the people who had made the beginnings of our country and had passed it on to us to continue their work. "Oh," she interrupted, "but America is all finished now!"

America finished! Until three years ago, it seemed merely amusing—the talk of such little girls—but now as we echo her words, we pause, realizing how seriously we have been put to it to find out not when was America finished, but what and where is America, and who are Americans? For even in Boston we have given up answering these questions by referring to the Mayflower. From every corner of the globe the answers had been coming in upon us, until we found ourselves in the midst of a civilization as difficult as it was rich; a civilization which presented the twin problems of how to conserve the riches and how to unify the peoples poured into our midst.

It is only a matter of course that museums stand ready to do their part toward these problems, for it is not by accident that a large proportion of museum visitors are foreign-born. The immigrant and his child want the museum. The Italian bride from her far-away quarter of the city comes there still in her orange blossoms, and the newly arrived Russian boy comes with his word or two of English; and a Madonna's smile or a brass icon with a bit of Russian inscription knit for them their past with this present. For where so clearly as in the museum can the immigrant be encouraged to believe that in this new world are continued the good things of his old one? Englishman, Frenchman, Japanese, Italian, Syrian—all may come to the museum and feel more at home than the native-born American, to so large an extent do their countries furnish the materials of which our art museums are made.

But it is not only because he finds there a familiar object that the immigrant comes to the museum; it is because he enjoys the things he sees. Appreciation and taste are his long inheritance; it is second nature to a Japanese to care for flowing line and to a Spaniard to revel in color. And the immigrant, ignorant and unlettered man that he is, has not yet learned the American way of spelling Art with a capital letter and setting it apart for women's clubs and moneyed connoisseurs. The eagerness of a class of little Russian Jewesses is a pleasant thing to see. "Oh," they exclaim, when the docent apologizes for keeping them a moment beyond the hour, "we could stay here seven hours". . . .

The museum is here to help voice the country's answer. "Let democracy, if need be, have its ready-made American clothes," one can imagine it saying as its doors swing open to offer its message to street and school, "but to love beautiful color, to embroider a tasteful pattern, to mould, to sing, to paint—these too are 'good American.' So good are they, that not only is there money in them, but opportunity and honor in the new country; so highly are they valued—the museum itself is evidence—that not only the state but private individuals spend their time and their money to cherish these things. America has need of the man who comes to make beautiful her paths as well as to dig her streets and lay her sewers." And if, so speaking, the museum can bring home to the immigrant his chance to help enrich the head and heart of his new country as well as her pockets, to serve the public and not merely the taskmaster on the job, will it not be giving him an inducement toward loyal citizenship to which he is eager to respond?

The concrete ways in which the museum tries to make clear its message are the habitual ways of its daily work, with merely a change of emphasis or an added effort at interpretation. At the Museum of Fine Arts in Boston, we have this winter been keeping in mind this work with the citizen. There is nothing startling to report, but a summary of what has been done may open up an exchange of ideas to further such work. . . .

Lectures to foreigners have been given in their own language, both in and outside the Museum, with the use of lantern slides illustrating the Museum collections. . . . A more intensive form of work has been done with high school pupils. As usual, large numbers of history classes have come to supplement the record of events in their books by the sight of related objects. In such docent work, the connection with the ideals of citizenship is a matter of stress and direction. When the high school girl answers, "Yes, I would like my history, only there is too much killing," the docent replies, "Yes, that is why you come to the Museum, to see the other side of history the lives of the people, their homes, the things they made and used and cared for: to see Charles I as Van Dyck saw him—the beauty-loving monarch, not the king who started a civil war."

But much more important is the work, now three years old, with pupils from high schools who are given vocational drawing in the Museum. By arrangement with the school committee, they are allowed to work in the Museum five afternoons a week, and the work done is credited to them as a school course. The instruction in drawing—free-hand and mechanical and from casts—and in design in color is given by members of the Museum school faculty. . . .

Again, both summer and winter, we have had our stories for children from city playground, settlement, or school. The summer work is always mainly significant because of numbers—six thousand eight hundred and thirty-six having come to us last summer; but some of the stories were chosen with a patriotic end in view. This winter the subject of the stories has been definitely America and citizenship. Their plan and scope was partly due to the stimulus given by the new civic work of the Woman's Education Association of Boston, and partly due to one of our most faithful boys: "I like best stories about America," he said.

Within the limitations set by the Museum collections, a series was planned called "The Long Journey to America: From Old Homes to New;" and from the first story, "The Age When Dreams Came True," the story of Columbus, we followed the different nations of settlers— Spanish, Dutch, French, English, Syrian, Italian, and Japanese—coming with each one from the setting and atmosphere of his old home and feeling the lure and effects of the new one. In most cases this has meant that the Museum material has been used as background and illustration rather than as subject-matter; as, for example, in the story of Pizarro— "From Spanish Towns to the Temple of the Sun"—when Spanish paintings and the Museum's Peruvian embroideries and pottery gave the setting. . . .

Such methods of work with citizens, actual or to-be, gain their import-ance, of course, because always behind the ways of using it, there stands the museum itself. . . . To such a child, whose experience of life would turn even the museum into a vast pawn-shop, it was a satisfaction to describe the spirit and purpose of givers and lenders to a museum and the reasons for the making of such a collection. For in most of our cities our museums stand as an example, through their lenders, donors, and admin-istrators of unqualified generosity and public-mindedness—an example of true American spirit.

# 33

# THE MUSEUM'S EDUCATIONAL CREDO

## Winifred E. Howe

*The Metropolitan Museum of Art Bulletin*, 13: 192–193, 1918

---

*The following educational credo, written by Winifred E. Howe, editor for publications at the Metropolitan Museum of Art, New York, represents the museum staff's collaborative effort to create a comprehensive institutional educational philosophy. Given the museum's position and influence this document had a wide and lasting impact on the museum profession.*

---

. . . We purposely limit our discussion to this Museum, inasmuch as the Metropolitan Museum through its history, location, and collections has a unique position and individual problems. Two things, at least, in its history are determining factors in the direction its development must take: first, the charter of the Museum, drawn up in 1870, which not only gives full warrant for the emphasis placed in recent years upon the educational side of museum activity but even definitely dictates such a policy in its wording "for the purpose of . . . encouraging and developing the study of fine arts, and the application of arts to manufacture and practical life, of advancing the general knowledge of kindred subjects, and to that end, of furnishing popular instruction"; and second, the amendment to the act of incorporation passed by the State Legislature in 1908 that forever classes the Museum among the educational institutions of the country. Its location, also, in the largest city in America with thousands of people of foreign birth within easy walking distance of its galleries presents to it the opportunity of striving to be "the melting pot of the artistic ideals of many peoples" and so a great "Americanizing force in the artistic development" of the country. Other art museums face a similar situation on a smaller scale; none has so vast an undertaking. Furthermore, the generosity of the friends of this Museum has placed within its walls collections more valuable and comprehensive than those entrusted to any other museum of art in America. The Metropolitan Museum is not only in name but in fact a metropolitan museum, national in scope, and must recognize its functions as such. Its educational ideals can be no less wide than those of the country itself, and no less inclusive of all classes of people than the ideals of democracy.

We may, then, formulate our creed as follows:

1. We believe that every human being is born with a potential love of beauty, and whether this capacity lies dormant or springs into activity depends largely upon his education, using this term to include not merely his acquirements in the schoolroom but all the influences at home and elsewhere that shape his character. Assuredly this latent power to find rest and happiness in those things that appeal to the eye is capable of development.

2. We believe that whether the cultivation of this faculty adds to the earning capacity of its possessor or not, it does unquestionably increase his happiness, and this in turn reacts upon his health of mind and body. Thus eyes that know how to see beauty and a mind that can appreciate its spirit are genuine assets to the individual, of greater value now than ever before, and through the individual to the community, the state, and the nation.

3. We believe that the Metropolitan Museum has an important role to play in the education of this innate love of beauty in all who come to its galleries or within the range of its influence.

4. We believe that it is possible through the breadth and comprehensiveness of the Museum collections to find in them some object or group of objects that may serve as a link between the present experience and interests of any visitor and the appreciation of such artistic qualities as form, color, surface, and imaginative content, and that the initial task of the museum instructor is to find this link.

5. We believe that through cooperation with the schools and correlation with the studies in the curriculum a generation of young Americans may grow up who will continue to come to the Museum as to a friend, feeling welcome and at home, and obtaining from their visits inspiration and help for their daily life, and who will know how to see beauty everywhere because they have learned its language here.

6. We believe that while museum teaching may have two legitimate functions, information and interpretation—in other words, that in which the objects are important in relation to some other subject,

and that in which they are important for themselves—the endeavor in this museum constantly is so to translate the message of the artist into terms intelligible to the visitor—be he child or adult—that in proportion to his ability he shall catch a glimpse of the artist's purpose.

7. We believe that the Museum may perform a two-fold service in the community; cultivating good taste in home decoration, dress, etc., on the one hand; and giving to salespeople, designers, and manufacturers, on the other hand, every facility for the study of the collections of decorative arts, for copying or adapting objects therein or gaining inspiration for new designs, thus helping to meet the demand that the Museum itself helped to create.

8. We believe that through its catalogues and Bulletins, through lectures given in schools and elsewhere, through groups of paintings lent to libraries, through its photographs for sale, and through its lending collections—photographs, post cards, textiles, prints, casts, and lantern slides—the Museum is extending its work of education and reaching many places where otherwise there would be little opportunity for cultivating a love of beauty.

9. We believe, finally, that in all these varied forms of educational work the Museum is performing a wartime service, the worth of which will be realized more fully when peace comes and brings with it a readjustment of values.

# SECTION V

## Museum Exhibition

The middle nineteenth to the early twentieth century was a dynamic period in the development of museum exhibition, as museum professionals began to separate the research and exhibit collections. The division created a boom in collecting, but it also gave rise to a revolution and renaissance on the public side of their institutions.

As early as 1869, Alfred Russel Wallace considered the possibilities for new methods of display in natural history museums. Though he still imagined systematic display, he envisioned exhibits in which lifelike taxidermied specimens would be placed in naturalistic settings. John George Wood agreed that systematic display of objects contributed to the "dullness of museums" and argued in favor of educational exhibits such as habitat groups. Half a world away at the Australian Museum, Gerard Krefft was developing a similar philosophy, heavily influenced by John Edward Gray, keeper of zoology at the British Museum in London, who was advancing the notion of popular instruction as a necessary component of the natural history museum.

Changes in the display of natural history objects sparked similar discussion concerning the display of ethnographic objects. In 1907, George A. Dorsey, curator of anthropology of the Field Museum of Natural History, and Franz Boas, assistant curator of ethnology at the American Museum of Natural History, engaged in an impassioned debate in the pages of the journal *Science*. Dorsey, a proponent for systematic display that emphasized the primitive or advanced nature of the objects, was highly critical of the new display methods employed by the American Museum of Natural History. Boas defended the American Museum, arguing in favor of arranging objects by tribe or culture. Henry L. Ward, director of the Milwaukee Public Museum, supported Boas and suggested the display of ethnographic material in dioramas to further enhance a contextual understanding of native cultures.

**Additional Readings**

Belcher, Michael. 1991. *Exhibitions in museums.* Washington, DC: Smithsonian Institution Press.

Dean, David. 1997. *Museum exhibition: Theory and practice.* New York: Routledge.

Lord, Barry, and Gail D. Lord. 2001. *The manual of museum exhibitions.* Walnut Creek, CA: AltaMira Press.

McLean, Kathleen. 1993. *Planning for people in exhibitions.* Washington, DC: Association of Science-Technology Centers.

Serrell, Beverly. 1996. *Exhibit labels: An interpretive approach.* Walnut Creek, CA: AltaMira Press.

———. 2006. *Judging exhibitions: A framework for assessing excellence.* Walnut Creek, CA: Left Coast Press, Inc.

Yanni, Carla. 2005. *Nature's museums: Victorian science and the architecture of display.* New York: Princeton Architectural Press.

# 34

## MUSEUM FOR THE PEOPLE

### Alfred Russel Wallace

*Macmillan's Magazine,* 19 (111): 244–250, 1869

*Alfred Wallace, British naturalist and codiscoverer of the Darwinian theory of natural selection, expounds on his design for the ideal natural history museum in the article excerpted below. Although he provides a detailed discussion of each of the various necessary departments, only zoology and ethnology are included here. Wallace promoted the new radical exhibit technique of displaying lifelike taxidermy groups in four-sided glass cases, which preceded the development of habitat dioramas. At the same time he saw a use for maintaining systematically ordered exhibits of detailed synoptic collections.*

Museums of Natural History should be, one would think, among the most entertaining and instructive of public exhibitions, since their object is to show us life-like restorations of all those wonderful and beautiful animals, the mere description of which in the pages of the traveler, the naturalist, or the sportsman, are of such absorbing interest. Strange to say, however, such is by no means generally the case; and these institutions rarely appear to yield either pleasure or information at all proportionate to their immense cost. We can hardly impute this failure to anything in the nature of Museums or of their contents, when we remember that good illustrated works on natural history are universally interesting and instructive; and that private collections of birds, shells, or insects are often very attractive even to the uninitiated, and at the same time of the highest value to the student. We must therefore seek for an explanation of the anomaly in the system on which public museums are usually constituted, in the quality of the specimens, and in the mode of exhibiting them, all which, it is now generally admitted, are equally unsuited for the amusement and instruction of the public and for the purposes of the scientific student.

Public museums of natural objects being such entirely modern institutions, we can hardly wonder that no generally accepted principles have yet been laid down for their construction or arrangement. They most frequently originated with private collectors, whose plan was naturally followed in their enlargement; and when they outgrew their original domicile, an architect was called in, who, according to his special tastes, designed a temple or a palace for their reception. However inconvenient or unsuitable the original mode of exhibition might turn out, or however ill adapted to its purpose the new building might prove, it would, of course, be exceedingly difficult and expensive to alter either of them, more especially as the modified plan might be found, after trial, to have defects as great as that which it replaced.

Quite recently, two eminent men (Dr. Gray and Dr. Hooker), both connected with great public museums, have made suggestions towards a more rational system; and as it is evident that museums will increase, and may be made an important agent in national education and the elevation of the masses, of the people, it seems advisable that the subject should be brought forward for popular discussion.

Accepting the few general principles that seem now to be pretty generally agreed upon, I propose to follow them out into some rather important details.

I shall consider, in the first place, what should be the scope of a Typical Popular Museum, and then sketch out the arrangements best adapted to make it both entertaining and instructive to the young and ignorant, and a means of high intellectual culture and enjoyment to such as may be disposed to avail themselves fully of its teachings.

Museums are well adapted to illustrate all those branches of knowledge whose subject matter consists mainly of definite moveable and portable objects. The great group of the natural history sciences can scarcely be taught without them; while mathematics, astronomy, physics, and chemistry make use of observatories and laboratories rather than museums. The fine and mechanical arts, as well as history, can also be illustrated by extensive collections of objects; and we are thus led to a broad division of museums, according as they deal mainly with natural objects or with works of art.

A museum of natural objects appears, for a variety of reasons, best fitted to interest, instruct, and elevate the middle and lower classes and the young. It is more in accordance with their tastes and sympathies, as shown by the universal fondness for flowers and birds, and the great interest excited by new or strange animals. It enables them to acquire a wide and accurate knowledge of the earth and of its varied productions; and if they wish to follow up any branch of natural history as an amusement or a study, it leads them into the pure air and pleasant scenes of the country, and is likely to be the best antidote to habits of dissipation or immorality. Such museums, too, offer the only means by which the mass of the working classes can obtain any actual knowledge of the wonderful productions of nature in present or past ages; and such knowledge gives a new interest to works on geography, travel, or natural history. Owing to the wide disconnexion of these subjects from the daily pursuits of life, they are so much the better adapted for the relaxation of those who earn their bread by manual labour. The inexhaustible variety, the strange beauty, and the wondrous complexity of natural objects, are pre-eminently adapted to excite both the observing and reflective powers of the mind, their study is well calculated to have an elevating and refining effect upon the character. . . .

Throughout the animal kingdom, at least one or more species of every Family group should be exhibited; and in the more important and interesting Families, one or more species of each Genus. The number of specimens is not, however, so important, as their quality and the mode of exhibiting them. A few of the more important species in each Order, well illustrated by fine and characteristic specimens, would be far better than ten times the number if imperfect, badly prepared, and, badly arranged. Let any one look at an artistically mounted group of fine and perfect quadruped or bird skins, which represent the living animals in perfect health and vigour, and by their characteristic attitudes and accessories tell the history of the creature's life and habits; and compare this with the immature, ragged, mangy-looking specimens one often sees in museums, stuck up in stiff and unnatural attitudes, and resembling only mummies or scarecrows. The one is both instructive and pleasing, and we return again and again to gaze upon it with delight. The other is positively repellent, and we feel that we never want to look upon it again.

I consider it therefore an important principle, that in a Museum for the People nothing should be exhibited that is not good of its kind, and mounted in the very best manner. Fortunately, specimens of a large number of the most beautiful and extraordinary animals are now exceedingly common, and every well-marked group in nature may be well illustrated without having recourse to the rarer and more costly species. Carrying out these views, we should exhibit our animal in such a way as to convey the largest amount of information possible. The male, female, and young should be shown together; the mode of feeding or of capturing its prey, and the most characteristic attitudes and motions, should be indicated; and the accessories should point out the country the species inhabits, or the kind of locality it most frequents. A descriptive tablet should of course give further information; and in the immediate vicinity, specimens showing any remarkable points of its anatomy, and any useful products that are derived from it, should be exhibited.

Each group of this kind would be a study of itself, and should therefore be kept quite distinct and apart from every other group. It should be so placed that it could be seen from several points of view, and every part of each individual composing it closely examined. To encourage such examination and study, seats should be placed conveniently near it—a point strangely overlooked in most museums, where it seems to be taken for granted that visitors will pass on without any desire to linger, or any wish for a more close examination. It would add still further to the interest of these typical groups if it were clearly shown how much they represented, by giving a list of all the well-known species of the genus or family, with their native country and proportionate size, and indicating, by means of a coloured line, which of them were exhibited in the museum. This would be an excellent and most intelligible guide to the collection itself, and would enable the visitor to judge how far it gave any adequate notion of the variety and exuberance of nature.

It would also, I think, be advisable, that as far as possible each well-mannered group of any considerable extent should occupy one room or compartment only, where it would be separated from all others, where the attention could lie concentrated upon it, and where the extent to which it was illustrated could be seen at a glance. This has not, I believe, been yet attempted in any museum; and when I come to speak of the building arrangements, I will explain, how it can be easily managed. In this room, a department would also be devoted to the comparative anatomy of all the more important species and groups exhibited; and a large map should be suspended, showing in some detail their geographical distribution. Here, too, we should place specimens or casts of the fossil remains of the family, with restorations of some of the more important species; and along with these, diagrams, showing the progress of development of the group throughout past time, as far as yet known. . . .

Connected with this there should be a students' department, to which all should have free access who wished to obtain more detailed knowledge. Here would be preserved, in the most compact and accessible form, all specimens acquired by the museum, which were not required or were not adapted for exhibition in the popular department. Here, too, should be formed a complete local or British collection of indigenous animals, according to the extent and means of the institution, with the best zoological library of reference that could be obtained. In this department, donations of almost any kind would be acceptable; for, when not required for popular exhibition, an immense number of specimens can, be conveniently and systematically arranged in a very limited space, and for purposes of study or for identifications museums are almost sure to be of value. One of the greatest evils of most local museums is thus got rid of—the giving offence by refusing donations, or being forced to occupy much valuable space with, such as are utterly unfit for popular exhibition. . . .

The chief well-marked races of man should be illustrated either by life-size models, casts, coloured figures, or by photographs. A corresponding series of their crania should also be shown; and such portions of the skeleton as should exhibit the differences that exist between certain races, as well as those between the lower races and those animals which most nearly approach them. Casts of the best authenticated remains of prehistoric man should also be obtained, and compared with the corresponding parts of existing races. The arts of mankind should be illustrated by a series, commencing with the rudest flint implements, and passing through those of polished stony, bronze, and iron—showing in every case, along with the works of prehistoric man, those corresponding to them formed by existing: savage races. Implements of bone and of horn should follow the same order.

Pottery would furnish a most interesting series. Beginning with the rude forms of prehistoric races, and following with those of modern savages, we should have the strangely-modeled vessels of Peru and of North America, those of Egypt, Assyria, Etruria, Greece, and Rome, as well as the works of China and of medieval modern Europe.

The art of scripture and mode of ornamentation should be traced in like manner among savage tribes, the Oriental nations, Greece, and Rome, to modern civilization. Works in metal and textile fabrics would admit of similar illustration. Characteristic weapons should also be exhibited; and painting might be traced in broad steps, from the contemporary delineation of a Mammoth up to the animal portraiture of Landseer.

This comprises a series of Ethnological illustrations that need not occupy much space, and would, I think, be eminently instructive. The clothing, the houses, the household utensils, and the weapons of mankind, can hardly be shown with any approach to completeness, in a Popular Museum; and many of these objects occupy space quite disproportionate to their intrinsic interest or scientific value. They could in most cases be sufficiently indicated by drawings or models. . . .

In his President's address to the British Association at Norwich, Dr. Hooker made some admirable remarks on the situation of museums. He observed: "Much of the utility of museums depends on two conditions often strangely overlooked, viz. their situation—and interior arrangements. The provincial museum is too often huddled away almost out of sight, in a dark, crowded, dirty thoroughfare, where it pays dear for ground rent, rates, and taxes, and cannot be extended. Such localities are frequented by the townspeople only when on business, and when they consequently have no time for sight-seeing. In the evening, or on holidays, when they would visit the museum, they naturally prefer the outskirts of the town to its centre. . . . The museum should be in an open grassed square or park, planted with trees, in the town outskirts; a main object being to secure cleanliness, a cheerful aspect, and space for extension. Now, vegetation is the best interceptor of dust, which is injurious to the specimens as well as unsightly, whilst a cheerful aspect, and grass and trees, will attract visitors, and especially families and schools." Evidently, then, the proper place for the museum is the centre of the park or public garden. This furnishes the largest and cleanest open space, the best light, the purest air, and the readiest access. With how much greater pleasure the workman and his family could spend a day at the museum, if at intervals they could stroll out on to the grass among flowers and under shady trees, to enjoy the refreshments they had brought with them. They would then return to the building with renewed zest, and would probably escape the fatigue and headache that a day in a museum almost invariably brings on. How admirably adapted for the National Museum of Natural History would be the centre of the Regent's or Hyde Park!

In designing museums, architects seem to pay little regard to the special purposes they are intended to fulfill. They often adopt the general arrangement of a church, or the immense galleries and lofty halls of a palace. Now, the main object of a museum-building is to furnish the greatest amount of well lighted space, for the convenient arrangement and exhibition of objects which all require to be closely examined. At the same time they should be visible by several persons at once without crowding, and admit of others freely passing by them. None except the very largest specimens should be placed so as to rise higher than seven feet above the floor, so that palatial rooms and extensive galleries, requiring proportionate altitude, are exceedingly wasteful of space, and otherwise ill adapted and unnecessary for the real purposes of a museum. It is true that side-galleries against the walls may be and often are used to utilize the height, but these are almost necessarily narrow, and totally unadapted for the proper exhibition of any but a limited class of objects. By this plan, too, the whole upper-floor space is lost, which is of great importance, because large proportion of objects are best exhibited on tables or in detached cases. . . .

Two of the great evils of museums are, crowding and distraction. By the crowding of specimens, the effect of each is weakened, destroyed; the eye takes in so many at once that it is continually wandering towards something more strange and beautiful, and there is nothing to concentrate the attention on a special object. Distraction is produced also by the great size of the galleries, and the multiplicity of objects that strike the eye. It is almost impossible for a casual visitor to avoid the desire of continually going on to see what comes next, or wondering what is that bright mass of colour or strange form that catches the eye at the other end of the long gallery. These evils can best be avoided, by keeping, as far as possible, each natural group of objects in a separate room, or a, separate compartment of that room—by limiting as much as possible the numbers of illustrative groups of species, and at the same time making each group as attractive and instructive as possible. The object aimed at should be, to compel attention to each group of specimens. This may be done by making it so interesting or beautiful at first sight as to secure a close examination; by carefully isolating it, so that no other object close by should divide attention with it; and by giving so much information and interesting the mind in so many collateral matters connected with it as to excite the observant and reflective as well as the emotional faculties.

The general system of arrangement and exhibition here pointed out does not at all depend on the building. It can be applied in any museum, and is, I believe, already to some extent adopted in our best local institutions. It has, however, never yet been carried out systematically; and till this is done, we can form no true estimate of how popular a Natural History Museum can become, or how much it may aid in the great work of national education.

# 35

# THE IMPROVEMENTS EFFECTED IN MODERN MUSEUMS OF EUROPE AND AUSTRALIA

**[Johann Ludwig] Gerard Krefft [with extensive quotes from John Edward Gray]**

*Transactions of the Royal Society of New South Wales, for the year 1868,* 2: 15–25, 1869

---

*Gerard Krefft, Australian zoologist, paleontologist, and museum adminis-trator, writes about his exhibition philosophy, which was greatly influenced by John Edward Gray, Keeper of Zoology at the British Museum in London, whom he cites extensively. Both were proponents of a museum design that allocated a public exhibition space with mainly synoptic collections that would enhance the educational experience of visitors. Their writings focus on the practical aspects of exhibition such as the most useful display case designs, effective use of instructive labels, and the destruction of exhibit specimens by insect infestation and exposure to light.*

---

The interest which all classes take in Natural History, has gradually changed the old fashioned curiosity shop of fifty years ago, into useful Museums—where rational amusement, combined with instruction, is offered to the mass of the people, and where students have every opportunity to examine and study the specimens, of which the Museum consists. With the British Museum for a model—we had, at first, adopted almost everything that is good and bad in that great Institution, till experience showed plainly that there was much room for improvement, and, this it appears has also been felt by Dr. J. E Gray. In a pamphlet sent to me by last mail, the principal

Keeper has suggested to the British Museum Trustees, certain alterations which I have advocated for years, and which, as far as it was possible, have long been adopted in our own Museum. . . .

I will now, with your permission, quote Dr. Gray, whose experience in the largest and most important Museum in the world, extends over a life time, and whose opinion should be well considered by those, who are about establishing private or public Museums in the colonies:

"It is easy to devise the plan of a Museum, which shall be the most interesting and instructive to general visitors, and one from which, however short their stay, or however casual their inspection, they can hardly fail to carry away some amount of valuable information.

"The larger animals, being of course more generally interesting, and easily seen and recognized, should be exhibited in the preserved state, and in situations where they can be completely isolated. This is necessary also, on account of their size, which would not admit of their being grouped in the manner, which I propose with reference to the smaller specimens.

"The older Museums were for the most part made up of the square glass-fronted boxes, each containing one, or sometimes a pair of specimens. This method had some advantages, but many inconveniences—among others, that of occupying too large an amount of room. But, I cannot help thinking, that when this was given up for the French plan of attaching each specimen to a separate stand, and marshalling them like soldiers on the shelves of a large open case, the improvement was not so great as many suppose; and this has become more and more evident since the researches of travellers and collectors, have so largely increased the number of known species, and of species frequently separated by characters so minute, as not to be detected without careful and close examination.

"Having come to the conclusion that a Museum, for the use of the general public, should consist chiefly of the best-known, the most marked, and the most interesting animals, arranged in such a way as to convey the greatest amount of instruction in the shortest and most direct manner, and so exhibited as to be seen without confusion; I am very much disposed to recur to something like the old plan of arranging each species, or series of species in a special case, to be placed either on shelves or tables, or in wall cases, as may be found most appropriate, or as the special purpose for which each case is prepared and exhibited may seem to require.

"But instead of each case, as of old, containing only a single specimen, it should embrace a series of specimens, selected and arranged so as to present a special object for study; and thus any visitor looking at a single case only, and taking the trouble to understand it would carry away a distinct portion of knowledge, such as, in the present state of our arrangements, could only be obtained by the examination and comparison of specimens distributed through distant parts of the collection.

"Every case should be distinctly labeled with an account of the purpose for which it is prepared and exhibited; and each specimen contained in it should also bear a label, indicating why it is there placed.

"I may be asked, Why should each series of specimens be contained in a separate case? but I think it must be obvious that a series of objects, exhibited for a definite purpose, should be brought into close proximity, and contained in a well-defined space, and this will best be done, by keeping them in a single and separate case. There is also the additional advantage, that whenever, in the progress of discovery, it becomes desirable that the facts for the illustration of which the case was prepared, should be exhibited in a different manner—this can easily be done by rearranging the individual case, without interfering with the general arrangement of the collection. I believe that the more clearly the object is defined, and the illustrations kept together, the greater will be the amount of, information derived from it by the visitor, and the interest he will feel in examining it.

"Such cases may be advantageously prepared to show—
The classes of the animal kingdom.
The orders of each class.
The families of each order.
The genera of each family.

"The sections of each genus, by means of one or more typical or characteristic examples of each class, order, or section.

"A selection of a specimen of each of the more important or striking species of each genus or section.

"The changes of state, sexes, habits, and manners of a well known, or an otherwise interesting species.

"The economic uses to which they are applied, and such other particulars as the judgement and talent of the curator would select as best adapted for popular instruction, and of which these are only intended as partial indications.

"No one, I think, who has ever had charge of a Museum, or who has noted the behaviour of the visitors while passing through it can doubt for a moment that such cases would be infinitely more attractive to the public at large, than the crowded shelves of our present Museums in which they speedily become bewildered by the multiplicity, the apparent sameness, and at the same time the infinite variety of the objects presented to their view, and, in regard to which, the labels on the tops of the cases afford them little assistance, while those on the specimens themselves are almost unintelligible.

"When such visitors really take any interest in the exhibition, it will generally be found that they concentrate their attention on individual objects, while others affect to do the same, in order to conceal their total want of interest, of which they somehow feel ashamed, although it originates in no fault of their own.

"I think the time is approaching, when a great change will be made in the arrangement of Museums of Natural History, and have therefore thrown out these observations as suggestions, by which it appears to me, that their usefulness may be greatly extended. . . ."

It will be seen from this that our great Museum authority has no longer any faith in the old fashioned arrangements, and if wall cases are found inconvenient in a cold climate like England, how much more dangerous must they be in Australia? The cabinets in the Melbourne Museum are arranged end on between the windows—the narrow part touching the wall, and leaving three sides free, so that back and front of the specimens can be inspected, and dangerous insects destroyed whenever they make their appearance. Where wall cases in particular those without glass tops are in use, the destruction from the attack of insects is very large, and the labour and expense to keep a collection well preserved, will amount to a considerable sum during the year.

The most useful cases, and those best adapted for our climate which I have seen, consisted of iron and glass only; they could be taken to pieces and removed without much labour—an advantage as well worth consideration, where, as often happens in young communities, the embryo Museum is only temporarily located in some vacant room, or it is desirable to shift the cases to an upper story.

I have already experienced the advantage of making the cabinets portable, and all the table cases now in use in the Australian Museum, can be taken to pieces.

Dr. Gray recommends that no specimens should be placed higher than about five feet from the bottom of the case, and this plan I have always endeavoured to carry out as much as possible. It is distressing to see visitors on tiptoe, trying to read the names of specimens raised above this level and the objects, thus become quite useless, except to the Curator, who requires a ladder when he wishes to inspect them.

Dr. Gray recommends the exhibition of specimens as follows: "Mammalia and their skeletons, being of a large size, require to have good-sized rooms.

"The birds and other animals, being small, are better seen in moderate-sized rooms, as large rooms dwarf the size of their specimens.

"The rooms and the cases in them need not be alike, as that tires the eyes of the visitors.

"Too much and too brilliant ornamentation of the rooms and cases kill the specimens; but, at the same time, they need not be like the rooms of a 'dock warehouse'. . . .

"If the skeletons of whales are exhibited, they are much better seen when placed in the middle of a room, or raised only slightly above the floor, so that they can be seen by persons walking, or at most, not raised higher than the skeleton of the Greenland whale now shown at the College of Surgeons. When suspended from the roof, they can only be very imperfectly seen or understood."

The plan to mount whale skeletons as Dr. Gray proposes to the Museum Trustees, is not to be recommended where visitors are so indiscriminately admitted as they are in Museums in Australia. I think specimens of this kind would not suffer much injury from being exposed, but it is always better to guard against accidents.

A whale skeleton with its lowest part, should be sufficiently high from the ground to enable a person to "walk beneath it, and, if there is no gallery, to view it from above, it would be well to erect a raised platform for this purpose. . . .

I now come to a very important subject, and that is, the desirability of having certain specimens kept in skins for the use of the student. Anybody who has inspected the first floor of the new wing, will remember the fine series of Australian and Indian birds kept in skins, and exhibited a pair of each in shallow glass cases. Their names, the locality where, and the date when they were shot, are neatly written, underneath each species, who brought this fine collection together, and arranged the series in such a manner, that every school-boy can easily find the bird he wishes to know.

In the same way the bones, and in particular the sterna of birds, so important in their classification, have been arranged; the fossil remains are also exhibited in this way, close to the mounted skeletons of several extinct birds.

In the Mammalian department there is also a series of mounted skeletons, besides a number of boards, each with a skeleton put down flat—a new way of arranging bones, which has since been adopted by many of my colleagues in England and on the continent of Europe.

A very important arrangement is, to have the teeth of animals mounted on glass slides, each species on a separate piece, besides reserving a skull in a stopper bottle. This plan answers excellently for comparison when classifying fossil remains.

I may also draw attention to the advantage glass has over wood or millboard, for mounting in particular delicate specimens; all the shells, the greater part of the smaller fossils, and other objects are thus exhibited in the collection. The paper upon which they rest never becomes dirty, and any color can be chosen, and removed if necessary without much trouble. . . .

I must now again quote Dr. Gray, to prove that almost every single proposition which he makes to the British Museum Trustees has been partially carried out in Australia years ago, and this assertion will be found further strengthened as soon as the necessary table cases are made, which will enable the Trustees to exhibit their collection to the best advantage, both for the student and for the general visitor.

Dr. Gray remarks: "What the largest class of visitors, the general public, want, is a collection of the most interesting objects, so arranged as to afford the greatest possible amount of information in a moderate space, and to be obtained, as it were, at a glance. On the other hand, the scientific student requires to have under his hands the most complete collection of specimens that can be brought together, and in such a condition as to admit of the most minute examination of their differences, whether of age, or sex, or state, or of whatever kind that can throw light upon all the innumerable questions that are continually arising in the progress of thought and opinion.

"Every scientific student requires the cases to be opened, to allow him to examine and handle the specimens, and in the stuffed state this cannot be often done without injury; and an artist always requires them to be taken out of the case for his purpose.

"In the futile attempt to combine these two purposes in one consecutive arrangement the modern museum entirely fails in both particulars. It is only to be compared to a large store or a city warehouse, in which every specimen that can be collected is arranged in its proper case and on its proper shelf, so that it may be found when wanted; but the uninformed mind derives little instruction from the contemplation of its stores, while the student of nature requires a far more careful examination of them than is possible under such a system of arrangement, to derive any advantage; the visitor needs to be as well informed with relation to the system on which it is based as the curator himself; and consequently the general visitor perceives little else than a chaos of specimens, of which the bulk of those placed in close proximity are so nearly alike that he can scarcely perceive any difference between them, even supposing them to be placed on a level with the eye, while the greater number of those which are above or below this level are utterly unintelligible. . . .

"The very extent of the collection renders it difficult even for the student, and much more so for the less scientific visitor, to discover any particular specimen of which he is in quest; and the larger the collection, the greater this difficulty becomes. Add to this the fact that all specimens, but more especially the more beautiful and the more delicate, are speedily deteriorated, and in some cases destroyed for all useful purposes, by exposure to light, and that both the bones and skins of animals are found to be much more susceptible of measurement and comparison in an unstuffed or unmounted state, and it will be at once apparent why almost all scientific Zoologists have adopted for their own collections the simpler and more advantageous plan of keeping their specimens in boxes or drawers, devoted each to a family, a genus, or a section of a genus, as each individual case may require.

"Thus preserved and thus arranged, the most and the most useful collection that the student could desire would occupy comparatively a small space, and by no means require *large and lofty halls for its reception.*"

The British Museum plan of exhibiting stuffed fishes and reptiles only, and keeping the spirit specimens in the cellar, has not been adopted by our Trustees, because the larger number of specimens being Australian, can be re-placed; duplicates are always kept in a dark room for this purpose, and as the Museum is well supplied by Professional and Amateur fishermen, we can always exhibit most of our genera and species.

The large fossil reptiles and fishes, I find, are best displayed on slanting platforms; in this manner the large "Plesiosaurus Cromptonii," above thirty feet in length, is shewn to great advantage, and at the least possible expenditure of space or money. This large fossil is screwed with bolts on to the boards, and the margin is then plastered with cement, gradually coming level with the board, so that it has the appearance of a large solid slab. Smaller objects, as skeletons of Crocodiles, Gavials, Fossil Fishes, &c; are fastened, on by wire.

Now, in the Dublin Museum, the original P. Cromptonii is arranged on a gigantic horizontal platform or table, taking up an immense amount of room, without showing much of the animal. . . .

# 36

# THE DULNESS OF MUSEUMS

## John George Wood

*The Nineteenth Century*, 21: 384–396, 1887

*Many of the ideas expressed in the article, excerpted below, by John George Wood, a popular British natural history writer, foreshadowed several developments in natural history museums worldwide. In particular, many of the necessary changes in museum exhibition that Wood outlines were incorporated into the "new museum" idea—a movement that gained momentum over the next two decades. While he believed in the value of habitat groups to create a more interesting exhibit, he demanded scientific accuracy.*

Oh! the dulness of museums!

I speak on behalf of the General Public. Full of interest to the expert, there is no concealing the fact that to the general public a museum, of whatever nature, is most intolerably dull, as I know by personal experience. To me, for example, a collection of blue china is dulness itself. I do not understand blue china, and its peculiar beauties are lost on me, while the experts cannot sufficiently feast their eyes on it, and are longing to nurse every teapot and stroke every plate in the collection.

Can anything be duller than a collection of coins when viewed by those who are absolutely ignorant of numismatics, know next to nothing of modern and nothing at all of ancient history, and can only appreciate a coin by its intrinsic value. They would perhaps admire a doubloon or a five-guinea piece, but would think very little of a daric.

A botanical collection would indeed be the *driest of dry subjects* to those who know nothing of botany, nor would an outsider be very much more interested if he were to walk for an hour in a botanical garden where the plants were absolutely growing.

Stay for a while in a geological museum, and watch the demeanour of those who pass through it. Putting aside the actual students of geology, who can be detected at a glance, there is not one in a hundred who is one whit wiser on leaving than on entering, nor, indeed, who has tried to be wiser. Stones, bones, and fossil shells, plants, and animals leave no further impression on the mind of the general visitor than that some of them are very big, and all of them are very ugly.

Even in art galleries, much of the same indifference prevails. Go to the National Gallery, or to the sculpture galleries of the British Museum, and watch the people as they wander among the priceless treasures of brush and chisel. The general visitors stroll listlessly through the building, utterly failing to appreciate a single beauty of canvas or marble, and sometimes openly avowing that they wonder why people should make such a fuss about faded pictures and battered statues. To their eyes the grand contours of the "Theseus" torso and the divine grace of the Milo Venus are invisible, while we have all read of the American visitors who derided the Medicean Venus as thick-waisted and splay-footed, their eyes having been accustomed to the distorted figures and crushed feet of their fashionable countrywomen.

The zoological galleries of a museum are scarcely less wearisome to the untrained eye. At first, perhaps, some amount of interest may be excited by the lions, tigers, leopards, some of the monkeys and a few eagles. But the interest soon cools, and the eye becomes painfully wearied by the monotony of long rows of beasts standing on flat boards, and of birds perched on short crutches, all "looking intensely nowhere, and staring with extraordinary earnestness at nothing."

Even the Zoological Gardens themselves soon pall upon the sight, and visitors abandon the beasts and gather round the band, tired even of watching the elephants and camels carry successive loads of children along the path and back again. There is, however, one exception, namely, "feeding time," when even the music yields to a greater attraction, and everyone rushes to see beasts and birds fed.

Now, this apparently unimportant proceeding gives a clue to the construction and organization of museums which will attract the general public, and, after attracting the people, will arouse their attention, and excite and retain their interest. The creatures which are exhibited in a museum which will be acceptable to the public must be represented as doing something, not as staring straight in front of them. Note, for example, the crowd which will throng the window of a shop in which is a wheel doing nothing but turn round and round. "Toddy's" demand to "shee the wheels go wound" is the natural expression of this universal craving for action. Not only must the creatures be represented in action, but they must be shown as acting their natural life. Thus it is that people are soon tired of seeing the elephants and camels acting as beasts of burden, but they are never tired of seeing the animals feed.

I have long thought that in the management of our museums we have too much ignored the wants of the general public. If people only visited museums for the purpose of study, there would be no difficulty in the matter. But scarcely one in a thousand enters the door of a museum as a student, the remainder doing so simply for amusement, and interfering terribly with those who go there for study.

If the nine hundred and ninety-nine could be altogether ignored and excluded, as Horace objected to and excluded the *profanam vulgus*, the management of a museum would be simple enough. But we cannot and ought not to ignore them, but to welcome them, to interest them, and try to lead them on to systematic study. For this purpose, it is evident to my mind that we ought to have three, if not more, absolutely different classes of museums, addressed to different mental conditions.

The first ought to be devoted entirely to purely scientific purposes, and to be secured from interruptions by outsiders, who should be considered as the *profanum vulgus*, and treated as such. Then there should be a second class of museum intended for those who are trying to learn the rudiments of science, and may in due time be promoted into the select band of regular students, lastly, and quite as important as the two others, there should be a museum intended for the general public, and teaching them in spite of themselves. . . .

Of the second order of museums we have, or rather we shall have, a nearly perfect example in the new departments of natural history at South Kensington. The bays which surround the great central hall are being fitted up so as to exhibit the outlines of the comparative anatomy of the creatures which are found in the various galleries. . . .

But where is the museum for the general public? We have none at present.

Professor Flower, to whose energy, guided by vast experience, we owe the gigantic strides which are being made in our national collection of zoology, considers that this systematic arrangement teaches the A B C of the science. So it may seem to him, whose mind has for years been saturated with the subject. But it is not so to the ordinary visitor, who must have made some progress in anatomy before he can appreciate the teachings which are presented to his eyes. . . .

Now, it must be evident that to well-educated persons who cannot see the distinction between a tiger and a leopard, who believe wild boars to be beavers, and who can deliberately mistake the slender, long-legged, huge-beaked stork of India for the short-legged, fat-bodied, stumpy dodo of

Mauritius, which has been extinct for at least two centuries, the wonderful modifications of the arm and tongue bones would convey no ideas whatever. Their eyes and their intellect would require a considerable amount of training before they could appreciate the treasures of knowledge which Professor Flower has offered to them.

It is easy enough to say that such persons have no business in museums, and that their opinion is of no consequence. In former days, I held that view myself, and was not very slow to express it as strongly as possible. I now advocate a very different theory, and would treat such persons as children, to be caught and taught. In most cases, their ignorance is not their own fault, but is due to the imperfection of their education.

If I were requested to take a number of children to the zoological galleries at South Kensington, I certainly should not try to interest their uninstructed minds by showing them the series of comparative anatomy, nor even weary their eyes and limbs by marshalling them along the rows of stuffed birds and beasts.

I should show them one or two of the monkey tribe, and point out the distinctions between the principal groups, giving at the same time a brief account of their distribution and life-history, so as to weave physical geography into the study of zoology. Then I should not allow them to range about as they liked, but should take them to the bats, carefully drawing their attention to the modifications of structure which enable a mammal to fly as swiftly as a bird. I should point out to them the common British bats which they may see on any summer evening, and then encourage them to find out for themselves the points wherein, putting size out of the question, the fruit bats and vampires differ from the bats of our own country. . . .

The general public is absolutely unable to appreciate the sublime works of the great masters, and to them a sonata by Beethoven or a fugue by Bach is simply wearisome in the extreme. They cannot appreciate any music that has not plenty of tune in it, and prefer a waltz or a polka to the masterpieces of the greatest composers. Yet these people are not ignored. On the contrary, they are encouraged, and every effort is made to attract them, so as to lead them to the appreciation of a better class of music. At certain hours there is dance music for those who like it, but interspersed with the dances are always pieces of a higher class, yet not so elaborate as to be above the heads of the audience. Then there are the Wednesday concerts where the music is of a mixed nature, and there are the daily concerts where selections from the highest class of music are always introduced. . . .

To return to our museums. Such teaching as I have mentioned would be very gratifying to the pupils, but would be horribly annoying to those who had passed the stage of pupilage and wanted the museum for the purpose of study. Moreover, the number of objects is greatly in excess of a pupil's requirements, and instead of helping him would only retard his progress. For pupils, of whatever age they may be, there ought to be a separate museum, where they could be interested and instructed without disturbing the regular students.

What kind of museum ought it to be? We all dwell in a small Utopia, and dream visions of perfection which we would fain see realized.

A very old Utopian dream of mine is a Natural History Museum for the public which would attract them and give them an interest in animal life. Attempts have been made in this direction, but they have all been on too small a scale, have little or no leading ideas, and are too often marred by errors so glaring that they convey false teaching and do actual harm to the science of which they are meant to be exponents. Nothing can be better than the, beautiful series of bird life which has already been noticed, and which marks a distinct era in the history of museums. But they are widely scattered, and do not attract one tenth of the notice which they deserve.

As familiar examples of false teaching, I may mention the groups in the Wurtemburg Gallery in the Crystal palace. As a rule the taxidermy is good, and the groups are spirited in their action, but they are marred by the most outrageous blunders. For example, there is a group representing a horseman carrying off some young tiger cubs and pursued by the infuriated parents. He has shot one of them and is turning round in the saddle to shoot the other. So far so good. But the man is a Moor, whereas the tiger is exclusively Asiatic, and is no more to be seen in Africa, than in England. Nothing would have been easier than to have placed an Indian chief on the horse, or, if the Moor were retained, to have substituted lions for tigers; in either of which cases the group would have been just as spirited, and the teaching would have been true instead of false. . . .

There are just as absurd mistakes in the ethnological groups. The figures, etc., are admirable, but the clothes and weapons seem to have been distributed at random. Women, for example, are represented as carrying weapons instead of burdens, as is the invariable custom among all uncivilized people. Tribes from various parts of the world, even such essentially different races as Abyssinians, Dyaks, Botocudos, etc., are alike armed with Zulu assegais. The crowning absurdity, however, is attained in the group of North American Indian warriors in council, where the speaker is wearing on his breast the bead head-dress of a Bechuana woman. . . .

Had I the good fortune to live in Utopia, I would construct a museum especially adapted to the despised Tom, Dick, and Harry, which should amuse them, should be of such a nature as to compel them to take an interest in the subject, and perchance to transform them into the Thomas H. Huxleys, Richard Owens, and P. Henry Gosses of the next generation.

Men of science are not born ready made, or, if we wish to be classical, do not spring into the world fully armed, like Pallas from the head of Zeus. It is true that naturalists are, like poets, born, and not made, but both naturalists and poets might have lived all their days without discovering their real vocation, had it not been revealed to them by accidentally meeting with some natural object or some piece of poetry to which their souls at once responded.

Museums occupy so vast a range, that I can only treat of those which illustrate the science of zoology. In the first place, such museums should be pre-eminently attractive. They should essentially deal with zoology in its true sense—i.e., the science of life—and not with necrology, or the science of death, as is too often the case.

For this purpose, four requisites are necessary. There must be plenty of space, plenty of money, time, and intimate knowledge of the subjects. I suggest then, on behalf of Tom, Dick and Harry, that their museum of zoology should consist not of isolated animals, but of groups, some large and some small, but all representing actual episodes in the life history of the animals exhibited. Neither scenery, trees, nor herbage should be conventional or evolved out of the inner consciousness of the maker. They should be truthfully copied from the many photographs or trustworthy sketches which are at our command. As far as possible, each group should be the reproduction of some scene which has actually been witnessed and described by travellers. . . .

This, however, is not all. Putting aside the absolute ignorance with which we have to deal, we must remember that the faculty of observation is almost in abeyance in many individuals, while that of generalization has never been developed. To each group, therefore, a placard should be attached, stating that it would be explained at a certain hour, and that the lecturer would remain for the purpose of answering questions. Such a course would attract thousands who otherwise would not set a foot inside a museum. I have often noticed that at museums, at the Zoological Gardens, and similar exhibitions, as soon as anyone begins to explain an object, an eager crowd begins to collect, all thirsting for information, and often showing themselves inconveniently unwilling to disperse. . . .

The object of language is to convey ideas, and I have always held that words are valuable in proportion to their power of conveying thought from one brain to another. A word therefore which can be understood by ten thousand hearers should always be used in preference, to one which only three or four individuals can be expected to comprehend. A lecturer should always bear in mind that his true object is to teach his hearers, and not to impress them with awe of his vast attainments. Nothing is easier than to employ the technical phraseology of science. The real difficulty lies in conveying the same information in language which everyone can understand. Could an institute such as I have sketched be established for the benefit of the general public, my dream would be realized. Would that it might take visible form among the permanent institutes which now seem likely to take the place of temporary exhibitions!

# 37

## THE ANTHROPOLOGICAL EXHIBITS AT THE AMERICAN MUSEUM OF NATURAL HISTORY

**George A. Dorsey**

*Science*, 25 (new series): 584–589, 1907

*In the following excerpted essay, George Dorsey, curator of anthropology at the Field Museum of Natural History, wrote a defense of the use of archival systemization—popular in American museums in the latter part of the nineteenth century (Jenkins 1994)—as a practical approach for exhibiting ethnographic artifacts, in response to the newly opened ethnographic exhibits at the American Museum of Natural History. In this type of exhibit, objects of a similar type are arranged in systematic order from the most "primitive" to the most advanced or "civilized," marking technological progression. The collection space became the exhibit space, with most if not all of the collection on display.*

. . . The activity of the department of anthropology in the American Museum of Natural History became very great ten or twelve years ago and continued with increasing strength until about two years ago, at which time there seems to have been a change in the administration. During the ten years above referred to, we find a systematic attempt on the part of those in charge to carry on investigations over an ever-increasing large area as fast as means would permit. As a result of this intelligently directed series of field operations there grew up in the American Museum one of the greatest departments of anthropology to be found in any museum in the world. The plan of exhibition was on the broadest and most liberal scale. One could for the first time in an American museum study in detail the essential and salient features of the culture of a very large number of tribes, especially those of North America and northeastern Asia; and it seemed it was only a question of time and the continuance of the same policy when all cultures, exclusive of that of Europe, would be found adequately represented. It seems doubtful if any institution ever acquired in the same period of time collections of such magnitude or ever accumulated material with such intelligence or exhibited it in an equally sound manner. Here one could really study the culture of tribes, one could study conditions as they exist; one felt that one was not looking at the illustrations of some elementary text-book, but that he had in front of him the data from which the history of the material culture of mankind might be written. One felt instantly in the halls of the department the spirit of investigation and it was everywhere apparent that this was prompted by the desire to advance science and not by the desire to find material which would fit into or harmonize with some ideal scheme of exhibition. One instinctively felt in the presence of these exhibits that one was in close contact with actual conditions and that one was studying people at close hand, for everywhere was present the evidence of intelligent direction. It was evident that the objects on exhibition were neither placed there with the idea of their beauty nor was their arrangement such as to present primarily a beautiful picture, but rather one felt that as one passed from the exhibit of one tribe to that of another that the dominating features of each culture were so presented that they were apparent, and of course this was due to the fact that the work of collecting and exhibiting had been performed in an intelligent manner. The collections revealed so far as possible the influence of environment both geographical and historical as the culture of one tribe upon that of another. This great series of exhibits properly excited the admiration of anthropologists both at home and abroad, and the wonderful growth of the department in such a short time deserved the admiration of all who were engaged in the study of anthropology.

It seems, however, that the point of view in the installation of this great mass of material was wrong, for on visiting the museum today one finds the condition so different from that which prevailed two or three years ago that one necessarily infers that the old point of view is no longer held. It seems, furthermore, that the present condition may be regarded as a visible manifestation of this complete change in policy. The first evidence of a change in the point of view became manifest when the great gallery containing the archeological collection from South America was thrown open to the public. The character of the scheme of installation of this collection was so singular that one felt that possibly an experiment was being tried and that the arrangement of the material might be only temporary and consequently a judgment of the merits of the scheme did not at the time seem justifiable. Since this gallery was thrown open to the public, however, the suspicion has become a conviction that the former ideals have been abandoned and new ones substituted. Thus it now appears that a great part of the ethnological collections are to be removed from exhibition and placed in storage, where, it is said, they will be available for students, and that in their stead will be placed on exhibition a series of type or standard or unit exhibits illustrating certain phases and areas of culture. Two such exhibits are fairly complete and are open to public inspection, namely, the Eskimo and the plains. We have then, on the one hand, the fact that the former scheme of installation has been abandoned, that by far the larger part of the material which was formerly exhibited in the halls devoted to ethnology has been or is soon to be removed and placed in storage, and on the other hand, we have in place of the old series of actual exhibits, certain systematic exhibits of which the Peruvian, the Eskimo and the plains, which are at present installed, may be regarded as typical.

First a word concerning the storage of material. Unquestionably in every institution occasions arise when it becomes necessary to withdraw from public exhibition for a longer or shorter period of time large collections. However necessary this may be, I am convinced that collections, especially those of ethnology, which are forced into retirement always suffer. There is not only the inevitable deterioration which always follows when ethnological specimens are packed away and which is always to be considered, but there is especially that loss of personal interest in such collections which can never be completely restored. The argument that such collections are always available for study is on the whole specious. As a matter of fact, at any rate in anthropology, these collections are rarely demanded for study. The reason for this is, of course, that one does not know what exists in the storage rooms; nor can a catalogue of storage material ever be of such a nature as to make such collections of any great value. When one visits a public institution like the American Museum, which from its size, wealth and position may be supposed to occupy a commanding position in American science, it is not for the purpose of finding what they have in storage but to see what they have on exhibition and to take advantage of the information which may be thus obtained. The student who desires to examine this material, having ascertained that it exists in the museum, might be reconciled to the idea of storage of the bulk of the collections if they were in glass cases, easily accessible, but it is quite impossible to reconcile the idea of study collections with the character of the storage cases which at the present time are to be found in this institution, for these storage cases are of the flimsiest material, from which it would seem impossible to exclude insects and dust and which apparently might be very easily destroyed by fire. The reasons why stored collections in ethnology lose their vital interest and deteriorate; from every point of view and especially fail in the purpose for which they were made are so obvious that it does not seem necessary to dwell longer on the subject.

Of the three collections above referred to, which represent the new ideals of installation in this museum, namely, the Peruvian, Eskimo and the plains, it may be noted first that while they all have certain elements in common they are not consistent one with another, for it seems that in the two ethnological exhibits it was the intention that no duplicate specimens should be shown, whereas in the Peruvian exhibit there is endless duplication. If the Peruvian exhibit is to conform to the other two it should be reduced to one tenth its present size. It is possible, however, that this is contemplated. As this exhibit even in other respects differs from the two ethnological exhibits it may be considered independently of them. Its essential defect is the fact that nowhere in the hall is emphasized the salient features of the culture of the Peruvians, namely, that they were a sessile, agricultural people, living in permanent habitations, possessing domestic animals. On the other hand, we are introduced to such categories as "objects in stone," "objects in wood," "objects in bone," etc., and this fortuitous principle of classification, of course, makes it exceedingly difficult for the student to obtain any idea of the true character of Peruvian culture. It would seem that in installing this collection an ideal scheme was held in mind, that the exhibition cases were conceived of as containing compartments, and each compartment received in advance its label, and that then the attempt was made to find specimens to fit the compartments. Where this was not possible the compartment was left vacant. The absurdity of this ideal scheme of installation, if carried to a logical conclusion, can be easily imagined. It only remains to add that the scientific interest of a great and valuable collection has been almost entirely lost. . . .

Upon examining the Eskimo and plains exhibit it seems that a similar ideal scheme was conceived of and that the great collections which existed in the museum from these two regions were searched to find specimens to fill in the pockets of this scheme. The two collections differ in many ways in detail and must be considered separately. The Eskimo exhibit as it stands conceives the Eskimo as a unit and makes such differences in culture as exist, for example, between that of the Greenlander and that of the Alaskan of very secondary importance. The very fact of any difference existing between the Eskimo of the east and of the west is practically lost sight of in the exhibit, and thus also is lost the opportunity to illustrate the influence of the contact of one culture upon another. Of course, if the culture of the Eskimo is a unit, it is quite unessential that one should know what tribe or tribes lie to the south of them or how they have been influenced by these tribes. It may be pointed out next that apart from this defect the collection gives an impression of the Eskimo which is false and misleading. Prominently displayed in the center of the exhibit is an Eskimo woman fishing in the ice. Owing to its position it might be taken as representing a typical phase of Eskimo culture. Thus a false impression is conveyed, as the Eskimo are not essentially fishers but hunters of sea mammals. Taking the fisherwoman on her own merits, however, the details of the group are misleading, to say nothing of the fact that men rather than women engage in such pursuits. Of nearly equal importance, owing to its position, is a house scene, bad in detail and misleading. The scene represents a woman by a lamp, the source of light and heat in an Eskimo house, completely clad in winter furs. Near her is a baby sprawling on the floor, also clad in furs. Both figures, of course, should be practically nude. The house is constructed after the manner of a temporary habitation, which is never lined. This house is lined. If the woman and child are properly costumed then the house must be regarded as a temporary structure, in which case its lining is entirely inappropriate. The assemblage of objects about the woman is also misleading and has been made without regard for actual conditions. Thus lying on the floor near the woman, who is cooking, is a man's knife, which is entirely inappropriate, and near by is a little toy kettle, which is, of course, entirely out of place. . . .

Such exhibits as those above characterized might with some degree of propriety be found in the lower grades of the public school, but they certainly do not seem worthy of an institution which claims to be foremost among American museums. If exhibits of this nature are advisable, it would seem that there is no reason for the concentration under one roof of large collections. If the purpose of the general public is to be served by such exhibits it would seem desirable that the great bulk of the collections which are now being stored should be distributed among some ten or twenty of the high schools of the city, for thus the ideal of this scheme might the more easily and cheaply be realized. Or, again, this type of installation might very well be adopted in a small institution with extremely limited resources, or it might even be adopted for a single one of the great halls of the American Museum; indeed, it is conceivable that one of the halls, such as the north hall of the main floor, might very appropriately, in this institution, be given up to an exhibit, in the briefest and most concise manner possible, which would attempt to represent the great general areas of culture which exist among the different peoples of the earth. Such a hall would indeed be of great value in a great institution like the American Museum and would amply repay the labor of preparing such an exhibit, for the material for such a hall could easily be selected from the duplicate specimens without making any considerable drain on the exhibit halls proper, which should be devoted to the ethnographic exhibit. But to adopt this as the type and standard of installation for the entire department seems, when one considers the greatness of the collections and the size of the building of this institution, utterly incongruous. In view of the commanding position which this institution holds in America, its example is bound to have a very great influence on all of our public institutions, and one has the right to expect from it work of the highest scientific value, and to expect that through its exhibition halls it shall appeal primarily to the intelligent scientific world.

# 38

# SOME PRINCIPLES OF MUSEUM ADMINISTRATION

## Franz Boas

*Science*, 25 (new series): 921–933, 1907

*Franz Boas, "Father of American Anthropology," wrote the following article, excerpted below, in response to George Dorsey's criticism of the new ethnographic exhibits at the American Museum of Natural History. Unlike Dorsey, Boas favored grouping objects by tribes or cultures to allow for the consideration of a broader context. He believed that civilization is not absolute and that a systematized progression was not representative of the complexities of cultural development (Jenkins 1994). Boas saw a clear philosophical distinction between anthropology and the other branches of natural history, and maintained that exhibition space in natural history museums should be designed with a distinct area for display of anthropological objects. He also recognized the tension between the use of museum objects in research and exhibition.*

Previously Dr. George A. Dorsey discusses in some detail the installation of the ethnological collections in the American Museum of Natural History, basing his criticism essentially on the point of view that the arrangement is an unsatisfactory attempt at popularizing the results of ethnological research. In his discussion he assumes that the essential object of a large museum must be research, not instruction, without, however, discussing the validity of this fundamental assumption.

I may be allowed in the following remarks to discuss what seems to me the vital question of the uses of museums as research institutions and as educational institutions. Since my own practical experience has largely been gained in ethnographical museums, I may be allowed to take my examples particularly from these, indicating at the same time in what respects ethnological museums seem to differ from natural-history museums.

Museums may serve three objects. They may be institutions designed to furnish healthy entertainment, they may be intended for instruction and they may be intended for the promotion of research.

The value of the museum as a resort for popular entertainment must not be underrated, particularly in a large city, where every opportunity that is given to the people to employ their leisure time in healthy and stimulating surroundings should be developed, where every attraction that counteracts the influence of the saloon and of the racetrack is of great social importance. If a museum is to serve this end, it must, first of all, be entertaining, and try to instill by the kind of entertainment offered some useful stimulant. The people who seek rest and recreation resent an attempt at systematic instruction while they are looking for some emotional excitement. They want to admire, to be impressed by something great and wonderful; and if the underlying idea of the exhibit can be brought out with sufficient clearness, some great truths may be impressed upon them without requiring at the moment any particular effort. The visitor of this class does not go to the museum to study the exhibits case by case and to follow a plan carefully laid out by the curator, but he strolls through the halls examining something that attracts his attention here and there without much plan or purpose.

It is a fond delusion of many museum officers that the attitude of the majority of the public is a more serious one; but a calm examination of the visitors passing through museum halls shows very clearly that the majority do not want anything beyond entertainment. This can easily be proved by following them through the halls and listening to their remarks, by the general tendency of visitors to go through all the halls of the museums from end to end in order "to have seen" the museum. It may be seen in the Sunday afternoon crowds in New York City when parents pass the hours after dinner with their children in pleasant surroundings, trying to take in the curious sights.

If this is true, then the very serious question arises, what can be done for this very large class of visitors? Obviously, a systematic exhibit will not appeal to them, and the best we can hope for is to bring home to them by single exhibits important points of view. Most of our museums are not built on a plan which promises success in this direction. To impress a point of view requires at least the possibility of concentration; while our large halls, built with a view to architectural impressiveness, do everything that is possible to distract the visitor, who, when just beginning to take in one exhibit, already looks forward to the next one, thus being prevented from ever concentrating his attention on any particular subject. Effectiveness must be based on the effort to concentrate attention, and on the unity of the idea expressed in each exhibit.

It seems essential that before deciding upon the selection of subjects to be presented to the public, the museum director should be clear as to the objects to be obtained by popular exhibits. Popularization of science has become of late years a kind of Shibboleth, and we are only too apt to believe that an effort to present in a simple way results of scientific inquiry is in itself a praiseworthy endeavor.

I fear that in this belief some of the fundamental objects of the popularization of science are overlooked. In the mass of lectures intended to popularize knowledge, in popular books, and not less in popular museums, intelligibility is too often obtained by slurring over unknown and obscure points which tend to make the public believe that without any effort, by listening for a brief hour or less to the exposition of a problem, they have mastered it. This I consider one of the serious dangers of popular presentation of science. It is a stimulus to the overestimation of one's own powers, which is so characteristic of many phases of our public life. It tends to stimulate the idea that the necessity for training for thorough work is an antiquated prejudice, and that good common sense with a little smattering of knowledge fits a man for any place in life, in business as well as in science and in public affairs.

What I understand by popularization of science is an endeavor to counteract these very influences, and to bring out the sublimity of truth and the earnest efforts that are needed to acquire it. Therefore every kind of inaccuracy should be most carefully avoided, and attempts to make all problems appear childishly simple by the elimination of everything that is obscure should not be tolerated.

This does not mean that the most complex problems should be selected for popular presentation, but the serious effort required to reach results should be emphasized. To apply this to the striking popular exhibits to which I referred before, enough should be given surrounding these exhibits to convey the impression that the visitor, by looking at the single thing, has not grasped all that is conveyed by the collections, and that there is more to study. . . .

There are only two methods possible to reach the visitors who come to the museum to be entertained. The one is to have only a very few exhibits of rare beauty and excellence, which by their own merit will prove attractive. However, this is avowedly neither the object nor the method of a large museum which endeavors to gather under its roof a great variety of objects, and to impose not only by a small selection of exhibits, but also by the comprehensiveness of subjects presented. Wherever this is true, it must be recognized that it is impossible to hold the attention of the people by the whole mass of exhibits, but that for every visitor the bulk of the material must merely give the background from which some subject that happens to strike his fancy will stand out in bold relief.

I think the experience of all large museums shows that this point of view, so far as the general public is concerned, is the correct one. When, for instance, the installation of a new immense mounted skeleton of some extinct animal is announced, people will flock in crowds to the museum to see the specimen, and the receptiveness of their minds is increased by the whole mass of material from which the new impressive specimen is set off, and by the striking difference of the atmosphere in the museum as compared with the ordinary everyday routine. The same is true when a large, beautiful group of birds is exhibited. The impression, however, is quite different if the museum should contain a great many mounted skeletons of immense size, or a great many groups of birds of similar character. The visitors will pass from one to another, but the amount of impressiveness of each will be correspondingly decreased. . . .

I believe the appreciation of the needs of the visitor who wants to be entertained has led most museums to lay much stress upon the preparation of groups in which certain objects are brought together, and which are generally intended to illustrate some important point. In the practice of group-making that has developed during the last fifteen years the need of the class of visitors for whom they are intended is often lost sight of. A group does not convey any more information than a picture in an ordinary picture-book might be made to convey. It differs from the picture-book in being more impressive by its size and surroundings. Therefore a series of groups, all of which illustrate different aspects of the same idea, are undesirable, because the impressiveness of each is decreased by the excessive application of the same device. I believe the effect of this undue multiplication of groups of the same type may be noticed in the collections of the United States National Museum. It is true that the multiplication of groups in the anthropological department of that museum is not due to a systematic endeavor on the part of the administration to present every Indian type in the form of a group. It is due rather to the onerous duty imposed upon the museum to send some new striking exhibit to every one of the endless series of national and international expositions, which, of course, are seen almost exclusively by sight-seers, who can not be reached by anything but such large exhibits as groups. Any one who will observe the visitors of the United States National Museum strolling through the Catlin Hall, which contains the Indian groups, will readily see how the first group seems very interesting, and how quickly the others appear of less and less interest and importance. For this reason it may safely be said that the method of bringing together large exhibits should be employed only sparingly and that the effect of each of these exhibits will be the greater the better it is set off against an indifferent background.

I have mentioned here large exhibits as those which will attract the general public. This is not quite correct, in so far as there will always be an appreciable number of visitors of a higher education, who may be attracted by the beauty and compact idea brought out by small special exhibits.

Museums may also be employed for the purpose of imparting systematic information. The number of people who visit the museum in search of such information is, comparatively speaking, small, but not by any means negligible; and the duty of the museum to supply such information to those who are in search of it must not be questioned. The question arises, however, in how far a very large museum is capable of supplying the needs of students of this type. Assuming a building like the American Museum of Natural History, which has at present eighteen halls and six galleries, with a floor space of from eight to ten thousand feet for the halls, and of from four to five thousand feet for the galleries, and imagining the various halls so arranged as to give a systematic presentation of the various sciences, we find that the whole becomes such a maze of separate and intercrossing systems, that the average visitor, even if desirous of obtaining systematic information, would be frustrated by the mass of material presented.

Here, obviously, the fundamental principle of elementary education has to be applied; namely, that effectiveness does not lie in diversity, but in the thoroughness of the material presented. *Multum, non multa.* So far as I am aware, the attempt at systematizing the collections of a very large museum according to a rigid scheme has never been made, obviously on account of the insuperable difficulties that present themselves. . . .

The impossibility of basing museum installation on a classification of objects from a single material point of view can be made clear best by the example of anthropological exhibits. At the same time this consideration will show in what the difference between anthropological collections and natural-history collections consists. An assemblage of material such as is found in anthropological collections consists entirely of things made by the various peoples of the world—their tools, household utensils, their ceremonial objects, etc. All of these are used in the daily life of the people, and almost all of them receive their significance only through the thoughts that cluster around them. For example, a pipe of the North American Indians is not only a curious implement out of which the Indian smokes, but it has a great number of uses and meanings, which can be understood only when viewed from the standpoint of the social and religious life of the people. It even happens frequently in anthropological collections that a vast field of thought may be expressed by a single object or by no object whatever, because that particular aspect of life may consist of ideas only; for instance, if one tribe uses a great many objects in its religious worship, while among another, practically no material objects of worship are used, the religious life of these tribes, which may be equally vigorous, appears quite out of its true proportions in. the museum collections. Another reason, namely the natural destruction of material, makes it quite impossible to make archeological collections systematic. Thus it happens that any array of objects is always only an exceedingly fragmentary presentation of the true life of a people. For this reason any attempt to present ethnological data by a systematic classification of specimens will not only be artificial, but will be entirely misleading. The psychological as well as the historical relations of cultures, which are the only objects of anthropological inquiry, can not be expressed by any arrangement based on so small a portion of the manifestation of ethnic life as is presented by specimens. Any one who has grasped this truth will recognize at once that an anthropological exhibit can not be cast into the single schematic mold which is to be repeated automatically the world over for every single people. With the wealth of interesting and important problems of anthropology, it is, however, perfectly easy to bring out in a popular manner one salient point here, another salient point there, according to the characteristics of the life of the people dealt with.

The difference between anthropological exhibits and those relating to natural sciences is only one of degree, because in no case do specimens alone convey the full idea that a collection is intended to express. This is particularly true in any exhibit intended to express function rather than form; as, for instance, in exhibits illustrating dynamic geology or facts relating to the physiology of plants and animals. The difference between anthropological and natural-history collections, however, consists in the trifling importance of the specimens as compared with their functional importance in anthropology, and to the fact that all the specimens are primarily incidental expressions of complex mental processes that are themselves the subject of anthropological inquiry. These latter are almost entirely missing in that field of biology which is ordinarily presented in museums.

For this reason anthropological collections should be treated like collections of artistic industry and art collections rather than like collections illustrating natural sciences.

It is therefore clear, that, so far as the public is concerned, the essential point of view of the anthropological collection and that of the natural-history collection are entirely distinct; and, if the attempt is to be made to bring out coherently the ideas underlying the anthropological exhibit, there ought to be no necessity for the visitor to come into contact with the natural-history exhibits while passing through the anthropological halls. On the whole, this end is difficult to attain in a large complex museum building; and the question may therefore be very well raised, whether it would not be better to separate entirely anthropological collections from those relating to natural history.

Still another consideration may be mentioned here, which has an important bearing upon the systematic arrangement of anthropological collections. It has been pointed out before that anthropology is essentially an historical science, and consequently not readily amenable to systematization; but, further than this, there is so much disagreement among the best anthropologists of our times in regard to the significance of anthropological data in a systematic presentation of the subject, that it seems hardly justifiable for any museum to assume to dictate by its arrangement what the approved system of anthropological science shall be.

Before further discussing the question of museum policy in regard to its relation to the public and to schools, it may be well to discuss the value of the museum as an institution intended to serve the progress of science.

The objection which is raised against the concentration of the work of the large museum in these lines rather than in educational lines is the old objection against serving the few rather than the masses. Serious educators have long since recognized that the education of the masses which we all desire is impossible without the most thorough and painstaking education of the teacher, and that the applicability of a sound educational system can not be confined to elementary schools, but that without secondary schools, colleges, universities and training schools for teachers, the whole system of public education falls to the ground. Therefore, we do not at all agree with the popular illusion that opportunities given to the few who advance science are opposed to the advancement of the masses, but we rather recognize in them an indispensable means of advancing public education.

I do not hesitate to say that the essential justification for the maintenance of large museums lies wholly in their importance as necessary means for the advancement of science. This is particularly clear in the case of the United States National Museum, which is the depository of all the government surveys, and whose duty it is to preserve the material on which the work of the surveys is based. The education of the masses can be infinitely better subserved by small museums.

What, then, is the function of the large museum? It is the only means of bringing together and of preserving intact large series of material which for all time to come must form the basis of scientific inductions. Every year shows more clearly that the loss of old collections, due to the lack of large museums until the middle of the last century, is one of the serious obstacles to the advancement of science. Museums are the storehouses in which not only must the material be preserved by means of which deductions of scientists can be checked, but they are also the place where scientific materials from distant countries, vanishing species, paleontological remains, and the objects used by vanishing tribes, are kept and preserved for all future time, and may thus be made the basis of studies which, without them, would be impossible. We are spending vast sums year after year to bring together evidences of life forms of distant countries and of past ages, to accumulate the monuments of the past and objects used by remote tribes. We collect these because they are the foundation of scientific study. Should we then be unwilling to provide adequate means for keeping intact the results of our expensive inquiries? It is the essential function of the museum as a scientific institution to preserve for all future time, in the best possible way, the valuable material that has been collected, and not to allow it to be scattered and to deteriorate.

Considering this point of view, there can be no greater misconception of the duties of a museum administrator than the belief that proper care of accumulated material is less important than beautiful exhibits. The lack of proper care of inflammable and perishable material, the constant shifting about of material not used for exhibits, the lack of conservatism in exchanging and giving away collections for elementary educational purposes, belong to the most inexcusable features of museum adminis-tration. Unfortunately the method of preservation of collections in our museums is in many cases not what it ought to be, partly from neces-sity, partly from choice. The crowded condition of the building, like that of the United States National Museum, the attempt to relegate vast amounts of material to rooms, as in the American Museum of Natural History, and the use of wooden receptacles for the storage of valuable material, endanger the safety of the collections and make their use tempo-rarily or permanently difficult. Serious scientists know perfectly well that in the study of biological and anthropological phenomena observations on a single specimen are generally misleading, and that one of the great advantages gained in modern times, and based to a great extent upon the improvement of museum methods, consists in the possibility of examin-ing long series rather than individuals. The reason for this is that the series alone can give us what is characteristic, while, when only an individual is available, characteristic traits may be overlooked, or we may be liable to consider an accidental trait as characteristic for a whole group. For this reason science is better served by the preservation of large series relating to the same question in one place rather than by scattering such series over a great many different places. This is true of all sciences, and this is the justification for the accumulation of extended material bearing upon the same point. In-roads that are made upon large collections in order to obtain scattering material otherwise not represented in the museum should be resisted by every conscientious scientist.

In order to make large series useful, the bulk of the material in a museum should be kept in such a manner that it is not only accessible at a moment's notice, but that it can also be examined from any point of view. While in zoological collections consisting of skeletons and skins, this end may be attained fairly adequately by storage in metal boxes systematically arranged and easily opened, other material can not be handled in the same manner. This is particularly true of anthropological material, which, on account of the difference in size, form and material of the objects, and on account of the multiplicity of the points of view from which the material can be viewed, can only be stored satisfactorily in such a way that each specimen can be seen. . . .

Bearing these points in view, the question arises, in how far the interests of the public and the interests of science can be harmonized. It is my opinion that the attempt at a thorough systematization of a large museum must be given up, because it is based upon a misconception of the function of the large museum. Systematic museums must be small museums.

It is very probable that in a large museum in which the systematization of the exhibit for the benefit of educational purposes is made the principal point of view the function of the individual curator will become more and more that of an officer who carries out the orders received from the general museum administration, so that there would hardly be room for investigators of the highest order in such an institution. That the systematization and popularization of the collections of a large museum does not agree with the best interests of science, has evidently been felt by the administration of the United States National Museum, in which, in the Biological Department, the work on the exhibit halls has been divorced completely from the scientific work on the collections.

The question then arises, What shall we do with our collections to make them useful to the public and at the same time useful for the advancement of science? Two methods are possible for reaching this end. Either we may have a complete separation of the collections intended for the public and of those intended for the scientist, or we may decide to make the entire collection equally accessible to the public and to the scientist. . . .

If a museum is planned like the American Museum of Natural History, the only thing to do is to acknowledge freely that the public is to be admitted to all the collections in the museum; to arrange the collections from scientific points of view, and to set off from these collections in conspicuous places those exhibits which are intended for the public. The central aisles of the large halls, for instance, lend themselves admirably for exhibits of this type, while the side alcoves may be used to furnish the indifferent background from which the popular exhibits should be set off.

I am not by any means convinced that this is the best solution of a difficult problem. The attempt to make accessible in this way the entire collections is unnecessarily expensive; and the work that must go on in the collections, if the museum is to be a live institution at all, will tend to distract from the dignity of the halls, which I consider, so far as the public is concerned, as one of the essential features of the museum. It seems to me that while the public is admitted to a museum hall, everything in the hall should be calculated to increase the impression of dignity and of aloofness from everyday life. No dusting, no mopping, no trundling-about of boxes, should be permitted in a hall visited by the public, because it disturbs that state of mind that seems best adapted to bring home the ideas for which the museum stands.

It has been proposed to overcome the economic difficulty involved in the necessity of having large collections accessible, and the expensiveness of exhibit halls intended for the public, by placing the study collections outside of the large cities, in suburbs, where land is inexpensive, and where unpretentious buildings can be erected. This proposition has been made in England, and has been carried out by the Ethnographical Museum in Berlin. Although the separation of the exhibit collections and the storage collections involves considerable administrative difficulties, and is open to scientific objections, it is not impossible that we shall necessarily be led to the adoption of this principle of administration. While however, the collections are concentrated in one large building, we must accept the principle that the collections must receive proper care, and must be available for scientific study. In our museum buildings with which we have to get along at the present time, this end might very well be attained by placing either in one wing or on one floor the exhibits intended for the general public, and also those intended for students in high schools, special training schools, colleges, and even for many students of universities. In collections of this kind the more advanced collections intended for students would give what I called before the indifferent background which is so necessary for the general public. A large number of halls, however, will have to be installed in a more condensed manner, perhaps by adding galleries to halls of unnecessary height, in which material could be made accessible to students. There is no reason why the public should not be admitted to halls of this kind, although presumably very few of the visitors would carry away any other impression than that of the magnitude of the field of work covered by the museum. A thorough reorganization of museum administration will not be possible until the plan of operation of the museum is decided upon before the museum building is erected, and until the small systematic educational museum, which serves as an adjunct to elementary instruction, is separated entirely from the large museum. Like the university, the large museum must stand first and last, in its relation to the public as well as in its relation to the scientist, for the ideals of science.

# 39

## MODERN EXHIBITIONAL TENDENCIES OF MUSEUMS OF NATURAL HISTORY AND ETHNOLOGY DESIGNED FOR PUBLIC USE

### Henry L. Ward

*Transactions of the Wisconsin Academy of Sciences, Arts, and Letters,*
16: 325–342, 1909

*Based on his long experience at Ward's Natural Science Establishment in Rochester, New York—founded by his father Henry A. Ward—Henry L. Ward, Director of the Milwaukee Public Museum, discusses the changing exhibit philosophy in American natural history museums at the turn of the twentieth century in the article excerpted below. He argues against the use of systematic exhibits in favor of taxidermy groups. Ward contends that displaying animals in a natural setting invites comparison and thus better attracts the interest of visitors, particularly children, while well-written labels that interpret the scientific knowledge known about the specimens on display could be used to augment this experience. Ward also indicates that although the group idea began as a technique to better understand zoological and botanical specimens, its scope was expanding to include geological and anthropological specimens.*

The modern museum is a complex institution; the product of many years of evolution in biology and geology taken in their most comprehensive senses and also of a special science, museology, that has but recently gained sufficient prominence to be designated by a distinctive name.

There have been many and profound changes during the last score of years in the relationships between museums and the public and these have had their principal outward expression in altered conditions in the exhibition rooms. Whether those have been most effected by a normal, internal evolution or by the reaction to external stimuli is worth considering in order to determine which has been the more potent factor.

Some museums have been established in a commercial spirit, either in expectation that the admittance fees would yield a profit or that they would prove valuable accessory attractions to some establishment of a different character, but these have naturally been in charge of men of mediocre or low scientific attainments and have had little apparent influence on museum development.

The important scientific museums have been in charge of reputable scientists each with his cabinet of curatorial specialists, and not a little of the speculative advancement of natural history and a large amount of systematic work has emanated therefrom. . . .

Aside from the rapidly growing public lecture courses of museums the exhibitional department is that which, most intimately touches the public and is that in which the science of museology finds its fullest expression; consequently it is very essential that those persons having to do with the arrangement of specimens for exhibition should be proficient museologists. This has not always been the case and the eminent specialist has sometimes shown himself a dismal failure in the exhibition department of the institution with which he is connected, a condition leading to a regrettable lack of harmony between himself and the efficient museum director.

Not many years ago little or no attempt was made to attract and hold the interest of the layman and, by arrangement and label, interpret to him some of the knowledge that scientists had learned concerning the specimens shown. Such a catering to the intellect was apparently not considered advisable and it almost seems, as we look back upon that period, as if the museums feared to lose the respect of the multitude if they stooped to be comprehensible. . . .

Most of the larger museums of today are to a considerable extent supported by public funds and more particularly is this so in their departments of public exhibition in which the people in general are naturally most especially interested. Also there is a growing movement in the establishment of municipal museums which is well marked here in Wisconsin so that a discussion of these matters before this assemblage, representative of the scientific associations of the state and presumably much interested in the scientific education of the masses, may not be untimely. The museum that receives little or no support from public funds naturally owes little or nothing in that direction and so, in the arrangement of its exhibits, is free to disregard their special needs; but when this support constitutes a material part of or, as in some cases, its entire income then the museum is under moral obligations to discharge its debt in the fullest possible degree by rendering special service to the public.

In order to set before you the change in attitude in the one matter of admission I will quote from a book published in 1778, by John and Andrew Van Rymsduck, entitled "Museum Britannicum," being a guide to the then 25 year old British Museum, in which the following directions are given for those wishing to view the collections: "Now in respect of knowing the method of applying to see the British Museum, it is by delivering in a list of the Christian and surnames of each Person, with their titles, rank, Profession, and places of abode, to the Porter's Lodge, at the left Entry within the Gate, who will enter them in a Book; the Principal Librarian orders the Day and Hour for the Tickets to be fixed upon, which when sent for are delivered.

"No more than fifteen Persons are permitted at one Time, and two hours allowed for viewing, and as most Company's love to go together, the fewer in Number, the list is, the easier, they will serve to compleat the Number of Fifteen, and the sooner they stand a chance of being admitted.

"Such as have obtained Tickets and cannot come, are earnestly desired to return them to the Porter as early as they can that others may be entered in their Stead.

"After a list has been entered in the Book, if the Tickets are not fetched away, at the latest by Ten in the Morning, the Day before the Time of admission, they will be otherwise disposed of; and no Regard will be paid to such Lists as require the Tickets to be sent to any of the Parties.

"If any one comes with another Person's Ticket, it is expected that they acquaint the Officers with it, in order to have the Name changed; and the Officers may turn away any one that shall presume to get Admittance under a fictions Name or Character."

These regulations, you will recollect, were enforced in restriction of the use of the nation's museum by the citizens thereof. There has been since then a progressive liberalizing of these matters, but I believe that it remained to very recent times to give the fullest practicable use of museum exhibits free to the public. In fact, to the best of my knowledge, the Public Museum of the City of Milwaukee was the first institution of this nature to throw open its doors for the free admission of the public on every day of the year, a regulation to that effect having been adopted and put into force in December 1905.

Only nineteen years ago an eminent naturalist, a curator in one of the largest museums in the world, replied to my question whether certain restrictions of exhibition were not rather hard on the public, with: "The public be damned." Such an attitude has long since been abandoned by those who have at heart the welfare of their institutions and great pains

and expense is lavished on those parts of museums designed for the especial use of the dear public and they are admitted at all reasonable times
with the least possible restrictions. In that former period of museum
evolution it was but natural that the ordinary visitor should be looked
upon as a necessary evil, a person who unfortunately had to be admitted
because he helped to pay the museum's running expense; but it would
have been too much to expect that he should be particularly considered
in the selection and labeling of the specimens placed on exhibition; and as
such a short time has elapsed since these days it is hardly to be expected
that a very general concordance of opinion would be reached as to just
what it is best to do for the public. . . .

There was a lack of homogeneity of ideas among museum workers as
to the proper aim of the exhibition series. The parting line has on one
side of it practically all of the directors of museums who have expressed
an opinion and a fair number of curators; while on the other hand are a
respectable number of curators whose scientific attainments are such as
to bespeak careful consideration for their views. By some of these latter
it is maintained for anthropology, that all specimens (including in many
instances scores of duplicates) should be placed on exhibition both to
insure their preservation and so that anyone wishing to make a detailed
study can see them without the necessity of applying for admission to
study rooms. Another feature is perhaps best epitomized by a leading
authority in anthropology in a private letter in which he writes: "Do not
make the mistake of arranging an exhibit to illustrate a theory as to man's
cultural development but show the facts as you find them."

There is very little to be urged in favor of the first of these propositions
but much that might be said in favor of the latter and yet it is not convincing because it seems applicable to a different phase of museum development than that under consideration. It appears to be more appropriate
for research museums, or perhaps we had better say University museums,
than for those that are to be mainly used by the unspecialized, and to a
great extent uninstructed public. . . .

In museums whose content, are to be used by scholars for study, any
interpretations of this sort are uncalled for and had better be omitted, for
in them the student is expected to elaborate his own theory. A research
museum is to be used for educational purposes but is not, like a public
museum educational; it is passive, not active. However, it is well to recollect that inasmuch as a museum can contain but a selected few of the
specimens obtainable in the field it must afterall reflect the ideas of the
collectors and curators as to which objects are worthy of preservation,
which are pertinent to some investigation; in other words the specimens
are almost without exception collected and selected with some theories
as to their desirability over many others which are rejected, and therefore

no arrangement of them could very well reflect conditions as they occur in nature. A collection made by an uneducated, indiscriminate gatherer of everything movable would probably most nearly meet this impracticable ideal. We can perhaps show an Indian grave, the immediate setting of a birds' nest or the layout of a fossil skeleton as it occurred in nature, but we can not hope to show the archeology of even one county of a state in all its possible relationships or the true avian ecology of a single township in the largest museum building ever constructed. Such studies, to be of value, must be made in the field. The museum can not supplant nature as a primal source of information, and while it probably should attempt to illustrate the manner of occurrence of many things, yet after all such exhibits must be for pedagogical convenience or popular education, and not for research, and consequently are probably oft' times improved by being made schematic in character. . . .

While museums for the public may be and undoubtedly are aids in the development of budding naturalists, yet the small number of these is a negligible quantity and as a general statement, it may be said that the making of naturalists is not the aim of such museums, but that it is rather to ameliorate the ignorance of the general public in a manner that will afford it thoughtful pleasure both in the museum and in its subsequent contact with nature. We doubt that this can be done by the exhibition of specimens bearing only name and place labels. The public is not educated to the point where it can get many orderly ideas beyond those that the curator has arranged for its assimilation; to them collections not so treated are largely conglomerations of curios. . . .

To be encyclopedic in treatment is to cease to be popular and results in repelling rather than in attracting the average man; and so with museums it is conceived that the way to be assured of conveying a fair knowledge of a subject is to limit, the ideas to a reasonable number that it is deemed worth while emphasizing and then by display and labels impressing these on the public so that the museum management may be confident that something more than a hazy idea of a conglomeration of curios is taken away by the visitor. Though the principle of selection was put into practice in this country about fifty years ago it apparently has until lately been ignored or lost sight of in many quarters while in a few others the idea has obtained that it was wrong in principle. Recently the question has come up for discussion in connection with the fundamental one as to the aim and object of such museums as we are discussing. The question involved may perhaps be stated succinctly as: Whether it is well for a museum designed for the public to be an undigested reflection of nature or whether it is not better to make it educational? If it is the one it can hardly be the other.

Some time since it was impressed upon my attention that here in Wisconsin it was generally believed by librarians that it was quite the proper thing for libraries to establish museums as departments of themselves and that anyone was capable of administrating them, so that when an invitation was given me to address the Wisconsin Library Association at La Crosse in February, 1907, I gladly embraced the opportunity to discuss before that important gathering some of the things that a museum should be, the wide and basic differences between libraries and museums and the special qualifications requisite in the museum man. The cause of this misappreciation of the museum idea by librarians apparently is that they have not followed the evolution of these institutions, conceiving them still to be what they were a few years ago—more collections of objects rather than educational institutions.

Having adopted a scheme of public education many methods have suggested themselves as how best to carry it out and catch and hold the public's attention and interest. In some instances it has been conceived that the conversion of a museum into a gigantic text book illustrated by specimens was the proper course to pursue; a system too literally in accordance with Goode's celebrated dictum: "An efficient educational museum may be described as a collection of instructive labels, each illustrated by a well-selected specimen." Paraphrasing this we might say that an efficient educational museum is a collection of important ideas illustrated by judiciously selected specimens whose import is indicated by carefully worded labels.

Some years ago it was common museum practice to exhibit series after series of natural history objects each accompanied by a label giving only name and provenience, and as if to accentuate the monotony, but in reality to facilitate comparison, the animals were all mounted in essentially the same pose, with the left side towards the beholder. A case of these was a tiring procession, all apparently marching to the left but going nowhere, and I might also add, leading nowhere. The idea seemed to be that taxonomy was the chief end of zoology and unfortunately the public failed to take a very lively interest in such displays. Ultimately the ambitious taxidermist conceived the idea that he was practicing an art rather than merely following a trade and he developed groups of animals which depicted something of their habits and habitats; but conservatism frowned on these early ambitions. As late as 1883 it was written: "We know that museum authorities persist in crying out against groups, but eventually they must give way and admit pieces that are at once interesting and instinctive." [The Taxidermists' Exhibition. Anon., *Ward's Natural Science Bulletin*, Vol. 2, No. 2, p. 13.]

The idea almost seems to have been that nothing could be instructive that was interesting, much as we have heard the parallel idea expressed that nothing that was palatable could be healthy; which undoubtedly has been evolved from the undeniable fact that most medicines are distasteful. Can it be that the old museums conceived that the public would stand for a dose of science as unpalatable as one of medicine? At all events, it seems to have been a rather recent inspiration for museums to attempt to interest and captivate the public and instruct it unawares. We do this with the miscellaneous reading of our children when we select for them books in which history or geography or some other school subject is interwoven and disguised in a fascinating story; and while many of the visitors of a free museum are still children the rest are after all only children grown up and the same kind of allurements will cause them to swallow the dose of instruction.

Having once grasped the advantages of taxidermic groups in bringing out zoological facts their use has rapidly become general, almost universal, and the idea has spread to other departments, until we even have petrological groups. Science has not suffered by this; the taxidermy of our museums has vastly improved in all details and as the making of a good group frequently involves more detailed knowledge of habits and habitats than can be found ready at hand, the studies necessitated have added to zoological and ecological science. Next to mammals and birds, anthropology has most availed itself of this style of installation. The result of group exhibition is that the visitor sees a certain object not as an isolated, unrelated thing; but in relation to other objects, in a reproduction of its natural environment and in connection with others of its kind. Only those who have the planning and making of such groups are apt to appreciate the many details in which not hazy generalizations but exact specific knowledge is necessary, and can therefore fully appreciate how much more such groups tell and suggest than does the individual specimen; but it must be apparent to any one that a good group makes a much stronger and more lasting impression on the popular visitor than does the single specimen, and that while very likely he fails at first view to carry away a consciousness of all that it depicts yet he certainly has gotten more than he would have received from the wearisome procession of older days. The striving after realism of environment has called into co-operation the artist and the mechanic. The scenic backgrounds of some groups are worthy of exhibition as works of pictorial art. . . .

There is also a noticeable striving after the abolition of the time honored shelf exhibit. It needs no argument to demonstrate the inartisticness of the apothecary-shop-like arrangement of specimens on wooden shelves. They must still be retained for some things but, many times, other methods of installation are greatly preferable and have been used in most modern museums, though the abolition of the shelf has not yet reached its maximum development. In line with this are a multitude of museum details as lighting, placement, style and construction of cases, color and texture of background, etc., etc., that, while requiring most careful attention from the museum man and going a long way towards making or marring the exhibits, are hardly proper subjects for discussion in this place.

The labeling of specimens is, however, such an important feature in modern museum development that I must say a few words upon it. The color and quality of paper, style and size of type, color of ink and make up of the label including; proportions, length of lines and spaces between them have much to do with its effectiveness irrespective of what it may say. The artists object to what they are pleased to term the spotted effect of an adequately labeled collection; and the criticism is not without weight; but the objects of museums of art and of natural history differ and this variance has been well expressed by an art museum man in a definition that ran about as follows: "The object of a museum of art is to afford thoughtful pleasure; that of a museum of natural history to afford pleasurable thought." Under the terms of this concept we presume no one, not even an artist, will presume to interdict the use of labels in natural history museums. . . .

A label must of course tell what the object is, preferably giving precedence to the common over the technical name. It must give the provenience of the object and if it be one having sex, state which; if subject to seasonal variation, the date when taken should be given. These are essentials that must be on all labels. Other features such as geographical distribution, food, (if an animal), migration periods, if a migratory bird, use, if a human artifact or useful object, etc., may be given or omitted as determined by the size allowed. For large specimens, classificatory divisions, and set groups, where larger labels are permissible, they should answer the questions that would likely occur to an intelligent, non-scientific person and should contain such other matter as the curator thinks should be known. The writer should remember that his readers are mostly untechnical, and he can tell in a clear way all that the ordinary student wishes to know. The growing attention being paid by museums to their labeling is indicative of their clearer grasp of their proper mission as educational institutions. . . .

Museums have entered on a period of accelerated evolution, and are rapidly forging ahead to their proper position on the crest of the wave of popular education and culture that is sweeping over all civilized nations. The subject is one that should interest us all, and although I have purposely limited this essay to but one of the various phases of museum activities, exhibition, and have necessarily treated that very superficially, I trust that I have succeeded in indicating the general trend of such institutions as belong to the restricted class under consideration.

# SECTION VI

## Museums and Universities

This section focuses on the relationship between universities and their museums. Even though both museums and universities see themselves as educational institutions, they accomplish their missions and deliver their programs in very different ways. The first four articles explore various aspects of the educational role of the museum within the university. Edward Forbes discusses the use of the campus museum in science education, Francis Greenwood Peabody creates a campus museum for use in social science education, and Edward Waldo Forbes sees a role for art museums as a powerful tool for teaching students to create art and appreciate art. Homer R. Dill, credited with creating the first continuously operating museum education program in the United States, discusses the history of museum training in natural history museums. In the final essay, Newton H. Winchell contends that research and publication should be the primary focus of campus museums.

### Additional Readings

Birney, Elmer C. 1994. Collegiate priorities and natural history museums. *Curator: The Museum Journal* 37: 99–107.

Conn, Steven. 1998. *Museums and American intellectual life, 1876–1926.* Chicago: University of Chicago Press.

Genoways, Hugh H. 2000. Challenges for directors of university natural science museums. *Curator: The Museum Journal* 42: 216–230.

Lanyon, Scott M., Gordon Murdock, and Donald Luce. 2000. Planning for a natural history museum in the university environment: A case study. *Curator: The Museum Journal* 43: 88–92.

Mares, Michael A. 2001. *A university natural history museum for the new millennium*. Norman: Sam Noble Oklahoma Museum of Natural History.

———. 2002. Miracle on the prairie: The development of the Sam Noble Oklahoma Museum of Natural History. *Museologia* 2: 31–50.

———. 2003. Did we help create the crisis in university natural history museums? *The Newsgram, Mountain-Plains Museum Association Newsletter* November, pp. 22–23.

Solinger, Janet W. (ed.). 1990. *Museums and universities: New paths for continuing education*. New York: Macmillan Publishing Company.

# 40

# ON THE EDUCATIONAL USES
# OF MUSEUMS

## Edward Forbes

Museum of Practical Geology, Metropolitan School of Science, Applied Mining and the Arts, Department of the Board of Trade. London: Longman, Brown, Green, and Longmans, 19 pp., 1853

*Edward Forbes, as lecturer in natural history at the Royal School of Mines, London, presented this opening address, excerpted below, at the school's Museum of Practical Geology. Forbes was a strong proponent of the college or university museum, because, he contended, they supported professional instruction and therefore were the "most useful museums." He regarded the British Museum as an "Encyclopedia of reference" and argued that for national museums to be useful to a general nonscientific public, they should adopt the design of a university museum and provide popular instruction to interpret the collections.*

. . . Museums, of themselves alone, are powerless to educate. But they can instruct the educated, and excite a desire for knowledge in the ignorant. The labourer who spends his holiday in a walk through the British Museum, cannot fail to come away with a strong and reverential sense of the extent of knowledge possessed by his fellow men. It is not the objects themselves that he sees there and wonders at, that make this impression, so much as the order and evident science which he cannot recognize in the manner in which they are grouped and arranged. He learns that there is a meaning and value in every object however insignificant, and that there is a way of looking at things common and rare distinct from the regarding of them as useless, useful, or curious, the three terms of classification in favour with the ignorant. He goes home and thinks over it; and when a holiday in summer or a Sunday's afternoon in spring tempts him with his wife and little ones to walk into the fields, he finds that he has acquired a new interest in the stones, in the flowers, in the creatures of all kinds that throng around him. He can look at them with an inquiring pleasure, and talk of them to his children with a tale about things like them that he had seen ranged in order in the Museum. He has gained a new sense, –a thirst for natural knowledge, one promising to quench the thirst for beer and vicious excitement that tortured him of old. If his intellectual capacity be limited and ordinary, he will become a better citizen and happier man; if, in his brain there be dormant power, it may waken up to make him a Watt, a Stephenson, or a Miller.

It is not the ignorant only who may benefit in the way just indicated. The so-called educated are as likely to gain by a visit to a Museum, where their least cultivated faculties, those of observation, may be healthily stimulated and brought into action. The great defect of our systems of education is the neglect of the *educating* of the observing powers, a very distinct matter, be it noted, from scientific or industrial *instruction*. It is necessary to say this, since the confounding of the two is evident in many of the documents that have been published of late on these very important subjects. Many persons seem to fancy that the elements that should constitute a sound and manly education are antagonistic, that the cultivation of taste through purely literary studies and of reasoning through logic and mathematics, one or both, is opposed to the training in the equally important matter of observation through those sciences that are descriptive and experiments. Surely this is an error; partisanship of the one or other method or rather than department of mental training, to the exclusion of the rest, is a narrow-minded and cramping view from whatsoever point to be taken. Equal development and strengthening of all are required for the constitution of the complete mind, and it is full time that we should begin to do now what we ought to have done long ago. Through the teaching of some of the sections of natural history and chemistry, the former for observation of forms, the latter of phenomena, I cannot but think the end in view might be gained, even keeping out of sight altogether, if the teacher holds it best to do so, what are called practical applications. For this branch of education museums are the best textbooks; but, in order that they should be effectively studied, require to be explained by competent teachers. Herein at present lies the main difficulty concerning the introduction of the science of observation into courses of ordinary education. A grade of teachers who should be able and willing to carry science into schools for youth has hardly yet appeared. Hitherto there have been few opportunities for their normal instruction. . . .

In their instructional aspect considered apart from their educational applications, the value of Museums must in a great measure depend on the perfection of their arrangement and the leading ideas regulating the classification of their contents. The educated youth ought, in a well-arranged museum, to be able to instruct himself in the studies of which its contents are illustrations, with facility and advantage. On the officers in charge of the institution there consequently falls a serious responsibility. It is not sufficient that they should be well versed in the department of science, antiquities, or art committed to their charge. They may be prodigies of learning, and yet utterly unfitted for their posts. They must be men mindful of the main end and purpose in view, and of the best way of communicating knowledge according to its kind, not merely to those who are already men of science, historians, or connoisseurs, but equally to those who as yet ignorant desire to learn, or in whom it is desirable that a thirst for learning should be incited. Unfortunately museums and public collections of all kinds are too often regarded by their curators in their scientific aspect only, as subservient to the advancement of knowledge through the medium of men of science or learning, and consequently as principally intended for the use of very few persons. This is not the main purpose for which the public money is spent on museums, though one of the very highest of their uses, and in the end of national consequence, since the surest measure of national advancement is the increase and diffusion of scientific and literary pursuits of a high grade. One of the signs of a spread of sound knowledge and intellectual taste in a country is the abundant production of purely monographic works by its philosophers, and the evidence of their appreciation by the general mass of readers, as indicated by the facility with which they find publishers. . . .

It has long been a subject of discussion, in what manner and to what extent can instruction by means of lectures and public teaching be advantageously associated with public collections. There are those who are opposed to such a course, holding that museums should stand on their own exclusive merits, and be mainly places of personal study and consultation. This, however, is the contemplation of them under their scientific aspect only; and although it may fairly be maintained, that a great central collection, such as the British Museum, may be rendered most serviceable by this course of action, holding that magnificent establishment as a general index for science, and, as it were, Encyclopedia of reference, I feel convinced, after a long and earnest consideration of the question for many years, that unless connected with systems of public teaching, museums in most instances are of little use to the people. The most useful museums are those which are made accessory to professorial instruction, and there are many of such in the incited. Unfortunately museums and public collections of all kinds are too often regarded by

their curators in their scientific aspect only, as subservient to the advancement of knowledge through the medium of men of science or learning,
and consequently as principally intended for the use of very few persons.
This is not the main purpose for which the public money is spent on
museums, though one of the very highest of their uses, and in the end of
national consequence, since the surest measure of national advancement
is the increase and diffusion of scientific and literary pursuits of a high
grade. One of the signs of a spread of sound knowledge and intellectual
taste in a country is the abundant production of purely monographic
works by its philosophers, and the evidence of their appreciation by the
general mass of readers, as indicated by the facility with which they find
publishers. . . .

It has long been a subject of discussion, in what manner and to what
extent can instruction by means of lectures and public teaching be advantageously associated with public collections. There are those who are
opposed to such a course, holding that museums should stand on their
own exclusive merits, and be mainly places of personal study and consultation. This, however, is the contemplation of them under their scientific
aspect only; and although it may fairly be maintained, that a great central
collection, such as the British Museum, may be rendered most serviceable by this course of action, holding that magnificent establishment as a
general index for science, and, as it were, Encyclopedia of reference, I feel
convinced, after a long and earnest consideration of the question for many
years, that unless connected with systems of public teaching, museums in
most instances are of little use to the people. The most useful museums
are those which are made accessory to professorial instruction, and there
are many of such in the country, but almost all confined to purposes of
professional education, and not adapted for or open to the general public. The museums of our Universities and Colleges are, for the most part,
utilized in this way, but the advantages derived from them are confined
to a very limited class of persons. In this Institution, an endeavour has
been made to render its contents subservient to the cause of education
and instruction; and the course which is here taken may be imitated with
advantage in the provinces, where there are not unfrequently collections
of considerable extent turned to small account for the benefit of the residents, a large proportion of whom in many instances are ignorant of their
very existence. Yet it is to the development of the provincial museums,
that I believe we must look in the future for the extension of intellectual
pursuits throughout the land.

In every museum of natural history, and probably in those devoted
to other objects, there gradually, often rapidly, accumulates a store of
duplicates that if displayed in the collection render it more difficult to be
studied than if they were away altogether, occupying as they do valuable

space and impeding the understanding of the relations and sequence of the objects classified. If, as is sometimes the case, they are rejected from the collection and stowed away in boxes or cellars, they are still in the way, for cellarage and storage—as we know here, from the want of them, to our detriment,—are indispensable for the proper conducting of the arrangements of museums. Yet out of these duplicates, more or less perfect sets of specimens might be made up, of very high value for purposes of instruction. A well-organized system of mutual interchange and assistance would be one of the most efficient means of making museums generally valuable aids to education. Much money, when money is at the command of curators or committees, is spent in purchasing what might be obtained for asking or through exchange. Some objects of great scientific interest, but equally costly, might be purchased by one establishment only, and made fully as useful, instead of being bought in duplicate by two or more contiguous institutions. The larger institutions might supply the smaller; and out of the national stores, numerous examples—to them almost worthless, but to provincial establishments highly valuable—might be contributed with facility and greatly to the public benefit.

It is in this way, viz by the contribution of authenticated and instructive specimens, that the museums supported by the State can most legitimately assist those established from local resources in the provinces; the scientific arrangements of the latter might also be facilitated through the aid of the officers attached to Government institutions. Money grants would do in many cases, more harm than good, destructive as they are of spirit of self-reliance, and apt to induce a looseness of expenditure and habits of extravagance. . . .

I cannot help hoping that the time will come when every British town even of moderate size will be able to boast of possessing public institutions for the education and instruction of its adults as well as its youthful and childish population, when it shall have a well-organized museum, wherein collections of natural bodies shall be displayed, not with regard to show or curiosity, but according to their illustration of the analogies and affinities of organized and unorganized objects, so that the visitor may at a glance learn something of the laws of nature, wherein the products of the surrounding district, animate and inanimate, shall be scientifically marshaled and their industrial applications carefully and suggestively illustrated, wherein the memorials of the history of the neighbouring province and the races that have people it shall be reverently assembled and learnedly yet popularly explained; when each town shall have a library the property of the public and freely open to the well-conducted reader of every class; when its public walks and parks (too many as yet existing only in prospect) shall be made instructors in botany and agriculture; when it shall have a gallery of its own, possibly not boasting of the most famous pictures or statues, but nevertheless showing good examples of sound art, examples of the history and purpose of design, and, above all, the best specimens to be procured of works of genius by its own natives who have deservedly risen to fame. . . .

# 41

# THE SOCIAL MUSEUM AS AN INSTRUMENT OF UNIVERSITY TEACHING

## Francis G. Peabody

Publications of the Department of Social Ethics in Harvard University,
4: 1–43, 1911

*Francis Peabody describes in the article excerpted below the Social Museum used to supplement the "social ethics" movement he founded at Harvard University. The museum contained collections of photographs, documents, and manuscripts displayed in didactic exhibits (Long 1999). The museum closed in 1931, and its collections were placed on permanent deposit at the Fogg Art Museum in 2002 (Harvard University 2003).*

University teaching is being rapidly revolutionized by new applications of the inductive method. The scientific habit of mind, trained to observe and to generalize from observation, has long been applied to the facts of nature, and museums of zoology, botany, anatomy and chemistry have been recognized as indispensable prerequisites of university instruction. Lectures on science, however suggestive they may be, are not of the essence of education in science. Not the ear, but the eye, is the primary organ of scientific knowledge; and next to the eye, the hand. To interpret nature one must, first of all, see, touch, scrutinize, and analyze. The laboratory, the dissecting table, the clinic, the microscope, the museum, are the instruments of sound learning. The schoolmaster of Do-the-Boys Hall in "Nicholas Nickleby" was a monster of vulgar brutality, but in a degree of which Dickens himself was perhaps not aware, Mr. Squeers was a prophet of scientific education. "C-l-e-a-n," he said, "clean, to make bright, to scour; w-i-n-d-e-r, winder, a casement. When the boy knows this out of book, he goes and does it." Is not this familiar method of the naturalist equally available for the sciences which concern themselves with human history and conduct? May not the phenomena of social evolution, like those of physical evolution, be inductively approached? Is not the chief hindrance of social progress to be found in the failure to apply to the facts and movements of society the method of science, as though emotion and sentimentalism could be substitutes for accurate observation and prudent generalization?

Should not, therefore, the museums of natural science be supplemented by similar collections designed to promote the study of the social sciences?

This transition in education may be illustrated by the development of Harvard University during the last fifty years. The Museum of Comparative Zoology was founded in 1859, and in connection with this museum were soon organized further collections and laboratories, of paleontology, botany, mineralogy, and geology. In 1866 was added the Museum of Archaeology and Ethnology, which now forms the anthropological section of the University Museum. In 1889 the inductive method was applied in a new direction by the endowment of the Semitic Museum, illustrating the history of Palestine, Assyria, Egypt and allied races; and the instruction of the University in the manners, customs, religions, and philosophies of these types of civilization has been stimulated and refreshed by this presentation of suggestive facts to the student's eye. A further step was taken in 1902 by the establishment, in large part through the princely gifts of the German Emperor, together with generous contributions from the King of Saxony, the Government of Switzerland, and a committee of scholars, artists and men of affairs in Berlin, of the Germanic Museum. This unique collection of models and reproductions sets before the visitor in a most impressive manner the story of German art and architecture from the fifth to the eighteenth century. The student of history finds himself confronted by the statue of Henry II from Bamberg, of Maximilian from Innsbruck, of the Great Elector from Berlin, and of Frederick the Great from Stettin; the student of religious art inspects with his teacher the bronze gates of Hildesheim, the golden gate of Freiberg, and the tomb of St. Sebald's at Nuremberg. What effect these graphical illustrations are likely to have on the vitality and attractiveness of Germanic studies may be readily conceived. The dignity and continuity of German art are perhaps nowhere more effectively exhibited, and many American students learn, for the first time, in the Germanic Museum the scope and refinement of German culture. Finally, in this series of collections, was begun in 1903 the Social Museum, to promote investigations of modern social conditions, and to direct the amelioration of industrial and social life. Such a museum is undertaken on the assumption that the most immediate need of students concerned with the social question is, not merely enthusiasm or sympathy or self-sacrifice or money, but wisdom, discretion, the scientific interpretation and comparison of facts; and that this application of the inductive method may be encouraged by setting before the student in graphical illustrations the evidences of progress in various countries and putting at his command the fund of experience accumulated in various parts of the world.

The remoteness of the United States from other countries and the brevity of its social history make this provision of illustrative material all the more necessary. Problems of the social order, which elsewhere represent gradual processes of social evolution, have presented themselves in the United States with startling abruptness and in dimensions of portentous magnitude, and put a sudden strain on political and social wisdom. The growth of the great cities, with its consequences of congested population, unsanitary dwellings, intermittent employment, and peril for childhood, is so modern a phenomenon that the principles of municipal government and municipal poor-relief have not unreasonably failed to keep pace with the new demands. The flood of a million immigrants a year, sweeping into the seaboard cities, and drawn for the most part from nationalities unfamiliar with the principles of democracy, threatens to overwhelm the traditions and ideals of the earlier stock. The collisions of labor with capital, of the white race with the blacks in the South, and of Orientals with Occidentals in the West, raise new questions both of self-preservation and of justice. These and many other social problems have in large measure taken Americans by surprise, and the science of society cannot safely proceed without new observation, comparison and appropriation of the experience of the world. The same demand for comparative sociology is laid, in various degrees, on other countries. Germany has much to teach the United States of municipal administration, but may learn much from America concerning the free conciliation of labor-disputes, the treatment of juvenile delinquents, or the work of social settlements. England offers to Americans instruction in trade-unionism and industrial cooperation, but must turn to the United States for lessons in the reform of the drink-traffic and the checking of the drink-habit. For all such purposes of comparative study the Social Museum provides what a museum of comparative zoology offers to the naturalist, and becomes the corrective of hasty judgments and the prerequisite of judicious conclusions. . . .

This Museum offers for the present hardly more than an outline of its complete intention, but it is already possible to appreciate the expansion of academic research which it represents. A student, for example, proposes an inquiry into the various schemes now advocated, both in Great

Britain and the United States, for the insurance of wage-earners, of which the German plan is the monumental example. He turns for assistance to the Social Museum, and finds there, through the munificent generosity of the German Government, and the courtesy of the Commissioner at the St. Louis Exposition, the exhibit made at the Louisiana Purchase Exposition of the Imperial Insurance System, consisting of one hundred and nine diagrams and statistical charts, together with a complete collection of reports and documents; to which by the generous cooperation of private corporations are added special exhibits from Bochum, Halle, Saarbrücken, Hanover and other German towns. It does not follow from this provision of material for study that the American student will find himself committed to a similar scheme under the different conditions of American life, but it must greatly fortify his social courage to see in pictorial and statistical representation the wonderful expansion of this administrative service in Germany, and the multiplication of institutions for the prevention and relief of disease which have been the consequences of this vast scheme of Imperial responsibility. A second student undertakes a special research in the problem, now gravely felt in the United States, of the systematic correction of mendicancy and vagrancy, and he finds in the Social Museum a collection of photographs, charts, and documents illustrating the labor colonies of Germany, Holland and Belgium, and is led to compare the various systems of detention, discipline and maintenance which have been approved by these countries as adequate to cope with the tramp-question. Still another student concerns himself with the problem of improved housing which, more than any other form of social amelioration, commends itself to the basic instincts of American citizens. He examines the various types of this new science, in which it is proposed that wise philanthropy shall coincide with reasonable commercial returns, and the Social Museum provides him with pictorial evidence, not only of successful enterprises in American cities, but of the best schemes of city-blocks and rural housing in Great Britain, France, Germany, Italy, Belgium, Switzerland, and New Zealand. The settlement-system, represented graphically by exhibits from one hundred and twenty-six settlements, the cooperative-system, the French Institutions Patronales and Syndicate Ouvriers; the provision in various countries for the insane, the defective, the sick, and the criminal—these and many other subjects of special inquiry lie before the student in the Social Museum, as though he were himself a traveller through many lands, observing the material which contributes to an inductive study of society. Incomplete as the present collection is, and fluid as it must always be under the rapidly changing circumstances and needs of social life, it at least brings the world near to the student and the student near to the world. Academic research is held close to facts, and social experiments are tested by experience. . . .

# 42

# THE RELATION OF THE ART MUSEUM TO A UNIVERSITY

**Edward W. Forbes**

Proceedings of the American Association of Museums, 5: 47–55, 1911

*Edward W. Forbes, director of the Fogg Art Museum at Harvard University, describes, in the article excerpted below, the function of a university art museum. Forbes believed that art instruction should include frequent exposure to original works of art when possible, and alternatively photographs and slides of works of art, and casts of ancient sculpture. Recognizing the limitations of university art museums to collect original works of art, Forbes recommends developing temporary exhibits to extend the quality and types of art that students can view and to give all visitors a sense that the museum is a dynamic part of the university world.*

. . . The relation of an art museum to a university is more complicated than appears at first sight, because the study of art is in many ways less easy to manage than the other studies in the university course. In history, literature, foreign languages, mathematics, and philosophy, books, documents, and men are all that are necessary; in chemistry and physics—laboratories; in botany and forestry—flowers and trees. But in fine arts, even granting the possession of a museum as expensively built as a scientific laboratory, a very intricate question arises—how shall it be filled and what shall be the purpose of its activities? The problem has some of the same difficulties that the problem of the geologist has, in that the great works to be studied are not accessible in themselves, and the effort must be made to make them interesting and real to the student by means of reproductions, or of smaller and less important specimens of the same kind. Probably few universities have ever felt justified in spending their funds for the purchase of objects of art. Usually, as in the case of Harvard, the works of art, and also the museums which hold them, have come as gifts.

Art, like most other studies, can be approached from the practical side or from the theoretical. As a rule, the college course is taken from the theoretical side. The student is taught the history of art in terms of words, but he does not take the charcoal and the brush himself. A man can learn something about the theory of riding, of football, of swimming, or of music by hearing lectures on the subject; but the men whose opinions are really valuable on those subjects are men who have practiced them, and not merely read about them.

Is this so in the case of art? In art we are confronted by the fact that there is involved the creative faculty and the critical faculty. It seldom happens that a man has both powers developed in a high degree. The man who has the critical faculty in large measure is not likely to be a creative genius. The man who has the power to conceive and execute great works of art must be satisfied with a weaker critical sense, for he has a greater gift.

Broadly speaking, the art school is the place for the man who is to paint—the university is the place for the man who is to learn to criticise and write on art. We must remember, too, that the average undergraduate student of fine arts does not propose either to paint or to criticise. His object is to get an intelligent appreciation of the subject for the purposes of general culture, but in this discussion I will rank this latter class with the critics. The object is largely the same; the difference is a matter of degree. The critic is the professional, the man of general culture is the amateur. But even the man who is to criticise should know how to paint. Or to put it more bluntly, he should know what he is talking about, just as the man who undertakes to know about swimming should be able to swim. No one but a trained engineer would pick an engine to pieces. The same principle holds in everything. The man who knows best what the difficulties are, understands best the skill of the master who overcomes them. The world has too many young critics who must earn their bread and butter by making a sensation. Much chaff is foisted into the literature of criticism by these immature experimenters. Kipling lashed them with reason in his lines:

When the oldest colors have faded And the youngest critics have died.

. . . The problem appears to be—how can a university fine arts museum be most useful under these conditions? The first obvious need for the purpose of teaching the history of art is a collection of slides and photographs. By means of these the lecturers can illustrate the history of art. In gathering a suitable collection of photographs the labor involved is great, particularly in a university like Harvard, where courses are given on a large variety of subjects and where, as time goes on, a larger and larger variety of courses will be given. The Fogg Museum now has about forty-three thousand photographs, but these are spread over the fields of architecture, ancient, medieval, and modern; of sculpture, including Egyptian, Greek, Italian, French, and German; and of the painting of many lands and centuries. I know a private collector in New York who has fifty thousand photographs of Italian paintings of the fourteenth, fifteenth, and sixteenth centuries alone. So it is clear that our collection can hardly be called complete. . . .

Our slide collection, numbering five thousand, is much smaller. The lecturer can pick out from the mass of photographs the few most significant ones to have made into slides for his lectures, while the student wants the greater wealth of material in the form of photographs which he can study at his leisure.

There is a difference of opinion about the value of casts. Many authorities say that an ancient statue can be studied better from a photograph than from a cast. . . . We have a small library attached to the Fogg Museum, and some of the most important art periodicals come to us regularly. Our students, however, have to depend for books largely on the college library.

Such is our equipment in the way of reproductions and historical and literary material. But we have something more—we have originals, I believe strongly that the first requisite in study is enthusiasm. Perhaps the two most effective ways of exciting enthusiasm are, first, by teaching the student himself to draw. . . . The second is the opportunity to look at original works of art. In this way we come into direct touch with the master himself. There is something about originals which has the power to stir interest where reproductions fail. Of course it is practically impossible to have originals by Michelangelo and Rembrandt, in fact, by most of the great men that we are studying. But the paintings by the masters or the pupils of these great men have a power of awakening interest. . . .

It is important to keep the students interested in the museum. The principle is clearly good of having a change of exhibitions. People will come to the museum if a well-advertised and attractive temporary show allures them. The impression is given that there is life in the place, and that the museum, like the rest of the university and the world, is a place of change and growth. Unfortunately, in the case of the Fogg Museum we are handicapped by having so little room. A temporary exhibition is expensive and troublesome to manage, as we have to get carpenters to remove some of our permanent exhibitions and make other changes.

. . . Here I want to bring up the question of whether the university art museum should contain the works of living men. There are two ways of doing this: first, by the temporary exhibitions; and second, in the permanent collections. It may even be possible to have exhibitions of the work of the students themselves, as is the case at Yale.

In the past the policy of the Fogg Museum has been to exhibit the work of men who are dead. This year we have made an innovation and have recently held an exhibition of works by Degas; and in the print room at present is an exhibition of etchings by modern masters, some of whom are alive. The advantages of exhibiting modern works of art are various. The students like it. The artists of today speak in a language the students readily understand. Art is not dead. It is not a memory of the past, nor a butterfly preserved in a glass bottle. It is among us, and is part of our life. We should be alive to the tendencies of our day.

The difficulty is, first, that all modern art is not good, and we wish to maintain a high standard. In having exhibitions of the work of living men we may subject ourselves to various embarrassments. Artists sometimes have feelings. We do not wish to be always in hot water, and make ourselves unpopular by refusing them if we do not think their work up to our standard. If we attempt to discriminate between the good and bad art of today, people will say: "Judge not that ye be not judged". . . .

In conclusion, I believe that the university should have a museum where the student is fired with enthusiasm by the teachers, who are the interpreters of art, by the awakening of new possibilities in himself when he finds that he too can paint and create, and by the inspiration which comes from contact with works of art.

If an art school and university are to combine, they should both be the gainers. The young artist should learn that technical skill is of little avail unless there is spirit; the student should liberate the sleeping powers of his hand. The courses should cover as broad a range of subjects as possible, including not only the historical side with its accompaniment of photographs, but the aesthetic, the technical, and the spiritual sides, going through the range of great thoughts and high ideals in many lands and centuries. Above all, the enthusiasm should be kindled and kept alive by the men and the works of art in the university, and the museum should do its utmost to collect the fairest flowers that are to be found, that tell the story of the artistic and imaginative possibilities of man.

# 43

# TRAINING MUSEUM WORKERS

## Homer R. Dill

Proceedings of the American Association of Museums, 11: 41–46, 1917

*In the article excerpted below, Homer R. Dill describes the origins of formal museum training in natural science museums. Although the training had an extensive practical component, it was supported by a broad academic education that led to a baccalaureate degree. In the summer of 1917, the University of Iowa established the first continuously-operating university museum training program in the United States. Dill makes an excellent case for the value of university natural history museums and considers the problem of orphan collections—a current issue in college and university museums.*

Before proceeding with what I have to say relative to museum training work, I should like to forestall any misunderstanding as to what I am trying to accomplish along this line. At the present time the work deals entirely with the science museum. The matters of administration, business methods, and policies which are essential in directing any institution, whether it is a museum, library, or school, are, for the time being, secondary to a thorough knowledge of technique, which I believe to be fundamental in successful museum building. A man may be a good manager and a diplomatic politician with tact and ability to handle a board of directors, and yet fail in the actual results as they appear in the museum. The first essential is a comprehensive knowledge of the work. In order to direct, one must know the technical side. It is upon this principle that a training course should be based.

There has been some speculation as to the cause of the deplorable conditions existing in many of the college museums. In a former report of the

Commissioner of Education, the following statement appears, based on data from the Directory of American Museums: "The founding of science museums by colleges and learned societies was a natural expression of the interest of the time in descriptive natural history. The displacement of that interest by the biology of the succeeding half century, with its emphasis upon laboratory studies in morphology and embryology is the fundamental reason for the large number of neglected and inactive college museums to-day." I believe it is not difficult to find some instances that would seem to verify these conclusions; but, despite this evidence, I am convinced that in the progressive colleges and universities of this country the science museum has a brilliant future.

There was a time when one man, known as a professor of natural history, taught all the natural science in college. This man also had charge of the museum. With the growth of the institution, professors in zoology, botany, and geology were required, and as an outcome of further growth the work in these fields at length became divided to such an extent that we have today a multitude of specialists in every branch of science, each one giving his full time and thought to some detail of the work. In a day of such specialists the general college museum has been naturally neglected. I am convinced that, while the scientific men all recognize the educational value of a good college museum, each one feels that he must devote all of his own time to his special line in order to accomplish necessary results. No one, in short, has come to fill the important function of the old professor of natural science which had to do with the building up of series of natural objects for study and exhibit. This necessary work leaves a wonderful field of opportunity to young men and women who are attracted in that direction.

As I have previously stated elsewhere, "In these days when wild life is rapidly disappearing, and when in many instances the specimens which we are placing in the exhibits of our museums are the last of their kind, the importance of preserving them permanently is brought home to us. The expert of the museum has an account to render with future generations, and no excuse will avail him for not keeping up with the times. During the past five years the authorities of the leading museums of the country have awakened to these facts, and consequently the demand for trained men and women in this line has far exceeded the supply. The effect has been two-fold: to open within the museum itself an entirely new field of opportunity; and to extend the efforts of collectors to the remotest corners of the world in search of new forms of animal life. Trained men are required also for this pioneer work which furnishes most congenial occupation to the lover of adventure and travel."

At the last meeting of this Association it was suggested that "the preservation and care of museum specimens" be considered at this meeting. I believe that the first requisite in this direction is a well trained man. While it is true that some of the larger museums have trained men to meet their special requirements in a satisfactory manner, a very large percentage of the museums of the country still have obvious need of trained men. The colleges themselves are waking up to a realization of their need in this direction.

Since the introduction of museum training work at the State University of Iowa, many letters of inquiry have come to us. The universal interest expressed is indeed gratifying. The requests for trained men who are strong in museum work and able to teach science have been so numerous, in fact, that we cannot furnish enough graduates to supply the demand for curators and other workers. What better evidence of genuine interest can we produce than these letters? Since certain of those who have expressed an interest in the subject have felt themselves unable to devote a year or even a semester to it, in order to accommodate such persons, we are offering a course of six weeks in our summer session. To determine whether the demand would be sufficient for this special course, a letter of inquiry was mailed to every science museum listed in the Directory and to the universities, colleges, and high schools that have to our knowledge any interest in this direction. A very large percentage of replies was received from the two thousand letters mailed. These replies were convincing as to the desirability of giving such a course; and surely they show better the real condition of the museums than can any statistics gathered from the Directory. It is, furthermore, to be regretted that some of the museums listed in the Directory do not actually exist at the present time, and some, indeed, are mere loan collections. In one case a so-called "college museum" lent to an institution by a wealthy man, upon his death was removed and divided among his several heirs, one of whom tried to sell his share of worthless specimens to our institution at reduced rates. I also remember, with a shudder, a trip to an attic room in a city building where the most horrible example of this kind was to be seen—strange, weird creatures covered with dust and so begrimed that they no longer bore the slightest semblance to the original animals. Not one specimen had a legible label. The collection had been presented to the city by a wealthy man with the understanding that it should have the care of a curator. The catalog published by this museum was quite elaborate; it contained the curator's name in large type, the names of a board of directors in smaller type, and a long list of the specimens that were supposed to be in the collection. When one had made due allowance for some of the unfortunate animals that were listed under the wrong scientific names, which in many cases were misspelled, this catalog made quite a good showing! In other words, this museum existed only on paper—a paper museum, the only excuse for its existence being the fact that it was a means of a curator's drawing a salary from the city. From such museums as these nothing can be proved as to the conditions that actually exist. . . .

A brief outline of the courses of training in museum work that we are offering is as follows: The first year is devoted to the fundamentals of freehand drawing and modeling; laboratory work in the museum is supplementary. Then the student is allowed to major in any one of the natural sciences, which seem most suitable as a preparation for one who is to make the building of museums his life work. He has, furthermore, a large practical experience in the museum laboratory, where all kinds of specimens are being mounted. An extensive zoological museum is at hand for study and comparison. New methods are continually being worked out for him. He is taught to handle old and difficult skins. In his English work the theory of museum methods is taken up. At the same time he may pursue allied courses, such as chemistry, drawing, and painting, all the time he is pursuing the broad course that leads to the B.A. or B.S. degree. The methods are such that the major part of the manual work may be delegated to a nontechnical man, while the one in charge is able to devote his thought and time to the directing of the work. As a result of this training a number of men have already gone out to fill responsible positions in the larger museums. . . .

We do not expect to revolutionize the museum world. We know that it is not possible to make a museum director of every student who registers for the work. But here and there we begin to see gratifying results. Each year shows a marked increase in the number of students who take the work, as well as a greater demand for trained men to fill museum positions. Once more, our argument is that such training, while it is indispensable to the man who is starting at the bottom, remains of service to him throughout the degrees of his advancement through the various stages leading to directorship.

I believe any man who has had experience in college and university administration knows well that with all the interests that are represented and the demands that must be met no department can accomplish anything without a good live man to look after its interest. When the college museum has the right kind of man to direct it, we need have no fears for its future.

# 44

# MUSEUMS AND THEIR PURPOSE

## N[ewton] H. Winchell

*Science*, 18: 43–46, 1891

*Professor Newton Winchell, state geologist of Minnesota, presented the lec-*
*ture excerpted below before the Academy of Sciences of St. Paul, Minnesota.*
*He begins with a history of museum origins and discusses the value of*
*university museums. Winchell also emphasizes the importance of collections-*
*based research and publication as the imperative functions of museums.*

. . . A museum was originally a temple in which the muses were wor-
shipped or invoked. At Athens, a hill near the Acropolis was called the
Museum because of the existence on it of such a temple. It was a place for
study and high contemplation. Although we have outgrown the myth-
ology of the Greeks, their literature and their institutions have so pervaded
our language and institutions that we find the germs of some of our choicest civil and social growths sunk deep into that old civilization. Those
germs have fruited, in part, in our day, and the fruit is somewhat different
from what the germs seemed to foreshadow. The germ of the museum at
Athens, fraught then with prophecy of poetry, art, and history, had but
little promise of science. The muse of astronomy was but one of the nine
whose shrines were in those temples. Scholars who sought the museum
were inspired with visions of the beautiful and the poetic, or of the light
and passionate frivolities of life. There was no muse of geology known,
though that science, by her aid, was to be a potent factor in preserving
and perpetuating the words "muse" and "museum" in the new civilization; nor any muse of biology, though the poetry of biologic science has
since been a prolific branch of modern scientific literature. There was no

muse of botany, nor of paleontology, nor of electricity. I think that if the Grecian Museum had continued to the present, the number of the inspiring muses would have been increased far beyond the mythical nine. That dynasty has passed away and with it has almost been lost the original idea of the museum.

The word, however, which is imperishably stamped on the language of all modern civilized nations, remains. It bears a weird, and to the original nine who gave it origin and character and authenticity, almost an unknown signification. Let us look into this a moment, and endeavor to learn what is the modern meaning of this word "museum." We shall find that it bears three interpretations, or dominant ideas. First, there are museums designed for entertainment; second, there are museums intended for the instruction of the visitor; third, there are museums for research.

The modern so-called "dime museum" typifies the museum designed for entertainment, although in many such may be found some of the characteristics of the second class. It is a place of "curiosities" and monstrosities, of cheap theatricals and legerdemain. Such have long been known, although under different names, in the principal cities of Europe and America, the most noted in this country being Barnum's Museum in New York City thirty-five or forty years ago. Here the visitor is wholly passive under the manipulation of the presiding genius of the place. He may enter the presence with any foreign, or even adverse sentiment. He simply is willing to be amused for half an hour.

The modern museum designed for instruction has a somewhat higher function and rank. Its purpose is to inspire in the visitor a thirst for knowledge, and in a degree to furnish that knowledge, at second hand. He seeks not that amusement may be lavished upon him, but he is at least willing to put forth an effort to obtain information. With this end attained he is satisfied. The instruction he has received remains in his mind unclassified and generally unassimilable. He knows more of the earth and of the things upon it when he retires from the place than when he approached it. Of his mental capacities his memory only is necessary thereafter to enable him to make useful that which he has seen. He is instructed and benefitted in so far as he appreciates and retains the ideas which the various objects have brought to his mind. Such museums are common. They accompany nearly all modern institutions of higher learning. They are patronized in proportion to the number of instructive objects they have on exhibition, or the variety and beauty of their specimens, or of the cases in which they may be contained. They serve, like travelling circuses, to attract the light-minded and the curious; but their service is higher than that of the circus, in the higher grade of information which they impart, and in the greater benevolence of the motive for which they are maintained. Such museums discharge an important function in education, and particularly in scientific education, and to this day they express the popular idea of a perfect museum. They may sometimes partake of the elements that characterize the third class, or the museum for research, and, in so far as they do, their sphere is raised nearer the true ideal. In general, however, they are far removed from the true museum, and from the germinal idea which was planted in the Grecian mind. You will note that the motive of the patron in both these cases is one of self-improvement or gratification. He has no object ulterior to that of being himself benefitted. There is, moreover, in the museum itself, no other purpose expressed, nor any possibility of any other purpose being accomplished by the visitor. . . .

The true museum is that which approaches nearest to the cardinal idea of the Grecian museum. Its aim is not to amuse, nor to instruct, but to afford that inspiration which shall enable the visitor to instruct others. The reverent devotee approaches such a museum with no selfish motive. He invokes his muse to inspire in him sentiments that shall benefit his fellow-men. When I say that there are but few such museums in our day, you will not question the statement. You will rather inquire whether there are any such in existence. Such a museum is based on a broader idea than the exhibition-museum, though its frequenters may be fewer. Scientific research, long-continued study, profound contemplation, and conference with the writings of others—these are the purposes of such a museum. In but few places is this carried out, but it is the fundamental and growing idea underlying some modern museums. The full fruition of this idea will be the culminating result of the germ which was planted in the early Grecian soil. Transferred to modern times, ripening in the sunlight of a new civilization, with its roots nourished by more genial influences, the germ of the Grecian museum produces in our day, or is beginning to produce, a fruit somewhat different, although generically it is identical with that which it bore under Athenian culture. . . .

It is only with the recent awakening of modern society to the usefulness and beneficence of modern science that the true idea of a true museum has become again apparent. This idea finds illustration in a few museums in all the great nations of Europe and America. The highest enlightenment is compatible with the highest efficiency of these organizations, for they are the great dynamos that keep the machinery of modern advancement continually moving. This, however, has been the result of a growth whose former stages were insignificant, and perhaps but faintly foreshadowed the form that the completed museum should take on. This growth had a natural philosophical as well as chronologic order. We might appeal to history to show this. From the lowest form of a museum meant for amusement simply, consisting of a collection of rare and grotesque objects, rose that which embraced the idea and purpose of education. With instruction, still variously larded with amusement, gradually came necessarily the last term of the series, viz., an eagerness for research. This last term, first put into ideal form by Lord Bacon in his "New Atlantis," near the end of the seventeenth century, in which he works the idea of a great national museum into his romance, was definitely recognized and enacted by parliament, in the establishment of the British Museum in 1753. The Louvre at Paris, containing the great national museum, was converted from a royal residence and playhouse when in 1789 it came into the possession of a republican government.

But I need scarcely mention, to this audience, those museums which exemplify the idea which I am trying to inculcate. If you call to mind those bee-hives of industry where are stored the choicest collections of years, or of centuries, representing all departments of knowledge, whether of natural science, or of history and antiquity, or of literature, or of art, in which the nations of the earth take the greatest pride, you see, perhaps, in Britain, the great British Museum with its numerous departments and its libraries, or the United States National Museum at Washington, or some of the great continental museums. These great collections subserve the ends both of instruction and of research, but chiefly their purpose is to aid the student in research, although this was not the prime object in their establishment. As already stated, however, when the second phase of museum-growth has been attained, viz., the idea of instruction, the last term of the series necessarily follows, and the museum takes on the last phase of its development—it becomes a place for research. It is by no means necessary that this last stage should exclude the functions of education and enlightenment. It is better that they co-exist. They aid each other. The instructed visitor may become an investigator, and the greater the number of enlightened visitors leaving its rooms, the greater the number of truth-seekers will be who frequent its laboratories and libraries.

As a museum takes on this highest function, however, it retires more and more from public gaze. Its cases and its drawers may be well filled with well-arranged and labelled specimens, and the casual visitor may imagine he has sufficiently seen the museum when he has passed through its public halls. But he has not seen the working of the museum in its highest departments. In the numerous laboratories are more specimens than those that are on exhibition. These are for the eye only of the true seeker after truth. The student-patron enters all the recesses, and has access to all the specimens. He alone invokes the muse in the spirit of the early Greek poet. Unobtrusively he solves his great problems. Unselfishly he proclaims the new truths to the world. His service is as sincere, and as necessary to the development of modern civilization, and to the apprehension of the laws of nature, whether they be the laws of gravitation or of brotherly kindness, as that of any truth-seeker or man-lover. The laboratories and recesses of these great museums, which are unseen by the public, are crowded with such devout truth-seekers. . . .

# SECTION VII

## Philosophy of Museums with Living Collections

This final section focuses on zoos, aquaria, botanical gardens, and arboreta—museums with living collections. Today, the American Association of Museums includes institutions with living collections in their definition of museums, but it was not until Charles H. Townsend, first director of the New York Aquarium, elucidated the shared philosophy among aquaria (and zoos) and museums of natural history—particularly regarding educational exhibits—that the first President of the American Association of Museums agreed to include these institutions under the museum rubric.

The works presented here reveal just this sort of understanding, facilitated by the fact that many of the authors had worked for natural history museums in their early careers. The essays by Nathaniel Lord Britton and Theodore Link examine broader topics about botanical gardens and zoos, respectively. The next four articles focus on specific development of prominent institutions in the United States, including the Missouri Botanical Gardens, Harvard's Arnold Arboretum, the New York Zoological Park, and the New York Aquarium.

### Additional Readings

Baratay, Eric, and Elisabeth Hardouin-Fugier. 2002. *Zoo: A history of zoological gardens in the West*. London: Reaktion.

Covins, Frederick. 1989. *The arboretum story: A social and historical record of the arboretum area of central Worcester.* Worcester, England: Arboretum Residents' Association.

Grove, Carol. 2005. *Henry Shaw's Victorian landscapes: The Missouri Botanical Garden and Tower Grove Park.* Amherst: University of Massachusetts Press.

Hanson, Elizabeth. 2002. *Animal attractions: Nature on display in American zoos.* Princeton, NJ: Princeton University Press.

Hay, Ida. 1995. *Science in the pleasure ground: A history of the Arnold Arboretum.* Boston: Northeastern University Press.

Hoage, R. J., and William A. Deiss. 1996. *New worlds, new animals: From menagerie to zoological park in the nineteenth century.* Baltimore: The Johns Hopkins University Press.

Kisling, Vernon N. (ed.). 2001. *Zoo and aquarium history: Ancient collections to zoological gardens.* Boca Raton, FL: CRC Press.

Langmead, Clive. 1995. *A passion for plants: From the rainforests of Brazil to Kew Gardens—The life and vision of Ghillean Prance, Director of the Royal Botanic Gardens, Kew.* Oxford, UK: Lion Publication.

Newman, Murray A. 1994. *Life in a fishbowl: Confessions of an aquarium director.* Vancouver, Canada: Douglas and McIntyre.

Rothfels, Nigel. 2002. *Savages and beasts: The birth of the modern zoo.* Baltimore: Johns Hopkins University Press.

Rudolph, Emanuel D. 1991. One hundred years of the Missouri Botanical Garden. *Annals of the Missouri Botanical Garden* 78: 1–18.

Weaver, Stephanie. 2007. *Creating great visitor experiences: A guide for museums, parks, zoos, gardens & libraries.* Walnut Creek, CA: Left Coast Press, Inc.

Wemmer, Christen M. (ed.). 1995. *The ark evolving: Zoos and aquariums in transition.* Front Royal, VA: Smithsonian Institution Conservation and Research Center.

# 45

# BOTANICAL GARDENS

## Nathaniel Lord Britton

*Proceedings of the American Association for the Advancement of Science,*
45: 171–187, 1896

*Nathaniel Britton, first director of the New York Botanical Garden,
explains the mission and work of a modern nineteenth-century botanical
garden. He explains that historically as botanical gardens moved from the
private to the public realm "four main elements" came to define the modern
botanical garden—the utilitarian or economic, the aesthetic, the scientific
or biologic, and the philanthropic (which is not well defined and might
better be described as an education or a research element mainly developed
through the establishment of a botanical library).*

## Origin and Development

The civilization of plants within small areas for their healing qualities by
the monks of the Middle Ages appears to have been the beginning of the
modern botanical garden, although these medieval gardens doubtless
took their origin from others of greater antiquity. Botanical gardens were
thus primarily formed for purely utilitarian purposes, although the aesthetic study of planting and of flowers most doubtless have appealed to
their owners and visitors. Their function as aids in scientific teaching and
research, the one which at present furnishes the dominating reason for
their existence, did not develop much, if at all, before the sixteenth century,
and prior to the middle of the seventeenth century a considerable number

existed in Europe in which this function was recognized to a greater or less degree, of which those at Bologna, Montpellier, Leyden, Paris, and Upsala were perhaps the most noteworthy. The ornamental and decorative taste for planting had meanwhile been slowly gaining ground, as well as the desire to cultivate rare or unusual species, and during the eighteenth century attained a high degree or development. Many persons of wealth and influence fostered this taste and became, through the employment of men skilled in botany and horticulture, generous patrons of science. The world was searched for new and rare plants, which were brought home to Europe for cultivation, and many sumptuous volumes, describing and delineating them, were published, mainly through the same patronage. The older gardens were essentially private institutions, but as the rights of the people became more and more recognized, many existing establishments and an increasing number of newly founded ones became, to a greater or less extent, open to the public, either through an admittance fee or without charge. The four main elements of the modern botanical garden have thus been brought into it successively:

1. The utilitarian or economic.
2. The aesthetic.
3. The scientific or biologic.
4. The philanthropic.

These four elements have been given different degrees of prominence, depending mainly upon local conditions, some gardens being essentially aesthetic, some mainly scientific, while in our public parks we find the philanthropic function as the underlying feature, usually accompanied by more or less of the aesthetic and scientific.

*The Economic Element.*—In the broadest extension of this department of a botanical garden there might be included, to advantage, facilities for the display and investigation of all plants directly or indirectly useful to man, and their products. This conception would include forestry, pharmacognosy, agriculture, pomology, pathology, and organic chemistry, and, in case the management regards bacteria as plants, bacteriology.

The display of the plants may be effected by growing such of them as will exist without protection in the locality in a plot, more or less individualized, commonly known as the Economic Garden, while those too tender for cultivation in the open are grown in the greenhouses, either in a separate house or section, or scattered through the several houses or sections, in the temperatures best adapted to their growth. The display of plant products, best accompanied by mounted specimens of the species yielding them, by photographs and by plates, is accomplished by the Economic

Museum, where these are arranged in glass or glass-fronted cases, suitably classified and labeled. It is believed that the most useful results are obtained by arranging this museum by the products themselves, and thus not in biologic sequence, but by bringing together all drugs, all fibres, all woods, all resins, where the same product is used in more than one industry the exhibit; may be duplicated, more or less modified, without disadvantage.

The investigation of economic plants and their products is accomplished through the Scientific Department, and few valuable results can be reached unless the scientific equipment is well developed. The two departments must work conjointly, both on account of the necessity of knowing just what species is under investigation, its structure, distribution, and literature, and in order that the most approved and exact methods may be used in the research. Any idea that the scientific element can be dispensed with in connection with economic studies is palpably untenable.

Teaching and research in agriculture, pomology, and plant pathology are so well organized in America, through our National Department of Agriculture and our numerous agricultural colleges and schools, that there is no great necessity for providing elaborate equipments for those branches in botanical gardens. But in case the endowment of a garden were sufficiently large to enable them to be successfully prosecuted, in addition to more necessary work, there can be no doubt that important additions to knowledge would be obtained. On the other hand, no such liberal allowances have been made with us for forestry or pharmacognosy, and research and instruction in these sciences must prove of the greatest benefit to the country.

*The Aesthetic Element.*—The buildings, roads, paths, and planting of a botanical garden should be constructed and arranged with reference to tasteful and decorative landscape effect. The possibilities of treatment will depend largely upon the topographical character of the area selected and, the natural vegetation of the tract. The buildings required are a fire-proof structure or structures for museum, herbarium, libraries, laboratories, and offices; a glass house with compartments kept at several different temperatures for exhibition, propagation, and experimentation, or several separate glass houses; and to these will usually be added dwelling-houses for some of the officers, a stable, and other minor buildings. The character, number, and sizes of the buildings generally depend on financial considerations. In placing the structures intended for the visiting public, considerations of convenient access, satisfactory water supply, and the distribution of crowds must be borne in mind, in connection with the landscape design. The planting should follow, as nearly as possible, a natural treatment, except immediately around the larger buildings and at the entrance, where considerable formality is desirable for architectural reasons. It is especially desirable that as much natural treatment as possible should be given to the areas devoted to systematic planting,—herbaceous grounds, fruticetum, arboretum. The rectilinear arrangement of plant beds found in most of the older gardens has become abhorrent to landscape lovers, and the sequence of families desired can usually be quite as well obtained by means of curved-margined groups.

The cultivation of decorative plants, and especially the fostering of a taste for them, and the bringing of unusual or new species to attention and effecting their general introduction, are important functions of a botanical garden. For the accurate determination of these plants, information concerning their habits and structure, and suggestions regarding the conditions of their growth, the aesthetic side must rely on the scientific.

*The Scientific or Biologic Element.*—The important relations of the scientific department to the economic and aesthetic have already been alluded to. The library, herbarium, museums, and laboratories are the sources whence exact information regarding the name, structure, habits, life processes, and products of plants are derived, and they are the more useful as they are the more complete and thoroughly equipped. It is practically impossible for any one library to have all the literature of botany and related sciences, any one herbarium to possess an authentic and complete representation of all species of plants, or any one museum to be thoroughly illustrative; absolute perfection along these lines cannot be obtained, but the more closely it is approximated the better the results. The research work of the scientific department should be organized along all lines of botanical inquiry, including taxonomy, morphology, anatomy, physiology, and paleontology, and the laboratories should afford ample opportunities and equipment for their successful prosecution.

The arrangement of the areas devoted to systematic planting, and the proper labeling of the species grown, are important duties of the scientific department. The sequence of classes, orders, and families is usually made to follow some "botanical system." It is highly desirable that this should be a system which indicates the natural relations of the families, as understood at the time the garden is laid out, and be elastic enough to admit of subsequent modification as more exact information relative to those relationships is obtained. The weight of present opinion is overwhelmingly in favor of an arrangement from the more simple to the more complex, and this will apply not only to the systematic plantations, but to the systematic museum and the herbarium.

The scientific possibilities of a botanical garden are the greater if an organic or co-operative relationship exists between it and a university, thus affording ready facilities for information on other sciences.

*The Philanthropic Element.*—A botanical garden operates as a valuable philanthropic agency, both directly and indirectly. Its direct influence lies through its affording an orderly arranged institution for the instruction, information, and recreation of the people, and it is more efficient for these purposes than a park, as it is more completely developed and liberally maintained. Its indirect, but equally important, philanthropic operation is through the discovery and dissemination of facts concerning plants and their products, obtained through the studies of the scientific staff and by others using the scientific equipment. . . .

# 46

# THE MISSOURI BOTANICAL GARDEN

## William Trelease

*Popular Science Monthly*, 62: 193–222, 1903

*William Trelease, writing as the first Director of the Missouri Botanical Garden, recounts the early history of the public garden, originally the private garden of Henry Shaw, in the article excerpted below. Trelease describes Shaw's plans for transforming his garden from a private to a public institution and how as director he came to emphasize the educational and research component of the mission by building an herbarium and library, and publishing annual reports. The garden came to exemplify the modern botanical garden described by Britton in the previous reading.*

In 1840, Henry Shaw, an Englishman who had settled in St. Louis in 1819, retired from business with the—for that time—large fortune of a quarter of a million dollars. Revisiting the land of his birth, he saw how Englishmen enjoy the fruits of labor such as that by which he had acquired this large sum of money. Traveling on the continent, he saw what the world of pleasure offers to those who are able to pay for it. But he returned to the land of his adoption, determined to make for himself there surroundings as nearly as possible comparable with those of his own countrymen; and he so far succeeded that the modest little garden with which he surrounded his country house in the suburbs of St. Louis came in time to be the pleasantest of the resorts of the residents of that city, and the one place to which they were all sure to wish to take their visiting friends.

If he had stopped with this, he would have caused his name to be long remembered by his fellow citizens, for he did not hold his home as his own exclusively, but admitted to the enjoyment of its beauties any who wished to share them with him. But while his grounds were developing and growing in beauty, he learned, through the helpful acquaintance of Sir William Hooker and of his own fellow townsmen, Dr. George Engelmann, that it might be possible to perpetuate his name in a surer and more lasting manner, and to cause the garden that he had planned and planted to become of use in the world of science and to grow in such usefulness through the centuries, while losing nothing of its beauty and attractiveness to those who cared to enjoy without using it. In 1859 he secured the passage of an act by the legislature of Missouri which empowered him to deed or will, as he might elect, such of his property as he wished, to trustees for the maintenance of "a botanical garden for the cultivation and propagation of plants, flowers, fruit and forest trees, and for the dissemination of the knowledge thereof among men, by having a collection thereof easily accessible; by the establishment of a museum and library in connection therewith, as also by establishment of public lectures and instruction upon botany and its allied sciences, when it shall be deemed advisable in furtherance of the general objects of said trust; and . . . for the purpose of maintaining a perpetual fund for the support and maintenance of said garden, its care and increase, and the museum, library and instruction connected therewith."

As the new and larger plans shaped themselves in Mr. Shaw's mind, they began to take form on the grounds, and its flower garden, arboretum, and fruticetum were quickly laid out and planted, and separated and fronted by rubble walls in the outermost of which a severe but rather impressive gate-house, bearing the chosen name of the establishment—Missouri Botanical Garden—was built. Not far from his house, Mr. Shaw put a small fireproofed building over the door of which the inscription "Botanical Museum and Library" was cut in the stone, and in which, largely through the interest of Dr. Engelmann, were soon installed a small but well chosen collection of books, and some 60,000 specimens of plants, consisting of the herbarium of the then lately deceased Professor Johann Jakob Bernhardi and a small local collection made by Riehl. The arrangement of these specimens, Mr. Shaw once informed me, was entrusted to "a young man named Fendler," whose name was already known as that of an expert collector and destined to be made still better known by subsequent work in the tropics. On the occasion of my introducing to him a gentleman who was making a study of tile flora of Missouri and who wished to consult the Riehl collection, Mr. Shaw expressed the regret with which he observed that though the flower garden was visited by thousands of people each year, and the contents of the small and miscellaneous museum attracted them, this was the only request for access to the herbarium or library that had been made by a botanist for years.

From time to time he turned his thoughts toward the fuller realization of his plans, apparently hesitating between leaving their inception to the trustees that he had provided for appointing by will, and making the beginning himself either alone or in conjunction with trustees—a possibility specifically provided for in the enabling act of the legislature. On the occasion of my first visit to him, in the early spring of 1885, he pointed out to me the place, on Flora Avenue, before the main gate of the garden, where he had seriously thought of building lecture rooms, laboratories and residences for a faculty of botany. It was somewhat earlier than this that he called the great botanist, Asa Gray, into his counsels, and largely because of the wise advice of Dr. Gray, who saw that the time was not yet come in St. Louis for an institution such as was contemplated, he decided to let its growth be a normal one from small beginnings—but without in the least modifying his provisions for the final attainment of the largest results he had ever contemplated. . . .

It was apparently the death of Engelmann, a resident of St. Louis and one of the greatest as perhaps the most accurately painstaking of American botanists, that caused the next step forward to be taken. Shortly after this, in 1884–5, Dr. Gray was once more, and this time rather urgently, called into consultation, that the city in which the plans were laid might not be entirely without a botanist; and the result was that in the spring of 1885 Mr. Shaw proposed to the directors of Washington University to endow in that institution a school of botany, with the understanding that by testamentary provision the best uses of his garden for scientific study and investigation should be ensured to its professor and students. The offer being accepted, the Henry Shaw School of Botany was formally inaugurated on the sixth of November following, and its single professor was thrown into a pleasant and frequent personal intercourse with Mr. Shaw which lasted until the death of the latter. . . . His will was found to provide for the administration of the garden by an independent board of trustees consisting of fifteen persons; ten named by the testator, and the other five holding office as trustees *ex officio*, in various capacities: The chancellor of Washington University, the bishop of the episcopal diocese of Missouri, the president of the public school board of St. Louis, the president of the Academy of Science of St. Louis, and the mayor of the city. . . .

The testamentary provisions for the carrying out of Mr. Shaw's purposes do not differ in any essential respect from the plan sketched in the enabling act of 1859—passed because there was at that time some uncertainty as to the possibility of otherwise milking the provisions that he wished to make in such manner as to ensure their permanence. . . .

Provision is made for the cooperation of the garden and the school of botany by the requirement that the professor or professors in the latter shall be the director of the garden or his chief assistant, or both, or that they shall be appointed on nomination of or subject to the approval of the trustees of the garden. The instruction of garden pupils is specifically indicated as a purpose of the institution, and among the subjects that are mentioned as forming a part of the purpose of its founder are horticulture, arboriculture, medicine and the arts, so far as botany enters into them, and scientific investigations in botany proper, vegetable physiology, the diseases of plants, the forms of vegetable life, and of animal life injurious to vegetation, and experimental investigations in horticulture, arboriculture, etc.; but the testator wisely adds: "I leave details of instruction to those who may have to administer the establishment, and to shape the particular course of things to the condition of the times."

The intention and obvious need of maintaining the establishment as an ornamental garden are evident in the many references to it as a fundamental idea, and Mr. Shaw very specifically states that he considers it "an important feature to always keep up the ornamental and floricultural character of the garden." Direction is given that the yearly net revenue from the endowment shall be applied "first to the payment of the salaries of the director, assistants, professors and gardeners, and the payment of the wages of the employees and laborers, in keeping up the grounds in good style and providing for the preservation and increase of the plants and trees, and preserving the buildings and enclosures of the grounds, and secondly to the purchase of plants, flowers, and trees, additions to the library, *the enlargement* and improvement of the garden when necessary or advisable, and such other expenditures as from time to time may be found necessary" in furtherance of the purposes of the testator. . . .

It is the lot of all living and growing institutions which give promise of prolonged existence, to have gifts of greater or less magnitude made to them. The Missouri Botanical Garden has not proved an exception to this rule. Even before the death of its founder, Dr. George J. Engelmann placed in the hands of the present director of the garden the invaluable herbarium of his father, the late Dr. George Engelmann, and shortly after the organization of the board of trustees this was formally transferred to them by Dr. Engelmann, together with the library of his father, which, however, had actually been placed at the garden and in part arranged before the death of Mr. Shaw. One of Dr. Engelmann's biographers expressed the great surprise occasioned by the vast amount of work that he, a busy physician, had found time to do. The number and minute accuracy of his unpublished notes, which form part of this gift from his son, were even more surprising. Over 20,000 of them exist, varying in character from a mere memorandum of the appearance of a plant which he had observed in a foreign garden, or a simple bibliographic reference, to accurate detail sketches of all of the specimens on which his conception of a species in a difficult group rested; and the sixty thick volumes in which they are now contained are counted among the choicest possessions of the institution. . . .

A herbarium is an uninteresting collection to the average person who does not need to use it, whether he be a botanist or not, in envelopes or glued or bandaged down on sheets of paper are thousands of more or less fragmentary plants, sometimes moldy or worm-eaten, for time works havoc with all organic matter, and usually much faded. And yet not even the library is more indispensable for the worker on the species that they represent; for they are the real plants, and not some one's interpretation of them. The choicest part consists always of the original specimens preserved by an author when describing and naming a species or genus, for however his description or figure may have erred, this type persists as a record showing the true generic and specific characters. An herbarium not always a conclusive source to which to turn for final information, for the other may have and often has had two or more related species under his eye when describing the one to which he gave recognition and a name, and herbarium study calls for some discriminating power; but notwithstanding the inherent difficulties, its value is real and lasting. Though the founder of the Missouri Botanical Garden did not specifically mention a herbarium in his will, his purchase of the Bernhardi collection in the early years of his planning shows his practical appreciation of the need of such a part of the equipment of the institution. . . .

But the great ultimate purpose of a botanical garden is the fostering of research with the purpose of adding to knowledge. This was recognized by Mr. Shaw, and repeatedly mentioned in his provisions for the future of his establishment. Opportunity for it lies in every plant in the collections, and in every book on the shelves. To get men to use the opportunities offered is the greatest problem of administration. So far, the garden has employed only the most necessary caretakers, and it would have been impossible for a single one of its employees to have been spared from the force without neglect of some essential. Yet, though over-work and a permissible if entirely undesirable neglect of details of convenience in use, but not of preservative care, have been necessary, each of the higher employees has every year found time to do something worth doing in the field of investigation. The achievements, it is true, are neither as many nor as great as the workers or the management of the establishment would have wished them to be, but considering the fact that the garden has been in course of transition from the pleasure grounds of a gentleman to a scientific establishment, and that what has been done has been carefully done, they are not insignificant or unworthy, and each of the thirteen annual reports on the institution thus far printed contains at least one scientific publication of original results, of permanent interest to botanical workers. What will come of the staff of capable investigators that it may shortly be expected to gather together, is a matter of conjecture only—but the conjecture refers rather to the success with which men may be selected than to the opportunities that they will enjoy for the most earnest and serious application of which they are capable.

Research is coming to be recognized as of greater value for the practical development of our natural resources, with the passage of every year. The investigator sometimes sees in his subject only a problem that he must solve whether its solution can ever be of value or not. Sometimes he appears to be so constituted that the suspicion that it can result in anything useful is deterrent to him. Sometimes his chief interest lies in the very possibility of its utilization. But, in any case, no fact well made out and properly correlated is valueless, and the results of the most unpractical of discoveries are often utilized in commerce or in the arts with surprising promptness. While the research thus far carried on at the garden has been dictated largely by consideration of the needs of botanical science alone, or the personal interest of the investigator. . . .

# 47

# THE ARNOLD ARBORETUM: WHAT IT IS AND DOES

## Charles Sprague Sargent

Cambridge, MA: Gray Herbarium of Harvard University. 8 pp., 1918

---

*Arboreta are often thought of as only a collection of trees and are often not included in the rubric of museums. However, the following excerpt of Director Charles Sargent's early history of the Arnold Arboretum at Harvard University—considered one of the most important arboreta in North America—reveals a complex mission that includes, as do all scientific museums, both research and education components.*

---

The question is often asked: What is the Arnold Arboretum and what is it expected to accomplish for the benefit of the world?

A department of Harvard University, the Arboretum is a museum of trees and other woody plants and its object is to increase the knowledge of such plants. This museum owes its origin to the imagination of George B. Emerson. In 1868 James Arnold, a merchant living in New Bedford, Massachusetts, died and at the suggestion of Mr. Emerson left $100,000 to trustees, of which Mr. Emerson was one, to be used by them for the advancement of agriculture or horticulture. Mr. Emerson had long been interested in trees and had prepared for the Commonwealth an excellent "Report on the Trees and Shrubs Growing Naturally in Massachusetts," which had been published by the state. Another of Mr. Arnold's trustees, John James Dixwell, was also interested in trees and had formed on his estate in Jamaica Plain a collection of trees which had in the middle of the last century few equals in Massachusetts. Mr. Emerson, therefore, was naturally supported by his fellow trustee in his idea of using the Arnold money to establish an Arboretum, and between them they made in 1872 an arrangement with Harvard University by which they turned over to it the Arnold bequest, the University in return agreeing to devote to the Arboretum a part of the farm in West Roxbury which had been left to it by Benjamin Bussey to be used for a Farm School. This agreement provided that the University should grow on this land every tree and shrub able to endure the climate of Massachusetts. One hundred and twenty-five acres of the Bussey Farm was at first included in this arrangement and several years later the University added seventy-five acres more to the Arboretum, the area of which was further increased, as will be explained, by the City of Boston.

It is safe to say that none of the men directly engaged in making this agreement had any idea what an Arboretum might be, or what it was going to cost in time and money to carry out the agreement to cultivate all the trees and shrubs which could be grown in Massachusetts, and certainly none of them were more ignorant on these subjects than the person selected to see that this agreement was carried out. He found himself provided with a worn-out farm partly covered with native woods nearly ruined by pasturage and neglect, with only a small part of the income of the $100,000 available, for it had been decided by the University that the whole income could not be used until the principal had been increased to $150,000 by accumulated interest. He was without the support and encouragement of the general public which knew nothing and cared less about an Arboretum and what it was expected to accomplish.

Fortunately the late Frederick Law Olmsted became interested in the project and suggested that the City of Boston might well include under certain conditions the Arboretum in its park system. This plan met with little favor and was strongly opposed by the University and the Park Commission of the City, and it took five years of exceedingly disagreeable semipolitical work to bring it about. In 1882, however, the consent of the Legislature having been obtained to such an arrangement, a contract was made between the University and the City which permitted the Park Commission of Boston to seize by right of eminent domain the land devoted to the Arboretum and then to lease back to the University for one thousand years all this land; with the exception of that to be occupied by a system of drives and walks which were to be built by the City after plans to be prepared by Mr. Olmsted and which were to be maintained by the City during the period of the contract. The City further agreed to add to the Arboretum land necessary for carrying out Mr. Olmsted's plan for the roads, to protect the Arboretum by its police and to assume any taxes which might be levied on it during the period of the contract. On its part the University agreed that the Arboretum should be open to the public every day during the continuance of the contract from sunrise to sunset. The City was slow in building the roads, and it was not until 1885 that the planting of trees in their systematic arrangement was begun. . . .

In 1882 Dr. Bretschneider, the learned physician of the Russian Embassy at Peking, sent to the Arboretum a small collection of seeds which proved one of the most important gifts it has ever received. . . . It was the success in Massachusetts of the plants raised from the Bretschneider seeds that turned my attention to the importance of more thorough botanical exploration in China than had yet been attempted and led to the Wilson expeditions to central and western China. These were undertaken first by a London nurseryman at the suggestion of the Arboretum on lines proposed by it, and later by the Arboretum itself. Mr. Wilson's travels have greatly increased the number of trees and shrubs which are now cultivated in the United States and Europe and have made the Arboretum the best place for the study of the ligneous vegetation of eastern Asia. . . .

The Arboretum endeavors to increase the knowledge of trees by arranging the living plants in what may be described as a Tree Museum. This Museum, which now contains, one of the largest collections of trees and shrubs of the Northern Hemisphere in the world, occupies two hundred and twenty acres of hill, valley and meadow contributed for the purpose by the University and in small part by the City of Boston. Part of this land is occupied by good native oak woods and by a fine grove of Hemlock-trees which cover the steep slopes of what is called Hemlock Hill, the crowning feature of the Arboretum. On the remainder of the ground the trees have been arranged in family groups and in botanical sequence, all the species of each genus being together. In the case of important native trees several individuals have been planted comparatively near together with a single individual of the species sufficiently far from any other tree to make possible its free and full development. For the trees of other countries only space has been found for a single individual of each. Hardy shrubs are arranged in parallel beds on the only piece of level ground in the Arboretum near the Forest Hills entrance. This arrangement has been adopted that students who want to see and compare the species of a genus of hardy shrubs can do so easily and in a short time. Everywhere else in the Arboretum the attempt has been made to so group the trees and shrubs that the natural features of the place may be preserved, and that, although a person going along the drives can see close to the road a representative of every genus of trees in the Arboretum, he can do so without being unpleasantly impressed with the idea that he is in a systematically arranged botanical garden. A visitor, however, who sees only what can be seen from the drives gets little idea of this museum and its collections which must be studied from the grass-covered paths which lead the student to all the groups and to the principal points of interest and beauty.

More important for the increase of knowledge than the cultivation and convenient arrangement of living plants is the work which is carried on in the laboratories of the Arboretum, for comparatively few persons can study and enjoy these growing plants; but from the laboratories material and information reach far beyond the boundaries of the United States. There are two departments of these laboratories, first the nurseries and second the herbarium and library. In the nurseries have been raised nearly all the trees and shrubs which now form the outdoor museum, and from them hundreds of thousands of rare plants, or plants entirely new to cultivation, have been sent out in exchange for other plants, to be tested in almost every civilized country of the world. In these nurseries, too, have been produced by hybridization a few plants of considerable value. . . .

In the library and herbarium the material gathered by agents of the Arboretum is studied, and in its library have been prepared the books through which the information about trees collected by the Arboretum has reached the public. . . . The herbarium is rich in the ligneous plants of North America, and of China and Japan. Those from other countries are fairly well represented, and it is the purpose of those who now administer the Arboretum that this herbarium shall eventually provide material for the critical studies, begun in North America and continued in Japan and China, of the trees of all other countries. . . .

# 48

# ZOOLOGICAL GARDENS, A CRITICAL ESSAY

**Theodore Link**

*The American Naturalist*, 17: 1225–1229, 1883

*Theodore Link, renowned German-American architect, argues in the following excerpt that American and European zoos in the late nineteenth century were failing their own stated missions—to gain knowledge of the natural habits of animals—given the deplorable conditions maintained in animal enclosures. The statement "enclosures—not cages" encapsulates his philosophy. He urges a new design for zoological parks that would merge landscaping with necessary protective enclosures to reproduce as near as possible the animals' natural settings. Link also discusses some of the reasons for failure in captive breeding and makes some interesting recommendations.*

There is a great deal more in and about zoological gardens, I believe, than most people are apt to imagine; indeed, a lamentable ignorance or indifference concerning the true philosophy of the subject seems to prevail, generally and individually.

Hence zoological gardens are probably the most conservative institutions to be met with. One may visit them, year after year, and while everything around them abounds with the healthful changes of our progressive age, they offer but few evidences of a proper spirit towards scientific advancement. It is certainly strange that some of the shining lights in natural history have never raised an indignant cry against the obvious defects and blunders thrust upon our vision at every step. Only occasionally we meet with some traces of what might be termed semi-humanitarian attempts at transcendental zoology; but while these efforts in the right direction are hailed with genuine satisfaction by every student of animal life, it is a pity that they should be confined to specimens of comparatively small importance and but little market value, such as deer and other native herbivores. The lions and tigers, etc., the acknowledged monarchs and nobility of the animal kingdom, are yet allowed to languish in dungeons and vaults.

Indeed, the noble beasts of the desert appeal particularly to our sympathy from their iron-grated cells, and their perpetual, uneasy walking to and fro is intensely distressing to every compassionate beholder. The superficial observer may not recognize such niceties of distinction, but to the mind trained in utilitarian pursuits, they are important considerations in the attainment of the highest possible state of mental and physical comfort for all concerned.

Before proceeding any further, let us first consider the real mission of zoological gardens in contradistinction to menageries or "shows." I have before me the constitutions and by-laws of the different zoological societies in the United States, and according to the language of these documents, this mission is ostensibly "the study and dissemination of a knowledge of the natural habits of the animal kingdom." This definition does not seem to me to cover the ground, for the reason that there must first be the necessary *opportunities* before we can study; and *these* the disappointed zoologist seeks in vain. In fact, in this respect, the zoological garden of to-day affords but few more advantages than any of those traveling "shows" that come to us every season. By way of example, I have passed days and weeks by many a lion's cage in European and American gardens, intent upon study and observation; but with the exception of having, by numerous sketches, impressed upon my mind the *anatomical* peculiarities of these interesting animals, I cannot say that in other respects my perseverance has been rewarded to any great extent. I have simply found that an animal, as closely confined as most of them are in zoological gardens, retains *none* of its *natural habits*; it only exists—mere automaton; and even this existence is seemingly under protest. Therefore, this aforesaid "study and dissemination of a knowledge, etc.," is "a delusion and a snare". . . .

It may not matter very much for "show" purposes if most of the carnivores are partially blind, and painfully stiff along the spinal column, since the public at large does not easily notice these defects; but taken in evidence as symptoms of premature physical decay, and in connection with the fact that all closely confined animals last oft an average not even two-thirds of their natural life, these considerations gain in importance and become powerful arguments in favor of a rational reconstruction of the animals' places of abode.

There is an impression among "animal men" that some animals will not breed in captivity. It would be strange, indeed, if they did under the existing circumstances. Yet I am convinced that it is not the sense of captivity which restrains them from propagating, but rather the incongruity between their artificial habitation and their natural habits. The black bear is a striking example. You will find him in the so-called bear pit. Why bears should invariably be kept in *pits* has never been quite satisfactorily explained to me. The pit idea was, I believe, first introduced in the Jardin des Plantes at Paris, but the savant, who originated it, died long ago without entrusting to posterity the leading thought which moved him to this achievement. Since that day all "zoological" bears are consigned to pits.

This brings us face to face with one of the most lamentable features of zoological gardens, one which has retarded their scientific and artistic development more than anything else. I mean this servile, wholesale copying after "old masters" without any apparent discrimination. Yet there is scarcely a better field for the exercise of all the originality and versatility of a creative genius than a zoological garden.

Let us now, for the sake of demonstration, examine why Mr. and Mrs. Bruin refuse to turn their pit into a nursery. The free black bear has an economical way of spending the snowy season—he hybernates. As a captive, however, he is up and about all winter, because he does not recognize the paved recesses and vaults of the conventional pit as proper places for retirement. The loss of his good long snooze seems to unsettle him completely, and lead him into disastrous irregularities in his mode of life. For instance, instead of mating during the second fortnight of the October term, as is his wont at liberty, I have known him to copulate as early as the end of July. Now, since in the natural state the periods of gestation and hybernation fall together, the logical conclusion would be that with bears a periodical suspension of animation is not only beneficial but quite necessary to the development of vigorous offspring. That captivity does not produce absolute sterility in bears, is evinced by the fact that a female in the St. Louis gardens recently miscarried about a month after conception. Such knowledge, added to some native ingenuity, should enable us to construct enclosures for bears, where, in all probability, they would breed successfully.

The landscape features of a zoological garden claim the full attention of the designer. The aim here must be to unite beauty with use. On the whole, I would like to see the ruling principle advocated in these pages for the care of the animals, extended to their surroundings, by imitating, as near as the climate permits, the scenic characteristics of the homes of the various specimens confined; this would be a *pleasant* delusion to both visitor and animal. These widely different styles of scenery should, of course, be blended into a harmonious and well-balanced composition by a very guarded and gradual transition, thus affording delightful surprises at every step.

I believe I have, in a general way, indicated the road upon which such a state of perfection could be reached. The foremost condition will be the rational construction of *enclosures*—not cages—liberal in extent, and in strict accordance with the respective habits and instincts of the animals to be confined. *Cages* cannot well be avoided by traveling menageries; in zoological gardens they are inexcusable. . . .

# 49

# THE MAKING OF A ZOOLOGICAL-PARK MASTERPIECE

**William T. Hornaday**

*A Wild-Animal Round-Up.* New York: Charles Scribner's Sons, pp. 348–368, 1925

---

*William T. Hornaday, world-renowned conservationist and long-time director of the New York Zoological Park, discusses his philosophy for establishing and maintaining a successful municipal zoological park through the combined efforts of philanthropy and civic support. Hornaday's ideal is based on his design for the New York Zoological Park in 1925, which he built from the ground up under the direction of Henry Fairfield Osborn, noted paleontologist and president of the New York Zoological Society.*

---

Every large American city in which the masses are intelligent and proud desires a good zoological park; but for all that, a city can be very proud and boastful without having sufficient energy to make one. The New York Zoological Park is an object lesson of which many American cities may well take heed. It points the way by which every city, large or small, may create and maintain a zoological park of a size suitable to its population and resources. That end is to be attained by a judicious union of private effort, and municipal support at the expense of the taxpayers. New York has clearly demonstrated the fact that the taxpayer is willing to be taxed in a reasonable way for something that will furnish free and perpetual entertainment both to his wife and children and to himself, and at the same time be a credit to his home city. Give the taxpayer a fair chance, and he will support the zoological-park idea, willingly and even gladly.

The prime essentials to success in the creation and maintenance of a joint-effort zoological park are few in number, but the demand for them is inexorable. There must be (1) a free site in a public park; (2) permanence of control; (3) absolute freedom from "politics" and "graft" of every description; (4) wise but energetic management by a zoological society; (5) a general plan of development based on the best expert knowledge; (6) the merit system in choosing employees; (7) all collections must be furnished by the Society; (8) and all improvements and costs of maintenance must be paid for by the taxpayers. Finally, the park must be free on five days of the week, but two week-days should be pay-days, unless the population of the city concerned is under 500,000.

The European plan for the creation and maintenance of live-animal collections differs from the above, in several important particulars. Rarely does the municipality furnish a free site, or even free water. Usually the creating society is compelled to purchase ground, and it is usually selected as near as possible to the heart of the city concerned, so as to be very easily accessible. The result is a zoological garden, of from twenty to sixty acres, surrounded by dwellings, and sadly limited in space for the animals. A huge and costly restaurant and concert hall provides entertainment that draws society members, and strangers, also, many times each year; and there is no admission for non-members without the payment of a fee at the gate. There is no municipal support, and the very poor never see the inside of the establishment, because they cannot afford the price. I think it may truly be said that, even with occasional days of admission for the equivalent of ten cents, the zoological gardens of Europe chiefly benefit the rich and the well-to-do classes, to the exclusion of the very poor masses. New York City builds no public institutions from which the Man-Without-A-Quarter is shut out.

Through a combination of private generosity and municipal support, wise provisions of Nature and good management, imperial New York created in ten years time, and now presents to her people and to the world, an institution that three distinguished foreign critics have openly declared to be the foremost vivarium of the world. Those critics were Lord Northcliffe, Sir Harry Johnston, the African explorer, and Mr. F. G. Mak, a qualified expert on zoological gardens, and author of outdoor books. It is for the purpose of furnishing a bill of particulars that the writer has been drawn into writing at this time.

Every perfectly appointed zoological garden is a haven of rest to overwrought nerves, with the gentle and healthful stimulus of restful interest in new and different lines of thought. At ten o'clock in the forenoon, when the housekeeping of the day has been finished, and before the daily crowd has begun to arrive, a well-appointed zoological garden—with a good showing of flowers—comes as near to being an earthly paradise as the skill of man ever can produce within reach of the busy haunts of men. Of all the nerve-weary business and professional men of New York, how many are there who know that during the forenoon of every day in the year, and all day on pay-days, the Jungle Walk in the Zoological Park offers nerve balm of rare quality?

On Sunday afternoons, even the sight of the crowd is inspiring. It is good to see, at one sweep of the eyes over Baird Court and the region below it on the west, fully twenty thousand well-dressed people, one-third of whom are well-behaved and attractive children, busily enjoying the beauties of the place, and the band music. It is good to see, on every Monday morning in summer, from the records of the turnstiles, that on the previous day between 50,000 and 70,000 people have enjoyed the temples and shrines of Nature that God and man together have created for the benefit of the working millions in South Bronx Park.

The correct building of zoological gardens and parks is an exact science, just as much so as is astronomy, and the building of observatories. In formulating principles, and in working out the general design of the New York Zoological Park, we diligently studied nearly all existing zoological gardens, partly to ascertain what errors to avoid, and partly to acquire ideas of practical use. Knowing well what all the world has done previously, and having in hand the ideal site of all the world, is it then any cause for surprise that the last-built institution for living wild animals is the best one for the health and comfort of its occupants? The writer has been persuaded that it is no violation of the proprieties frankly to state, for the information of the American public, just wherein we think we have improved upon the work of our predecessors.

It must be counted as actually providential that the New York Zoological Society was founded in 1895 by Madison Grant; that it immediately attracted the support of Doctor Henry Fairfield Osborn; that for twelve years both those gentlemen dedicated an important portion of their lives to the Society's work; that South Bronx Park was acquired by New York City in 1884 and had remained an unspoiled wilderness; that the administration of Mayor Strong accepted in good faith the partnership proposal of the Zoological Society, and that every Mayor and Comptroller and Board of Estimate since 1897 has faithfully supported the Zoological Park undertaking.

The Zoological Park represents a perfectly harmonious joint effort on the part of a powerful philanthropic organization and the taxpayers of the City of New York. By reason of the first large financial sacrifice of the Zoological Society, justly regarded as a pledge of good faith, from the inception of the undertaking, the city government has relied absolutely upon the men and methods of that organization. In the plans and their execution, and in the selection of a permanent working force of 145 persons, there never has been even a hint of interference, or pressure, "political" or otherwise. In working out its own systems of economy in money, and in the saving of time, the Zoological Society has been permitted a degree of freedom of action that is probably without precedent in such matters. . . .

The eleven years of construction were years of intense, unremitting, and at times exhausting effort; but they produced a succession of triumphs. Even the "hard times" did not stay the Society's progress by more than a few months on our two final improvements for animals. We say to-day that the Park is practically "complete," because, for such an institution as ours, that term is accepted by all sensible persons in a comparative sense. We do not say that the Park is no longer open to improvement, or that further beautification is impossible. It is entirely possible that, during the next ten or twenty years, some other animal buildings may be found desirable. . . .

As the stranger passes through one of our turnstiles, there spreads before him the most magnificent composition of land and water that ever was dedicated to zoology. Its qualities were well summed up in one sentence by an English critic, F. G. Aflalo, when he described it as being "at once the envy and the despair of all European makers of zoological gardens."

If we could have modeled a site with our own hands, and said to the trees, the rocks, the valleys and the meadows—"Be thou here!"—I am sure we could not have produced the ideal result that the cunning hand of Nature fashioned for us in that marvelous site. Our total area is 264 acres; and it is all that we desire. . . .

First, then, of all our advantages we must place our marvelous grounds, which, for such purposes as ours, are in a class by themselves, and incomparable. Because of the tremendous advantage they gave us at the outset, it is hardly fair to compare our establishment with others that are handicapped by small grounds, on a dead level.

Second in line we place our open-air animal dens, aviaries and ranges, generally. Opportunities for outdoor life are available to about seven-tenths of all our vertebrates. It is only the serpents and a few other reptiles, some of the smaller monkeys, and about three-fourths of the birds in the Large-Bird House that in summer are not quartered outdoors. The open-air ranges for our hoofed and horned animals are from two to eight times as spacious as such animals can be allowed in even the largest Old-World zoological garden. . . .

The third feature in this enumeration is our House of Primates, unofficially called the Monkey House. It is notable because it is a house in which apes and monkeys can live long and happily, and because it is free from sickening monkey odors. The undenied success of our Monkey House is due to its new and practically perfect schemes of heating, ventilation, cage arrangements, lighting and sanitation. . . .

Our Lion House is the only lion house in the world that employs wire netting for cage fronts instead of heavy prison bars; that has balconies in its cages, and beautiful green tiles on its cage walls instead of whitewash or paint. It is also the only animal building that contains a studio for painters and sculptors. . . .

Let all those who are interested in making comparative studies of the zoological gardens and parks spend a few moments in considering our provisions for bison. The "zoological-park idea" is well illustrated by our herd of 16 American Bison, roaming over two spacious ranges with a total area of about 20 acres. There are some zoological gardens that as a whole contain only that area! When you see the breeding-herd—about 25 head of cows and "young stock"—either grazing contentedly on the knoll in the centre of the main range, or galloping toward the corrals at feeding-time, you are thrilled by the feeling that this is an adequate representation of the great American Bison as he lived and throve on his native plains. It was from this herd that the Zoological Society founded the Wichita National Bison Herd, as a contribution to the perpetual preservation of the species by our government. The nucleus herd was taken out of our ranges in October, 1907.

After all is said, it is not alone the fine buildings of brick and stone, or the fine corrals and ranges, that make a zoological establishment great or commanding. It is the living creatures themselves. I have seen some fine animal buildings that were poorly filled with animals, and others that were fully filled with poor *animals*. If the exhibits do not frequently compel visitors to exclaim, "How fine your animals look!" you may know that something is wrong. . . .

Our Elephant House and its adjacent yards represent high-water mark in wild-animal buildings. It is the crowning feature of the Zoological Park—spacious, beautifully designed, well built, perfectly lighted, heated and ventilated, and generously provided with open-air yards for all its animals. The keepers say that the elephants, rhinoceroses and hippo greatly enjoy their fine quarters, winter and summer; and where has New York City ever acquired elsewhere so fine a building for so little money as $157,000? But the finest Elephant and Rhinoceros House is of small interest unless the collection under its roof is also of commanding importance. We are extremely fortunate in being able to exhibit a collection of elephants and rhinoceroses in every way worthy of the new building. . . .

If we are to be fair to ourselves, we must call attention to the labelling of the Zoological Park collections, particularly the descriptive labels, the maps of distribution, the charts, keys and picture-labels in endless profusion, to inform and entertain the visitor, and render the collections of the utmost value.

On June 1, 1925, the total number of living specimens in the Park was 8,363, and they represented 1,079 species.

The tale is told. The Zoological Park and its collections must now speak for themselves. In 1924 they spoke to 2,572,050 visitors. The common people hear them gladly, but as yet the scientists of America, as a mass, do not seem to know that the New York Zoological Park has arrived.

# 50

# ADMINISTRATION OF THE PUBLIC AQUARIUM

## Charles H. Townsend

*Proceedings of the American Association of Museums*, 11: 106–113, 1917

*As natural history museum administrators began to professionalize in the early twentieth century, Charles H. Townsend argued for the inclusion of directors of aquaria (and zoos) into the newly formed American Association of Museums (1906). Townsend underscored the similarities between the institutions, particularly in function and mission, while downplaying the differences—mainly that aquaria acquired, cared for, and exhibited living organisms, as opposed to preserved specimens. As Director of the New York Aquarium, one of the earliest and largest of the world's metropolitan aquaria, Townsend faced and met many challenges in caring for living organisms. His experiences, elucidated in the following excerpted essay, are still relevant for today's aquaria and other collections of living animals.*

The public aquarium, with its exhibits of living aquatic animals, which has come into existence in many of the larger cities of the world during recent years, may well be classed as a museum of natural history, since it exists for the education and recreation of the people.

In some cities the aquarium is maintained as a feature of the zoological garden, while in others it is a separate institution. An aquarium is sometimes established in connection with the work of a biological laboratory. The aquarium in New York is maintained by the city, its entire management being in the hands of the New York Zoological Society which provides all exhibits from its private funds. The aquariums in Boston and Detroit are city institutions, controlled in each case by a department of parks. There are small aquariums in American and European cities which are conducted entirely as private business enterprises. There are probably not less than thirty aquariums in various parts of the world to which the public is admitted, exclusive of several very small ones connected with biological laboratories. . . .

The living collections of the larger public aquariums consist usually of both marine and freshwater animals. It is the character of the exhibits, whether of marine or freshwater forms, which determines the cost of maintenance in an institution of this kind. An aquarium with exhibition tanks requiring nothing more complicated than mere connections with a city water system, can obviously be operated at less expense than one requiring pumps for the circulation of sea water. It would be possible for any inland city not too remote from lakes or rivers to maintain excellent collections of freshwater fishes and amphibians at small cost as compared with marine exhibits requiring stored sea water. The flow of fresh water being practically automatic, the equipment for operation can be reduced to very simple terms. With the introduction of marine exhibits, the equipment, management, and cost of maintenance would be altogether different. . . .

The public aquarium is an institution which exists under the necessity of procuring its living exhibits directly from nature's sources of supply, the animal dealer having but a limited list of aquatic forms of life to offer. The collector for the aquarium must be prepared to go afield whenever specimens are needed for exhibition, and in northern latitudes enough collecting must be done in summer to provide against accidents that may occur in winter. Freshwater forms cannot be had when lakes and streams are frozen, and the winter season is unfavorable for the transportation of collections from the tropics.

Exchanges of specimens with other aquariums are helpful only in varying the exhibits, since each must do its own collecting, and aquariums in the United States are few in number and so located as to be under similar geographic limitations.

The collecting of aquatic animals involves their transportation in weighty tanks of their natural element, which moreover must be kept pure in transit. This compulsory procedure is always expensive. Experience has shown that the handling of fishes and other strictly aquatic creatures intended for exhibition alive can seldom be entrusted to fishermen. The untrained collector fails to appreciate the importance of taking those precautions in capture and shipment which are necessary for success. Aquatic animals must reach their destination not merely alive, but able to endure the conditions of captivity, always more or less unfavorable to wild creatures.

In addition to the necessity of guarding the water supply of an aquarium every hour of the twenty-four, and the daily care of the living exhibits, the staff of a large aquarium has the added duties of a public museum. There are crowds of visitors to be looked after, supplies to be purchased, machinery to be renewed, and a heavy correspondence with the public, the press, and with zoologists working in many lines. There are also labels, circulars, and pamphlets to be prepared. The duties of clerk, book-keeper, stenographer, etc., are, of course, similar to the duties of such employees in other museums.

In the matter of assistance to teachers of biology alone, the New York Aquarium has stocked small marine aquaria in more than three hundred school houses in Greater New York. The seashore collecting for this work goes on summer and winter.

Much of the work in an aquarium is not different from that of the average curator in a large museum of natural history, but we believe the duties of an aquarium curator to be more difficult, as all the exhibits in his department are living, moving creatures, to be catered for according to their special needs.

The feeding of as large a collection of fishes as that maintained at the New York Aquarium is a matter involving no small amount of labor and expense. The food consists of meat, fish, clams, sliced, chopped, or minced as may be necessary to Suit the size of the specimens. The whole collection is fed carefully in order that there may not be an unnecessary amount of food left unconsumed, which would have to be removed to prevent its affecting the water. Much of the food used in an aquarium is obtainable in the markets and consists largely of food fishes such as cod and herring. Preference is naturally given to the cheaper kinds of fish when the supply of such is abundant and when they are of such a character that they can be cut and prepared to advantage. Very little meat is required, but clams are used in great quantities. In addition to such foods as are procured in the markets, a considerable supply of natural live food is brought in from the adjacent bays and shores by the aquarium collector, consisting of minnows, shrimps, mussels, crabs, marine worms, small soft clams, and beach fleas or amphipods. More or less live food is always kept on hand in reserve tanks. In summer when live food is easily obtained, a great deal of it is used, being better for the collection in general, while in winter a larger amount of market food is necessarily consumed. . . .

The natural food of most fishes consists chiefly of other fishes, which may at times be their own young. Fishes in general are feeders on animal life, and their food supply includes practically the whole aquatic fauna. Fishes may be described as not only piscivorous and insectivorous, but as feeders on crustaceans, mollusks and worms. Plants do not constitute much of their food, although a few kinds feed freely on them, such as buffalo fishes, carps, and minnows. The young of many fishes nibble at tender plant shoots.

The New York Aquarium, apparently the largest institution of the kind and having about one hundred exhibition tanks, usually exhibits about two hundred kinds of fishes and other aquatic vertebrates. The total number of specimens in the building usually exceeds four thousand. The aquarium is open every day in the year, and its attendance for many years has exceeded five thousand persons a day. There are generally twenty-five or more employees on regular duty. The library, attached to the director's office, contains about one thousand volumes and is limited to works relating to fishes and aquatic life in general.

# REFERENCES

Adler, Cyrus. 1897. Goode memorial meeting. *Science* 5: 365–369.

Alexander, Edward P. 1983. *Museum masters.* Nashville, TN: American Association for State and Local History.

———. 1997. *The museum in America: Innovators and pioneers.* Walnut Creek, CA: AltaMira Press.

American Association of Museums. 1925. *Code of ethics for museum workers.* Washington, DC: American Association of Museums.

American Federation of Arts. 1952. *American art directory.* New York: American Federation of Arts.

Anonymous. 1945. Edward W. Forbes and Paul J. Sachs. *Burlington Magazine for Connoisseurs* 86: 152.

Argyle, A. W. 1974. The ancient university of Alexandria. *The Classical Journal* 69: 348–350.

"B., C. M." 1938. Retirement of Dr. Townsend from the directorship of the New York Aquarium. *Scientific Monthly* 46: 100–102.

Baker, Frank C. 1911. *The Lymnaeidae of North and Middle America, Recent and fossil.* Chicago: Chicago Academy of Sciences Special Publication.

———. 1928. *The fresh water Mollusca of Wisconsin.* Madison, WI: Academy of Sciences, Arts, and Letters, 2 vols.

Baker, Frank C., and Harley J. Van Cleave. 1945. *The molluscan family Planorbidae.* Urbana: University of Illinois Press.

Baker, Lee D. 1999. Columbia University's Franz Boas: He led the undoing of scientific racism. *Journal of Blacks in Higher Education* 22: 89–96.

Banks, Miriam A. 1937. Mr. Rowe: The Director of the Museum. *Bulletin of the Rhode Island School of Design* 25: 23–37.

Barbour, Edwin H. 1899. *Wells and windmills in Nebraska.* Washington, DC: Government Printing Office.

———. 1914. Mammalian fossils from Devil's Gulch. *University of Nebraska Studies* 14: 185–202.

———. 1916. The natural fuels of Nebraska. *Publications of Nebraska Geological Survey* 4: 337–346.

Benedict, Ruth. 1931. Professor Franz Boas, President of the American Association for the Advancement of Science. *Scientific Monthly* 32: 278–280.

———. 1943. Franz Boas. *Science* 97: 60–62.

Berrol, Selma C. 1970. Health education and welfare: The progressive impulse in the New York City Public Schools. *Elementary School Journal* 71: 134–142.

Black, R. D. Collison. 2004. Jevons, William Stanley (1835–1882). Oxford: Oxford University Press. Oxford Dictionary of National Biography Online. https://www.oxforddnb.com.library.unl.edu:80/view/article/14809 (accessed August 2, 2007).

Boas, Franz. 1911. *The mind of primitive man.* New York: Macmillan Company.

———. 1930. *The religion of the Kwakiutl Indians.* New York: Columbia University Press, 2 vols.

———. 1940. *Race, language and culture.* New York: Macmillan Company.

Bolton, Herbert. 1921–1922. *A monograph of the fossil insects of the British coal measures.* London: Palaeontolographical Society, 2 vols.

Britton, Nathaniel L. 1881. *Preliminary catalogue of the flora of New Jersey.* New Brunswick, NJ: Office of the Survey.

Britton, Nathaniel L., and Adisson Brown. 1896–1898. *Illustrated flora of northern United States and Canada and the British possessions.* New York: Charles Scribner's Sons, 3 vols.

Brower, Jacob V., Alfred J. Hill, Theodore H. Lewis, and Newton H. Winchell. 1911. *The aborigines of Minnesota.* St. Paul, MN: Pioneer Company.

Buchholz, J. T. 1945. William Trelease, 1857–1945. *Science* 101: 192–193.

Carlton, Grace. 1949. *Spade-work: The story of Thomas Greenwood.* London: Hutchinson & Company.

Chase, Evelyn. 1937. Mr. Rowe and the library. *Bulletin of the Rhode Island School of Design* 25: 21–23.

Clarke, John M. 1914. Newton Horace Winchell. *Science* 40: 127–130.

Clarke, Katherine. 1997. In search of the author of Strabo's *Geography. Journal of Roman Studies* 87: 92–110.

Cleevely, R. J. 2004. Gray, John Edward (1800–1875). Oxford: Oxford University Press. Oxford Dictionary of National Biography Online. https://www.oxforddnb.com.library.unl.edu:80/view/article/11344 (accessed November 2, 2007).

Cole, Fay-Cooper. 1931. George A. Dorsey. *American Anthropologist* 33: 413–414.

———. 1934. Frederick Starr. *American Anthropologist* 36: 271.

Cummings, Kevin. 2007. Frank Collins Baker. Illinois Natural History Survey. www.inhs.uiuc.edu/~ksc/Malacologists/BakerF.C.html (accessed July 16).

Cushman, Karen. 1984. Museum studies: The beginnings, 1900–1926. *Museum Studies Journal* 1: 8–18.

Dana, John Cotton. 1917a. *The new museum*. Woodstock, VT: Elm Tree Press.

———. 1917b. *The gloom of the museum*. Woodstock, VT: Elm Tree Press.

Davies, Helen. 2004. Robinson, Sir John Charles (1824–1913). Oxford: Oxford University Press. Oxford Dictionary of National Biography Online. https://www.oxforddnb.com.library.unl.edu:80/view/article/35795 (accessed July 25, 2007).

Dill, Homer R. 1952. The University Museum of Natural History. *The Palimpsest, State Historical Society of Iowa* 33: 33–64.

Dorsey, George A. 1925. *Why we behave like human beings*. New York: Harper & Brothers.

———. 1931. *Man's own show: Civilization*. New York: Harper & Brothers.

Encyclopedia Britannica. 2007. Varro, Marcus Terentius. Encyclopedia Britannica Online. https://search.eb.com.library.unl.edu:80/eb/article-9074866 (accessed March 13, 2007).

Epplett, Christopher. 2001. The capture of animals by the Roman military. *Greece & Rome* 48: 210–222.

Erickson, Robert F. 1999. Trelease, William. Oxford: Oxford University Press. American National Biography Online. https://www.anb.org.library.unl.edu:80/articles/13/13-01684.html (accessed May 21, 2007).

Erskine, Andrew. 1995. Culture and power in Ptolemaic Egypt: The Museum and Library of Alexandria. *Greece & Rome* 42: 38–48.

Farrington, Oliver C. 1897. Observations on Popocatepetl and Ixtaccihuatl. *Fieldiana: Geology* 1: 71–120.

———. 1903. *Gems and gem minerals*. Chicago: A. W. Mumford.

———. 1915. *Meteorites*. Chicago: Privately published.

Fink, Erin. 2005. Blooming purple and gold: The tradition of LSU's landscape. LSU Highlights. www.lsu.edu/highlights/051/landscape.html (accessed August 23, 2007).

Firth, Edith G., and Curtis Fahey. 2000. Scadding, Henry. Dictionary of Canadian Biography Online, University of Toronto/Université Laval. www.biographi.ca/EN/ShowBio.asp?BioId=41177 (accessed May 28, 2007).

Fletcher, Kate. 2004. Flower, Sir William Henry (1831–1899). Oxford: Oxford University Press. Oxford Dictionary of National Biography Online. https://www.oxforddnb.com.library.unl.edu:80/view/article/9766 (accessed July 29, 2007).

Flower, William H. 1883. On the characters and divisions of the family Delphinidae. *Proceedings of the Zoological Society of London* pp. 466–512.

———. 1891. *The horse: A study in natural history*. London: Kegan Paul, Trench, Trübner & Company.

Flower, William H., and Richard Lydekker. 1891. *An introduction to the study of mammals living and extinct.* London: A. and C. Black.

Forbes, Edward. 1841. *A history of British star-fishes, and other animals of the class Echinodermata.* London: J. Van Voorst.

Forbes, Edward, Sylvanus C. T. Hanley, and John C. Jay. 1848–1853. *A history of British Mollusca and their shells.* London: J. Van Voorst, 4 vols.

Gale, Robert L. 1999. Thwaites, Reuben Gold. Oxford: Oxford University Press. American National Biography Online. https://www.anb.org.library. unl.edu:80/articles/20/20-01014.html (accessed May 10, 2007).

Genoways, Hugh H., and Mary Anne Andrei. 1999. John Cotton Dana, Museum Master: An annotated bibliography of selected museum writings. In *The new museum: Selected writings by John Cotton Dana,* ed. W. A. Peniston, pp. 235–255. Newark, NJ, and Washington, DC: Newark Museum and American Association of Museums.

Gilman, Benjamin I. 1904. *Manual of Italian renaissance sculpture.* Boston: Riverside Press.

———. 1908. *Hopi songs.* Boston: Houghton Mifflin Company.

———. 1914. The day of the expert. *Science* 39: 771–779.

———. 1916. Museum fatigue. *Scientific Monthly* 2: 62–74.

———. 1920. *Museum of Fine Arts, Boston, 1870–1920.* Boston: Museum of Fine Arts.

Gilman, Roger. 1937. Mr. Rowe: The Director of the School. *Bulletin of the Rhode Island School of Design* 25: 18–20.

Giltinan, Katherine B. 2008. The early history of docents in American art museums: 1890–1930. *Museum History Journal* 1: 103–128.

Godkin, Edwin L. 1853. *The history of Hungary and the Magyars.* London: Cassell.

———. 1895. *Reflections and comments, 1865–1895.* New York: Charles Scribner's Sons.

———. 1896. *Problems of modern democracy.* New York: Scribner, 3rd edition.

Goode, George B. 1876. Catalog of the fishes of the Bermudas. *Bulletin of the United States National Museum* 5: 1–82.

———. 1888. *American fishes.* Boston: Estes and Lauriat.

Goode, George B, and Tarleton H. Bean. 1896. Oceanic ichthyology. *Special Bulletin of the United States National Museum* 2: 1–553.

Gray, John E. 1857. *Guide to the systematic distribution of Mollusca in the British Museum.* London: Trustees British Museum.

———. 1869. *Catalogue of the carnivorous, pachydermatous, and edentate Mammalia in the British Museum.* London: Trustees British Museum, 398 pp.

———. 1872. *Catalogue of ruminant Mammalia (Pecora, Linnæus) in the British Museum.* London: Trustees British Museum, 102 pp.

Greenwood, Thomas. 1886. *Free public libraries: Their organization, uses, and management.* London: Simpkin, Marshall & Company.

———. 1888. *Museums and art galleries.* London: Simpkin, Marshall & Company.

———. 1902. *Edward Edwards, the chief pioneer of municipal public libraries.* London: Scott & Greenwood.

Grinnell, Hilda W. 1940. Joseph Grinnell: 1877–1939. *The Condor* 42: 2–34.

Grinnell, Joseph. 1933. Review of the Recent mammal fauna of California. *University of California Publications of Zoology* 40: 71–234.

———. 1943. *Joseph Grinnell's philosophy of nature.* Freeport, NY: Books for Libraries Press.

Grinnell, Joseph, Joseph S. Dixon, and Jean M. Linsdale. 1937. *Fur-bearing mammals of California.* Berkeley and Los Angeles: University of California Press, 2 vols.

Grove, Richard. 1978. Pioneers in American museums: John Cotton Dana. Museum News 56(5): 32–39, 86–88.

Hagen, Hermann A. 1855–1860. *Monographie der termiten.* Berlin: Posen und Bromberg, 3 vols.

———. 1861. *Synopsis of the Neuroptera of North America.* Washington, DC: Smithsonian Institution.

———. 1862–1863. *Bibliotheca entomologica.* Leipzig: W. Engelmann, 2 vols.

Hall, E. Raymond. 1939. Joseph Grinnell (1877–1939). *Journal of Mammalogy* 20: 409–417.

Harvard College. 1957. *Fiftieth anniversary report of the class of 1907.* Cambridge, MA: Harvard College.

Harvard University. 2003. Classified documents: The Social Museum of Harvard University, 1903–1931. Harvard University, press release.

Hicks, Ellen C. 1978. The AAM after 72 years. *Museum News* 56(5): 44–48.

Hixson, Richard F. 1999. Godkin, Edwin Lawrence. Oxford: Oxford University Press. American National Biography Online. https://www.anb.org. library.unl.edu:80/articles/16/16-00633.html (accessed May 21, 2007).

Hornaday, William T. 1885. *Two years in the jungle.* New York: Charles Scribner's Sons.

———. 1887. The extermination of the American bison. *Report of the National Museum for 1887* pp. 367–548.

———. 1931. *Thirty years war for wild life.* Stamford, CT: Permanent Wild Life Protection Fund.

Horres, Alan D. 1984. Physiology Department, Medical University of South Carolina, Charleston, South Carolina. *The Physiologist* 27: 385–389.

Howe, Winifred E. 1948. An appreciation. *Metropolitan Museum of Art Bulletin*, new series 7: 49–50.

Howe, Winifred E., and Henry W. Kent. 1913. *A history of the Metropolitan Museum of Art with a chapter on the early institutions of art in New York*. New York: Gilliss Press.

———. 1946. *A history of the Metropolitan Museum of Art. Volume II. 1905–1941, Problems and principles in a period of expansion*. New York: Columbia University Press.

Hubbell, Harry M. 1935. Ptolemy's zoo. *The Classical Journal* 31: 68–76.

James, Edward T., Janet W. James, and Paul S. Boyer (eds.). 1971. *Notable American women, 1607–1950: A biographical dictionary*. Cambridge, MA: Harvard University Press.

Jenkins, David. 1994. Object lessons and ethnographic displays: Museum exhibitions and the making of American anthropology. *Comparative Studies in Society and History* 36: 242–270.

Jevons, William S. 1865. *The coal question*. London: Macmillan Company.

———. 1871. *The theory of political economy*. London: Macmillan Company.

———. 1874. *The principles of science: A treatise on logic and scientific method*. London: Macmillan Company, 2 vols.

Josten, C. H. 1960. Elias Ashmole, F.R.S. (1617–1692). *Notes and Records of the Royal Society of London* 15: 221–230.

King, John. 2007. When it comes to the tops in architecture, it's all about how it makes people feel. *San Francisco Chronicle* February 3, p. F-1.

Kohlstedt, Sally G. 1991. *The origins of natural science in America: The essays of George Brown Goode*. Washington, DC: Smithsonian Institution Press.

———. 1999a. Goode, George Brown. Oxford: Oxford University Press. American National Biography Online. https://www.anb.org.library.unl.edu:80/articles/13/13-00626.html (accessed August 11, 2007).

———. 1999b. Winchell, Newton Horace. Oxford: Oxford University Press. American National Biography Online. https://www.anb.org.library.unl.edu:80/articles/13/13-01836.html (accessed July 28, 2007).

Krefft, Johann L. G. 1869. *The snakes of Australia*. Sydney, Australia: T. Richards.

———. 1871. *The mammals of Australia*. Sydney, Australia: T. Richards.

———. 1873. *Catalogue of the minerals and rocks in the collection of the Australian Museum*. Sydney, Australia: T. Richards.

Langley, Samuel P. 1897. George Brown Goode. *Science* 5: 369–372.

Lee, Paula Y. 1997. The Musaeum of Alexandria and the formation of the "Muséum" in eighteenth-century France. *Art Bulletin* 79: 385–412.

Link, Theodore C., and Bertram A. Atwater. 1895. *The St. Louis Union Station: A monograph*. St. Louis, MO: National Chemigraph Company.

Long, Grace D. C. 1999. Peabody, Francis Greenwood. Oxford: Oxford University Press. American National Biography Online. https://www.anb.org.library.unl.edu:80/articles/08/08-01154.html (accessed May 21, 2007).

Lowie, Robert H. 1943. Franz Boas, anthropologist. *Scientific Monthly* 56: 182–184.

———. 1944. Franz Boas (1858–1942). *Journal of American Folklore* 57: 59–64.

Lucas, Frederic A. 1901. *Animals of the past.* New York: McClure, Phillips & Company.

———. 1921. *The story of museum groups.* New York: American Museum of Natural History.

Lucas, Frederic A., and Henry F. Osborn. 1933. *Fifty years of museum work.* New York: American Museum of Natural History.

Manning, Martin J. 1999. Dana, John Cotton. Oxford: Oxford University Press. American National Biography Online. https://www.anb.org.library. unl.edu:80/articles/20/20-00253.html (accessed July 19, 2007).

Marankou, Anna G. 2000. *The Consul Luigi Palma di Cesnola, 1832–1904: Life and deeds.* Nicosia, Cyprus: Cultural Center of the Popular Bank Group.

McFadden, Elizabeth. 1971. *The glitter & the gold.* New York: Dial Press.

Meritt, Lucy S. 1984. *History of the American School of Classical Studies at Athens, 1939–1980.* Princeton, NJ: American School of Classical Studies at Athens.

Miller, Lillian B. 1983–2000. *The selected papers of Charles Willson Peale and his family.* New Haven, CT: National Portrait Gallery, Smithsonian Institution, by Yale University Press, 6 vols.

———. 1999. Peale, Charles Willson. Oxford: Oxford University Press. American National Biography Online. https://www.anb.org.library.unl. edu:80/articles/17/17-00654.html (accessed August 1, 2007).

Mills, Eric L. 2004. Forbes, Edward (1815–1854). Oxford: Oxford University Press. Oxford Dictionary of National Biography Online. https://www. oxforddnb.com.library.unl.edu:80/view/article/9824 (accessed May 15, 2007).

Morse, Edward S. 1873. *On the systematic position of the Brachiopoda.* Boston: Press of A. A. Kingman.

———. 1886. *Japanese homes and their surroundings.* Salem, MA: Peabody Academy of Science.

———. 1917. *Japan day by day.* New York: Houghton Mifflin Company, 2 vols.

Nutting, Charles C. 1917. Museum methods. *Transactions of the American Microscopical Society* 36: 13–19.

Obituary. 1899a. Sir William Flower. *Science* 10: 90–91.

———. 1899b. Sir William Flower, K.C.B., F.R.S. *The Geographical Journal* 14: 217.

———. 1933a. Benjamin I. Gilman dies in Boston at 81. *New York Times* March 19, p. 32.

Obituary. 1933b. O. C. Farrington, Field Museum curator, dies. *Chicago Daily Tribune* November 3, p. 30.

———. 1966. Winifred E. Howe. *New York Times* August 16, p. 39.

Osborn, Henry F. 1897. Goode as a naturalist. *Science* 373–378.

Parry, Graham. 2004. Wood, Anthony (1632–1695). Oxford: Oxford University Press. Oxford Dictionary of National Biography Online. htt://0-www.oxforddnb.com.library.unl.edu:80/view/article/29864 (accessed August 12, 2007).

Peabody, Francis G. 1909. *The approach to the social question: An introduction to the study of social ethics.* New York: Macmillan Company.

———. 1914. *The Christian life in the modern world.* New York: Macmillan Company.

———. 1927. *Reminiscences of present-day saints.* Boston: Houghton Mifflin Company.

Peniston, William A. (ed.). 1999. *The new museum: Selected writings by John Cotton Dana.* Newark, NJ, and Washington, DC: Newark Museum and American Association of Museums.

Perkins, Agnes F. (ed.). 1910. *Vocations for the trained woman.* Boston: Women's Educational and Industrial Union.

Prichard, R. J. 1981. *Thomas Greenwood: Public library enthusiast.* Biggleswade, England: Clover Publications.

Pryor, Sara A. 1903. *The mother of Washington and her times.* New York: Macmillan Company.

———. 1907. *The birth of the nation, Jamestown, 1607.* New York: Macmillan Company.

———. 1911. *The colonel's story.* New York: Macmillan Company.

Quatrefages de Bréau, Armand de, and Frederick Starr. 1895. *The pygmies.* New York: D. Appleton & Company.

Radcliffe College Alumnae Association. 1931. *Radcliffe College Alumnae Directory.* Cambridge, MA: Radcliffe College Alumnae Association.

Rea, Paul M. 1910. *A directory of American museums of art, history, and science.* Buffalo, NY: Buffalo Society of Natural History.

———. 1930. What are museums for? *Journal of Adult Education* 2: 265–271.

———. 1932. *The museum and the community.* Lancaster, PA: Science Press.

Richards, G. C. 1941. Strabo: The Anatolian who failed of Roman recognition. *Greece & Rome* 10: 79–90.

Robinson, Sir John C. 1862a. *Italian sculpture of the Middle Ages and period of the revival of art.* London: Chapman and Hall.

———. 1862b. *Catalogue of the special exhibition of works of art of the mediæval, Renaissance, and more recent periods, on loan at the South Kensington Museum, June 1862.* London: George Eyre and William Spottiswoode.

Robinson, Sir John C. 1870. *A critical account of the drawings by Michel Angelo and Raffaelo in the University Galleries, Oxford*. Oxford: Clarendon Press.

Sanders, Albert E., and William D. Anderson. 1999. *Natural history investigations in South Carolina: From colonial times to the present*. Columbia, SC: University of South Carolina Press.

Sargent, Charles S. 1894. *Forest flora of Japan*. Boston: Houghton Mifflin Company.

Sargent, Charles S., and Charles E. Faxon. 1891–1902. *Silva of North America*. Boston: Houghton Mifflin Company, 14 vols.

Sargent, Charles S., Charles E. Faxon, and Mary W. Gill. 1905. *Manual of North American trees*. Boston: Houghton Mifflin Company.

Scadding, Henry. 1873. *Toronto of old*. Toronto, Canada: Adams Stevenson & Company.

Scales, Laura W. L. 1922. *Boys of the ages, their dreams and their crafts*. Boston: Ginn & Company.

Schrimper, George D. 1992. The University of Iowa Museum of Natural History: An historical perspective. *Journal of the Iowa Academy of Science* 99: 86–97.

Schwartz, George M. 2004. Newton Horace Winchell: A tribute. Newton Horace Winchell School of Earth Sciences, Department of Geology and Geophysics, University of Minnesota. www.geo.umn.edu/Winchell.html (accessed July 28, 2007).

Sellers, Charles C. 1980a. *Mr. Peale's museum: Charles Willson Peale and the first popular museum of natural science and art*. New York: W. W. Norton & Company.

———. 1980b. Peale's Museum and "The New Museum Idea." *Proceedings of the American Philosophical Society* 124: 25–34.

Sihler, E. G. 1923. Strabo of Amaseia: His personality and his works. *American Journal of Philology* 44: 124–144.

Siple, Ella S. 1927. The Fogg Museum of Art at Harvard. *Burlington Magazine for Connoisseurs* 50: 306–307, 309–311, 314–315.

Slack, Nancy G. 1999. Britton, Nathaniel Lord. Oxford: Oxford University Press. American National Biography Online. https://www.anb.org.library.unl.edu:80/articles/13/13-00197.html (accessed June 3, 2007).

Smith, Charles H. 2004. Wallace, Alfred Russel (1823–1913). Oxford: Oxford University Press. Oxford Dictionary of National Biography Online. https://www.oxforddnb.com.library.unl.edu:80/view/article/36700 (accessed July 16, 2007).

Smocovitis, Vassiliki Betty. 1999. Sargent, Charles Sprague. Oxford: Oxford University Press. American National Biography Online. https://www.anb.org.library.unl.edu:80/articles/13/13-01456.html (accessed May 21, 2007).

Sorensen, Lee. 2007. Forbes, Edward Waldo. Dictionary of Art Historians. www.dictionaryofarthistorians.org/ (accessed May 7, 2007).

Starr, Frederick. 1908. *In Indian Mexico*. Chicago: Forbes & Company.

———. 1918. *Korean Buddhism*. Boston: Marshall Jones Company.

———. 1922. *Catalogue of an exhibition of objects relating to Mount Fuji*. Chicago: Geographic Society of Chicago.

Starr, Raymond J. 1992. Silvia's deer (Vergil, *Aeneid* 7: 479–502): Game parks and Roman law. *American Journal of Philology* 113: 435–439.

Sterling, Keir B. 1999. Hagen, Hermann August. Oxford: Oxford University Press. American National Biography Online. https://www.anb.org.library. unl.edu:80/articles/13/13-00674.html (accessed May 24, 2007).

Thomas, Phillip D. 1999. Hornaday, William Temple. Oxford: Oxford University Press. American National Biography Online. https://www.anb.org. library.unl.edu:80/articles/13/13-00789.html (accessed July 29, 2007).

Thwaites, Reuben G. 1902. *Daniel Boone*. New York: D. Appleton Company.

———. 1905. *France in America, 1497–1763*. New York: Harper & Bros.

———. 1908. *Wisconsin*. Boston: Houghton Mifflin Company.

Townsend, Charles H. 1925. The Galapagos tortoises in their relation to the whaling industry. *Zoologica* 4: 55–135.

———. 1928. *The public aquarium: Its construction, equipment, and management*. Washington, DC: Department of Commerce, Bureau of Fisheries.

———. 1935. The distribution of certain whales as shown by logbook records of American whaleships. *Zoologica* 19: 1–50.

Trelease, William. 1913. Agave in the West Indies. *Memoirs of the National Academy of Science* 11: 1–298.

———. 1917. *Plant materials of decorative gardening*. Urbana, IL: Privately published.

———. 1924. The American oaks. *Memoirs of the National Academy of Science* 20: 1–255.

Van Cleave, Harley J. 1942. Obituary: Frank Collins Baker. *Science* 95: 568.

Van Rensselaer, Mariana A. 1888. *Henry Hobson Richardson, and his works*. Boston and New York: Houghton Mifflin Company.

———. 1893. *Art out-of-doors: Hints on good taste in gardening*. New York: C. Scribner's Sons.

———. 1909. *History of the city of New York in the seventeenth century*. New York: Macmillian Company, 2 vols.

Wallace, Alfred R. 1869. *The Malay Archipelago*. New York: Harper & Bros.

———. 1876. *The geographical distribution of animals*. London: Macmillan and Company, 2 vols.

———. 1889. *Darwinism: An exposition of the theory of natural selection*. London: Macmillan and Company.

———. 1905. *My life*. New York: Dodd, Mead & Company, 2 vols.

Waterston, C. D., and A. Macmillan Shearer. 2006. Biographical index of former Fellows of the Royal Society of Edinburgh, 1783–2002. Part I: A-J. Royal Society of Edinburgh, Edinburgh, Scotland, 496 pp. www.royalsoced. org.uk/archive/index.htm (accessed July 21, 2007).

Wayman, Dorothy G. 1942. *Edward Sylvester Morse: A biography.* Cambridge, MA: Harvard University Press.

Whitley, G. P., and Mary Rutledge. 2006. Krefft, Johann Ludwig Gerard (Louis) (1830–1881). Australian Dictionary of Biography Online, Australian National University. www.adb.online.anu.edu.ay/biogs/A050051b. htm (accessed July 24, 2007).

Whitmore, Elizabeth M. 1925. *John Taylor Arms: Notes on the development of an American etcher.* New York: privately printed.

———. 1927. *Prints for the layman: Their use and enjoyment in the average home.* Boston: C. E. Goodspeed and Company.

Who's Who. 1942. *Who was who in America, 1897–1942.* Chicago: A. N. Marquis Company, vol. 1.

———. 1950. *Who was who in America, 1943–1950.* Chicago: A. N. Marquis Company, vol. 2.

———. 1960. *Who was who in America, 1951–1960.* Chicago: A. N. Marquis Company, vol. 3.

———. 1967. *Who was who in America: Historical volume, 1607–1896.* Chicago: A. N. Marquis Company, revised edition.

Winchell, Alexander N., and Newton H. Winchell. 1909. *Elements of optical mineralogy.* New York: D. Van Nostrand.

Winchell, Newton H. 1875. *Geological report on the Black Hills.* Washington, DC: Government Printing Office.

Winchell, Newton H., Warren Upham, Leo Lesquereux, and Edward O. Ulrich. 1884–1901. *The geology of Minnesota.* Minneapolis, MN: Johnson, Smith & Harrison, 6 vols.

Wisconsin Historical Society. 2007. Thwaites, Reuben Gold 1853–1913. Dictionary of Wisconsin History. www.wisconsinhistory.org/dictionary/ (accessed May 10, 2007).

Wood, Anthony à. 1691–1692. *Athenae Oxonienses.* London: Tho. Bennet, 2 vols.

Wood, Anthony à, and John Gutch. 1674 [1786–1790]. *History and antiquities of the University of Oxford.* Oxford: Clarendon Press, 2 vols.

Wood, John G. 1851. *The illustrated natural history.* London: George Routledge & Company.

Woodward, B. B. 2004. Wood, John George (1827–1889). Oxford: Oxford University Press. Oxford Dictionary of National Biography Online. https://www.oxforddnb.com.library.unl.edu:80/view/article/29883 (accessed June 1, 2007).

# ABOUT THE AUTHORS

**Frank Collins Baker** (1867–1942) was born in Warren, Rhode Island. He was educated at Brown University, the Philadelphia Academy of Natural Sciences, and finally received his B.S. from Chicago School of Science in 1896. After working for Ward's Natural Science Establishment in Rochester, New York, he received an offer to be curator in the Chicago Academy of Science, where he worked from 1894 to 1915. He worked for three years in College of Forestry at Syracuse University (1915–1917) and then became a curator in the University of Illinois Museum of Natural History from 1917 until his retirement in 1939. He was president of the American Malacological Union in 1942. Baker's bibliography contains 360 titles (Cummings 2007; Van Cleave 1942; Who's Who 1950: 38). Among his most important works are Baker (1911, 1928) and Baker and Van Cleave (1945).

**Erwin H. Barbour** (1856–1947) was born near Oxford, Ohio. He did his undergraduate work at Miami University and received his Ph.D. from Yale University in 1882. From 1882 to 1888 he worked as an assistant paleontologist with the United States Geological Survey and then taught for two years at Grinnell College in Iowa. He came to the University of Nebraska in Lincoln in 1891, where his career continued until his death. He had numerous achievements at the university, including forming the University of Nebraska State Museum, serving as its director, and overseeing the construction of two homes for the museum with the most recent, Morrill Hall, still housing the museum. He formed the Nebraska Geological Survey and served as the State Geologist. His research was primarily focused on fossil mammals, with a particular interest in fossil elephants. He was the Nebraska representative to Columbian Exposition in Chicago in 1893, superintendent of mining, forestry, and university education at the Trans-Mississippi in Omaha 1897–1898, and superintendent of education, mining, and resources at the Louisiana Purchase Exposition in St. Louis in 1903. Besides publishing in paleontology (see, for example, Barbour 1914), he also published on a wide variety of topics, including windmill construction (Barbour 1899) and natural resources (Barbour 1916).

**Franz Boas** (1858–1942) is considered by many people to be the father of modern American anthropology. He was born (1858) and educated in Germany, receiving his doctoral degree from the University of Kiel in 1881. While working at the Royal Ethnographical Museum in Berlin, he began ethnographic studies in Canada of the Central Eskimos and Pacific Coast Indians. He came to the United States in 1888, working at Clark University until 1892. He became the chief assistant in anthropology for the Chicago World's Fair in 1893, and at the close of the fair, he took charge of moving much of the collection to the new Field Columbia Museum where he was named a curator. In 1896, he moved to the American Museum of Natural History to work as the Assistant Curator of Ethnology and Somatology. When he moved to New York, he also took a position at Columbia University, becoming a professor of anthropology in 1899, where he worked until his death in 1942. He left his employment at the American Museum of Natural History in 1905 (Benedict 1943; Lowie 1943, 1944). He made major scientific contributions through his "research in ethnology, linguistics, and in problems of race and of human growth" (Benedict 1943). In recognition of his contribution, he received many honors, notably being elected to National Academy of Science in 1900 and serving as president of American Association for the Advancement of Science in 1931 (Benedict 1931). He work diligently for racial understanding and is credited with the undoing of scientific racism (Baker 1999). Some of his significant contributions include Boas (1911, 1930, 1940).

**Herbert Bolton** (1863–1936) was born in Lancashire, England. He attended the Royal College of Science, London, and Owen's College, Manchester, completing a M.Sc. He was trained in paleontology and geology and took his first positions at the Manchester Museum, serving as assistant keeper from 1890 to 1898 and curator from 1898 to 1911. He moved to become Director of the Bristol Museum and Art Gallery from 1911 to 1930, while he simultaneously held the position of Reader in paleontology at Bristol University (Waterston and Shearer 2006). Bolton published extensively in paleontology, particularly on fossil insects, where one of his major contributions was the two-volume work *A Monograph of the Fossil Insects of the British Coal Measures* (1921–1922).

**Nathaniel Lord Britton** (1859–1934) was born in Staten Island, New York, and educated at Columbia College in New York. He first received an E.M. degree (1879) as an engineer of mines and then a Ph.D. in 1881. For five years Britton worked for the Geological Survey of New Jersey, publishing the *Preliminary Catalogue of the Flora of New Jersey* (1881). He became instructor of botany and geology in 1887 and then in 1891 professor of botany at Columbia College. In 1896, he became the first director of the developing New York Botanical Gardens, a position that he held until 1929. One of his major publications was a three-volume contribution, *Illustrated Flora of Northern United States and Canada and the British Possessions* (Britton and Brown 1896–1898). Britton was elected a member of the National Academy of Sciences in 1914 and president of the Botanical Society of America in 1898 and 1920. The botanical garden journal *Brittonia* was named in his honor (Slack 1999).

**Luigi Palma di Cesnola** (1832–1904) is one of the most colorful and controversial figures in late nineteenth-century museology in America. He was born into a minor noble family in the Piedmont (Piemonte) region of northwestern Italy in 1832. He served with the British in the Crimean War before emigrating to the United States in 1860. During the Civil War, he served with distinction as the Colonel of the 4th New York Cavalry. He was captured at the Battle of Aldie, Virginia, on June 17, 1863, and held for several months in Libby Prison in Richmond. After being exchanged, he returned to his old command, serving in the opening of Grant's overland campaign in 1864 and was then transferred to the Shenandoah Valley Campaign. Following the war he was appointed Consul to Cyprus, and during the voyage he assumed the title of General, which he used during the remainder of his life, saying that President Lincoln had promised him the promotion the day before his assassination. In Cyprus, he became involved in collecting antiquities. His collecting methods and export of materials were heavily criticized even at the time. The majority of the collection was sold to the developing Metropolitan Museum of Art in New York, and in 1879 Cesnola was elected the first director of the museum, a position that he held until his death in 1904 (Marankou 2000; McFadden 1971).

**John Cotton Dana** (1856–1929) was born in Woodstock, Vermont. Dana was educated at Dartmouth College, graduating in 1878. He passed the bar exam in Colorado and New York and held a variety of jobs including surveying, practicing law, editing a newspaper, preaching for a Unitarian church, and working as a construction superintendent. In 1889, he was appointed the first librarian for the Denver School District, which later became the Denver Public Library. Dana was highly successful with the library, instituting creative ideas such as open stacks and starting a loan collection of photographs and museum objects. Dana went to the City Library of Springfield, Massachusetts, in 1898, and to the Free Public Library of Newark, New Jersey, in 1902. He made the library widely known and highly popular in Newark, and in 1909 he founded the Newark Museum Association, which led to the development of another popular institution, the Newark Museum (Grove 1978; Manning 1999). Alexander (1983) placed Dana among his "museum masters." Dana's writings are scattered in small, obscure publications, but there is a recent bibliography of his work (Genoways and Andrei 1999) and a reprinting of most of his important works (Peniston 1999). The two most well-known of his books on museums are Dana (1917a, 1917b).

**Homer R. Dill** (1877–1959) trained in taxidermy work with William Temple Hornaday and served as the curator of the Maine State Museum from 1901–1905 (Schrimper 1992). In 1906, he came to the University of Iowa Museum of Natural History, taking up the positions of taxidermist and assistant professor of zoology and serving under C. C. Nutting, director of the museum. Dill led at least nine major expeditions collecting in Hawaii, Mexico, and several states within the mainland United States. His most famous work was probably the expedition to Laysan Island and the resulting Laysan Island cyclorama at the museum (Nutting 1917). Dill is credited with beginning in 1907 at the University of Iowa the oldest continuously-operating museum training program in the United States (Cushman 1984; Dill 1952; Schrimper 1992). The following year, Dill was made Director of Exhibits and Vertebrates, and from 1926 until 1949 he served as director of the museum (Dill 1952; Schrimper 1992).

**George A. Dorsey** (1868–1931) was born in Hebron, Ohio, in 1868, took undergraduate degrees at Denison (1888) and Harvard (1890), and received his Ph.D. from Harvard University in 1894. While still in graduate school, he traveled to South America to gather ethnological collections for the Chicago World's Fair in 1893, and in 1896 he became the curator of anthropology at the Field Museum of Natural History, where he remained until 1915. He conducted field studies all over the world but is best known for his research on the Plains Indian tribes such as the Arapaho, Arikara, Cheyenne, Osage, Pawnee, and Ponca. He became a major supporter of President Woodrow Wilson in the 1916 election and was named the Assistant Naval Attaché to Lisbon during World War I. After the war, he served as a newspaper correspondent and tried popular writing. His writing career was slow to develop, but in 1925 he had considerable success with *Why We Behave Like Human Beings*. At his death in 1931, he had just completed a volume titled *Civilization* (Cole 1931; Who's Who 1942: 333).

**Oliver C. Farrington** (1864–1933) was born in Brewer, Maine, and was educated at the University of Maine (B.S. 1881; M.S. 1888) and Yale University (Ph.D. 1891). After graduation, he worked as an assistant at the United States National Museum in 1893 and the following year became the first chair of the Department of Geology in the Field Museum of Natural History, a position he held until his death. He published widely in geology, including such papers as Farrington (1897, 1903), but he was most widely known for his work on meteorites, and his work *Meteorites* (1915) is still a classic study. He served as president of the American Association of Museums from 1914 to 1916 (Obituary 1933b; Who's Who 1942: 387).

**Sir William Henry Flower** (1831–1899) was born in Stratford upon Avon, England. He studied at University College London, Middlesex Hospital, and finally graduated with a Bachelor of Medicine degree from London University in 1851. He practiced surgery for several years, including spending 1854 serving in the Crimean War, before being appointed curator of the surgical museum of Middlesex Hospital and in 1858 adding a lectureship in comparative anatomy. In 1861, he moved to the position of the conservator of the Hunterian Museum of the Royal College of Surgeons, and here he added the position of Hunterian chair of comparative anatomy and physiology in 1870. Finally, in 1884, he became the director of the new British Museum (Natural History) in South Kensington. Flower was elected to the Royal Society (1864), president of the Anthropological Institute (1883–1885), president of the British Association for the Advancement of Science (1889), president of the Museum Association (1893), and receiving knighthood (1892) (Fletcher 2004; Obituary 1899a, 1899b). Among his important publications are Flower (1883, 1891) and Flower and Lydekker (1891).

**Edward Forbes** (pronounced "fourbees") (1815–1854) was born on the Isle of Man. In 1831, he went to the University of Edinburgh to study medicine but switched to the study of natural history. He made contributions in a wide range of natural history topic including living and fossil invertebrates, biogeography, and geology, becoming one of the most prominent naturalists of the pre-Darwinian period. He moved to London, taking a series of positions including chair of botany at King's College (1842), curator of the collections of the Geological Societies collections (1843), paleontologist of the Geological Survey of Great Britain (1844), and finally lecturer in natural history for the survey's School of Mines with the Museum of Practical Geology (1851). In early 1854, Forbes realized his dream, moving to the chair of natural history at the University of Edinburgh, but he unexpectedly died on November 18. Many of Forbes' philosophical works were quite abstract even in his own day, and they were quickly pushed aside with the publication of the *Origin of Species* (Mills 2004). Among Forbes' more important works on the taxonomy of invertebrates were Forbes (1841) and Forbes, Hanley, and Jay (1848–1853).

**Edward Waldo Forbes** (1873–1969) was born into a prominent Boston family. His father organized Bell Telephone Company with Alexander Graham Bell, and his mother was the daughter of Ralph Waldo Emerson. He attended Harvard University and traveled in Europe following his graduation in 1895. Forbes was appointed to the Board of Trustees of the Museum of Fine Arts, Boston, in 1903, and the following year he joined the visiting committee of the Fogg Art Museum at Harvard University. In 1909, he was appointed the second director of the Fogg and immediately recruited his fellow Harvard graduate and lifelong friend, Paul J. Sachs, to be the assistant director of the museum. They held these positions until December 1, 1944, when they both resigned and retired (Anonymous 1945). During their tenure at museum, they built the collections and endowment for the museum, instituted a museum training program (Alexander 1997), and in 1928 developed a Department of Technical Studies, the first program for scientific research in conservation (Siple 1927; Sorensen 2007).

**Anna Billings Gallup** (1872–1956) was born in Ledyard, Connecticut. She graduated from the Connecticut State Normal School in 1893. After four years of teaching biology, she entered MIT and in 1901 received a B.S. degree. In 1902, she became assistant curator of the Brooklyn Children's Museum—a division of the Brooklyn Institute of Arts and Sciences, now considered the first children's museum in the world. She was promoted to curator in 1904 and served as curator-in-chief from 1924 until she retired in 1937. Gallup worked tirelessly for her own institution but also championed the children's museum movement around the world. Gallup received the gold medal from National Institute of Social Sciences for her "distinguished service to humanity" and the William Hornaday Memorial Award for service and leadership in the junior museum field in 1930 (Who's Who 1960: 310). Edward Alexander (1997) listed Gallup among the "Innovators and Pioneers" of museums in America.

**Benjamin Ives Gilman** (1852–1933) was born in New York and studied at Williams College, graduating in 1872. He attended a series of graduate programs, focusing primarily in psychology, before serving as a lecturer at Princeton, Columbia, and Harvard in 1890 and 1891 and as an instructor in psychology at Clark University the following year. In 1893, Gilman became secretary of the Museum of Fine Arts, Boston, a position that he held until his retirement in 1925. Gilman received an honorary M.A. from Johns Hopkins University in 1902, and he served as president of the American Association of Museums from 1913 to 1914 (Obituary 1933a; Who's Who 1942: 458–459). Gilman wrote on museums but also in psychology and Native American and Asian music. Besides the book from which our selection was taken, he also wrote Gilman (1904, 1908, 1920). Students of museology also will be interested in reading Gilman's AAM presidential address (1914) and the article (1916).

**Edwin Lawrence Godkin** (1831–1902) was born near Dublin, Ireland, of English heritage. He graduated from Queen's College in Belfast in 1851. In 1853, he went to the Crimean War as the special correspondent for the London *Daily News*. Following the war, he returned to Ireland, becoming the editor of the *Northern Whig* in Belfast, but in late in 1856 he moved to New York. He studied law, passing the bar in 1858, and traveled extensively in the United States and Europe writing for the *Daily News*. In 1862 he returned to New York, working as the editor of the *Sanitary Commission Bulletin* and writing for the *New York Times* and *North American Review*. In 1865, Godkin became the editor-in-chief for the new newspaper *The Nation*, and by the end of the first year Godkin and two friends had taken ownership of *The Nation*, which they held until 1881, when they sold to the New York *Evening Post*. He served as the editor of the *Evening Post* until his retirement in 1900. In his position as editor, Godkin worked for many liberal causes to improve the lives of the poor and working classes (Hixson 1999; Who's Who 1942: 463). Some of his ideas can be found in Godkin (1853, 1895, 1896).

**George Brown Goode** (1851–1896) was born in New Albany, Indiana. He was one of the most innovative museum thinkers in the late nineteenth century. Kohlstedt described Goode "as an ichthyologist, genealogist, historian, curator, and museum administrator" (Kohlstedt 1991). Goode graduated from Wesleyan University in 1866 and then attended Harvard University, where he worked briefly under Louis Agassiz before returning to Wesleyan to be in charge of the new natural history museum. In 1877, Goode moved to the Smithsonian Institution as curator and then as assistant director of the U. S. National Museum. He remained in this position until he was promoted to director after the death of Spencer Fullerton Baird in 1887. He held this position until his untimely death at age 45 on September 6, 1896 (Alder 1897; Kohlstedt 1999a; Langley 1897; Osborn 1897). Alexander (1983) placed Goode among his "museum masters." Among his major scientific contributions were Goode (1876, 1888) and Goode and Bean (1896). Kohlstedt (1991) has edited a volume of writings by Goode that includes articles on the history of American science and education and two on museums.

**John Edward Gray** (1800–1875) was born in Staffordshire, England, but grew up in London. He had no formal education but was taught to read and write by his parents. He received training in pharmacology and chemistry and attended lectures in medicine. He found his true calling when he worked with W. E. Leach at the British Museum, although he failed to obtain a position on his first attempt. He took a temporary position at the British Museum in 1824, then moved to assistant keeper in zoology in 1837 and keeper in 1840. His first interests were in molluscans and botany, and he returned to them from time to time, but most of his work was on vertebrates, especially mammals. According to one of his biographers, the growth of the collections of the British Museum was "wholly due to Gray's efforts despite opposition from the administration and lack of finances." He received an honorary doctorate from the University of Munich in 1854 because he "formed the largest zoological collection in Europe." Gray's reliance on external features has invalidated much of his taxonomic work, but his catalogues remain useful to scientific researchers. In failing health from 1869 onward, he did not retire until 1874, shortly before his death. Besides his interests at the museum, he made contributions to the study of postage stamps and supported many social causes, such as prison discipline, treatment of lunatics, and sanitary reform (Cleevely 2004). Among his important scientific contributions are Gray (1857, 1869, 1872).

**Thomas Greenwood** was born into a family with modest means in Cheshire in northwest England in 1851 (Prichard 1981). He rose by producing technical publications, until he was eventually described as the "leading trade journalist" in England at the end of the nineteenth century (Prichard 1981). He credited his success to self-education gained by reading in public libraries; consequently, he became one of the leading advocates of expanding the public library system and creating a library profession in England (Carlton 1949). In addition to being an excellent editor and journalist, he authored numerous books including Greenwood (1886, 1888, 1902).

**Joseph Grinnell** (1877–1939) was born in Fort Sill, Oklahoma, and received his undergraduate education at Throop Polytechnic Institute in 1897. His graduate studies were conducted at Stanford University (A.M. 1901; Ph.D. 1913). Grinnell was a vertebrate zoologist and natural historian (Grinnell 1940; Hall 1939), who served as the original director of the Museum of Vertebrate Zoology at the University of California, Berkeley, founded by Miss Annie M. Alexander in 1908. He served in this position until his death in 1939 (Who's Who 1942: 490), publishing widely on variation and geographic distribution of birds and mammals of California. Among his important writings are Grinnell (1933, 1943) and Grinnell, Dixon, and Linsdale (1937).

**Hermann August Hagen** (1817–1893) was born in Königsberg, East Prussia, the modern Russian enclave of Kaliningrad, located on the Baltic Sea. He was educated as a medical doctor at the University of Königsberg, graduating in 1840. He showed an early interest in entomology, publishing his first paper at age 22. From 1843 to 1866, he worked as a surgeon in Königsberg while pursuing his studies of insects such as termites (1855–1860) and lacewings (1861). His most enduring contribution was *Bibliotheca Entomologica* (1862–1863), a comprehensive compilation of works in entomology written to that time, based on his visits to many of Europe's libraries and museums. In 1867, he moved to the United States and was hired by Louis Agassiz to join the staff of the Museum of Comparative Zoology at Harvard University. He held a progression of positions at Harvard, becoming professor of entomology in 1870 until 1890, when illness prevented him from working (Sterling 1999; Who's Who 1967: 294;).

**William Temple Hornaday** (1854–1937) was born in Indiana but spent most of his childhood in Iowa. He attended what became Iowa State University in 1872 and 1873 before taking a position in 1874 with Ward's Natural Science Establishment in Rochester, New York, to pursue a career as a taxidermist. He traveled for Ward's, collecting in Florida, Cuba, and Bahamas, before undertaking an around-the-world trip visiting India, Ceylon, Malaya, and Borneo, which led to the writing of his first book (1885). He became chief taxidermist at the U. S. National Museum in 1882 and served as president of the Society of American Taxidermists in 1883 and 1884. He is credited as being one of the important forces in creating what became known as habitat groups for natural history museum displays. In 1886, Hornaday lead an expedition to the American west to gather specimens for the museum, with special interest in the American bison. His experience alerted him to the fact the bison was quickly disappearing and set the course for the remainder of his life as one of the leaders of early conservation efforts. His concerns for the bison were documented in his book *The Extermination of the American Bison* (1887). He was the driving force in establishing the National Zoological Park, being named its director in 1889, but in a dispute in 1890 he quit. Six years later, he accepted the position of director of the New York Zoological Park (known as the Bronx Zoo), and over the next thirty years he built the zoo into a world-class facility. Hornaday worked for many conservation causes, notably the Migratory Bird Act, which provided federal protection to migratory birds (Thomas 1999). He described many of his conservation efforts in Hornaday (1931).

**Winifred Eva Howe** (1877–1966) was a 1901 graduate of Boston University (Obituary 1966). She joined the staff of the Metropolitan

Museum of Art in New York, working under the direction of Henry W. Kent, organizing and writing an early history of the museum (Howe and Kent 1913). Following the publication of this book, Howe served as a docent in the museum's education department and later editor of publications, a post that she held until 1941. Howe then moved to the position of editorial consultant and historian of publication while completing work on the second volume of the history of the museum (Howe 1948; Howe and Kent 1946).

**William Stanley Jevons** (1835–1882) was born in Liverpool, England. He attended University College London from 1851 to 1853, studying mathematics and chemistry, before he accepted the position of assayer at the Royal Mint in Sydney, Australia. He took training in assaying before going to Australia in late 1854, where he worked until 1859. In Australia he began an interest in philosophy and political economy. On his return to England, he took up his studies at University College, finishing his B.A. in 1860 and an M.A. in 1862, studying mental philosophy and political economy. Because of his nonconformist religious beliefs, he was able to take a position only at Owens College in Manchester, where he remained until 1876. In 1866, he took the new position of chair of logic, mental and moral philosophy, and political economy, areas in which he would build a national and international reputation. He made his initial reputation for his studies of the coal question in England. He was elected to the Royal Society in 1872. In 1876, Jevons moved to University College in London, taking the chair in political economics. During the same year, he received an honorary L.L.D. from the University of Edinburgh. He died in 1882 in a drowning accident (Black 2004). He published numerous books; among the most important were Jevons (1865, 1871, 1874).

**Johann Ludwig Gerard Krefft** (1830–1881) was born in the Duchy of Brunswick in what is now Germany. He went to the United States in 1850 and on to Victoria in Australia in 1852. He worked in the goldfields until 1857, when he joined a scientific expedition and was hired to catalogue it for the National Museum in Melbourne. In 1860, he was appointed assistant curator of the Australian Museum in Sydney, and in 1864 he was made curator. He published over 200 papers in natural history, achieving distinction for his work on snakes, fossils, and the discovery of the Australian lungfish. In 1873, a conflict arose between Krefft and the museum's trustees, and he was fired. In 1877, Krefft won a court case against the museum, but he was unable to return as director or find employment elsewhere (Whitley and Rutledge 2006). His important scientific contributions include Krefft (1869, 1871, 1873).

**Theodore Carl Link** (1850–1923) was born in Bad Wimpfen in Germany. He came to St. Louis, Missouri, in 1873 and pursued a career in architecture. Of the hundreds of buildings he designed, Link's most famous building was the massive, Romanesque St. Louis Union Station (Link and Atwater 1895), which was recently selected to 40th place on the list of "America's Favorite Architecture" by the American Institute of Architects (King 2007). Other important projects that he designed include Mississippi State Capitol, 1901–1903; Metallurgy Building for the St. Louis World's Exposition, 1904; Louisiana State University, 1920s. The architecture of the original buildings at the current site of LSU reflects Link's Italian Renaissance-style architecture (Fink 2005). He is credited as the first architect to use electric light decoratively. Link was elected a Fellow of the American Institute of Architects in 1889.

**Frederic Augustus Lucas** (1852–1929) was born in Plymouth, Massachusetts. Lucas worked for Ward's Natural Science Establishment 1871–1882. He next held a series of positions in the Division of Comparative Anatomy of the U. S. National Museum moving from osteologist (1882–1887) to assistant curator (1887–1892) and finally curator (1893–1904). Lucas moved to the Brooklyn Museum of Arts and Science as curator-in-chief, in essence the director, from 1904 to 1911 and then became director of the American Museum of Natural History from 1911 to 1923. Lucas served as member of the fur seal commission. He received an honorary Sc.D. from the University of Pittsburgh in 1909. Lucas served as the president of the American Association of Museums 1909–1910 (Who's Who 1942: 751). Books written by him include Lucas (1901, 1921) and Lucas and Osborn (1933).

**Edward S. Morse** (1838–1925) was born June 18, 1838, in Portland, Maine. At Bethel Academy in Maine, he developed an interest in the natural sciences, especially biology. Later, he went on to study conchology under Louis Agassiz at Harvard University. He settled in Salem, Massachusetts, where he spent most of the remainder of his life. He served as a lecturer at Harvard from 1871 to 1874, the chair in comparative anatomy and zoology at Bowdoin College, and published widely in zoology (Morse 1873). In 1877, he traveled to Japan searching for new shells to study. He took a position at Tokyo Imperial University and stayed until 1880. He became fascinated with Japan and collected Japanese pottery, wrote books (including Morse 1886, 1917), and maintained professional contacts throughout his life. In 1880, he took up the position of director of the Peabody Academy of Sciences, now the Peabody Essex Museum, for the remainder of his career. Morse received many honors during his life, including election to the National Academy of Science in 1876, president of the American Association for the Advancement of Science in 1885, president of the American Association of Museums in 1911, and from Japan the Order of the Rising Sun, Third Class, in 1898 and Order of the Sacred Treasure, Second Class, in 1922. Morse died in Salem on December 20, 1925, at the age of 87 (Wayman 1942; Who's Who 1942: 870).

**Francis Greenwood Peabody** (1847–1936) was born in Boston. He was educated at Harvard University (A.B. 1869; S.T.B. 1872; A.M. 1872) and studied at the University of Halle in Germany. Peabody was a chaplain and teacher at Antioch College for one year (1873) before serving as the Unitarian minister of the First Parish in Cambridge from 1874 to 1879. Peabody joined the Harvard Divinity School, where he held a succession of positions as lecturer in ethics and homiletics (1880–1881), professor of theology (1881–1886), preacher to the university (1886–1906), professor of Christian Morals (1886–1912), and Dean of the Divinity School (1901–1906). He was the first professor to teach Social Ethics as a separate academic discipline, and in this area his efforts ultimately resulted in the formation of the Department of Social Ethics in 1906 (Long 1999). Among his important books were Peabody (1909, 1914, 1927).

**Charles Willson Peale** (1741–1827) was born in Queen Anne's County, Maryland. His formal education ended at age 9, but he was apprenticed to a saddler from 1754–1761. He then established his own business, but it failed, and Peale decided to take up painting. He worked hard to teach himself painting and receive early instruction from John Hesselius. He left Maryland for Boston where he participated in some Stamp Act protests and received some encouragement in his painting from John Singleton Copley. From 1767 to 1769, Peale worked in the London studio of Benjamin West and visited many other London studios. He was able to work in many media, including portraits, miniatures, sculptures, and engraving, but his portraits of Revolutionary War and early American leaders are probably his best-known works. Peale joined the Pennsylvania militia rising to the rank of captain during the Revolutionary War, participating in the battles of Trenton and Princeton and smaller engagements around Philadelphia. In 1782, he began exhibiting his portraits and other paintings in his home in Philadelphia, and by 1786 he was adding natural history objects to what would be called Peale's Museum. Peale, credited with beginning the first popular museum in the United States, moved his museum to the American Philosophical building in 1794 and to Independence Hall in 1802. Peale had eleven children who survived to adulthood, and at least five of them followed him into work in art and natural history

(Miller 1983–2000, 1999; Sellers 1980a). Alexander (1983) placed Peale among his "museum masters."

**Sara Agnes Rice Pryor** (published as Mrs. Roger A. Pryor) (1830–1912) of Halifax County Virginia, moved to Charlottesville in 1839, where she gained her education from tutors at the University of Virginia. She married Roger A. Pryor, a lawyer, who was elected to the U. S. Congress from Virginia in 1859. He resigned from Congress at the outbreak of the Civil War and was made a Colonel in the Third Virginia Infantry. Sara traveled with his company, serving as a nurse, until he was attached to General Fitzhugh Lee. Roger was captured in 1864 and released the following year. They had little success following the war until they moved to New York City, where Roger established a law practice and ultimately was elected to the New York State Supreme Court. Sara led an active social life working for charities and founded the National Society of the Daughters of the American Revolution (Who's Who 1942: 999). Late in life, Sara wrote prolifically about life in the South and during the Civil War in a series of books, including Pryor (1903, 1907, 1911).

**Carolyn Morse Rea** (published as Mrs. Paul M. Rea) (?–1913) of Medford, Massachusetts, graduated from Wellesley College in 1900, after which she took courses at the Marine Biological Station at Woods Hole, Massachusetts, and taught at Western College in Oxford, Ohio. In 1904, she married her college sweetheart, Paul M. Rea, who was then the newly appointed director of the Charleston Museum. The museum was cramped, and the burgeoning collections had been poorly cared for, but her experience in biology was crucial to her husband's efforts to revitalize and improve the museum. In 1913, Carolyn Rea contracted typhoid fever and died after a short illness on May 11. Her obituary in the *Charleston Museum Bulletin* declared that "her sound judgment and untiring efforts on behalf of the Museum have contributed in large measure to its present development" and credited her solely for the mounting and labeling of the museum's mineral exhibits (Sanders and Anderson 1999: 123).

**Paul Marshall Rea** (1878–1948) of Cotuit, Massachusetts, was a graduate of Williams College in 1899. He received an M.A. in biology in 1901 from the same institution, writing a thesis on the anatomy and relationships of an aquatic worm, *Alma nilotica*. In 1903, he became director of the Charleston Museum in South Carolina and professor of biology at the College of Charleston. In 1913, he became the professor and head of the Department of Physiology and Embryology at the Medical University of South Carolina (Horres 1984). Rea was active in the early history of the American Association of Museums, serving as secretary (1907–1917) and president in 1919 and 1921 (Hicks 1978). As secretary, he compiled the first directory of American museums (Rea 1910). He served as the first director of the Cleveland Museum of Natural History from 1920 to 1928. Rea promoted the educational uses of museums (Rea 1930). He served as a consultant from 1930 to 1932 to the advisory group on museum education for the Carnegie Corporation of New York and wrote the report for the Advisory Group on Museum Education (Rea 1932). Rea also served as director of the Santa Barbara Museum of Natural History from 1933 to 1936 (Who's Who 1950: 439–440).

**Sir John Charles Robinson** (1824–1913) was born in Nottingham, England. He received training in painting in the studio of Michel-Martin Drolling in Paris, where he gained a broad knowledge of the fine and decorative arts before returning to England in 1847. On his return, he taught at the School of Design in Hanley, Staffordshire, until he moved to London, taking up the position of curator of the Museum of Oriental Art at Marlborough House in 1852. In 1857, this collection was moved to new quarters in the Victoria and Albert Museum, where Robinson worked until 1867. Robinson was an indefatigable collector and scholar, publishing a major book on Italian sculpture and organizing an immense special exhibition of medieval and Renaissance art in 1862. By the age of thirty-six he had amassed his own immense collection that included "paintings, drawings and prints, sculpture, medals and gems, ceramics, tapestry, and embroidery." From 1882 to 1901, Robinson was surveyor of the queen's pictures, and he was knighted in 1887 and made Knight of the Bath (CB) in 1901. He remained an active art critic to the end of his life (Davies 2004). Three of his important publications are Robinson (1862a, 1862b, 1870).

**Louis Earle Rowe** (1882–1937) was born in Providence, Rhode Island, and attended Brown University, graduating in 1904 and receiving an M.F.A. in 1906. He became a docent in the Museum of Fine Arts, Boston, in 1907 and took the position of assistant in the Egyptian Art Department in 1910. He took the position of director of the Rhode Island School of Design in 1912. The School included a small art museum, which he greatly enhanced, as he did many other programs of the School. Because of failing health, he took a year's leave of absence in 1928, but he returned the following year to take up half of his old job, becoming director of the Museum, with another person serving as Education Director. He held the position of Museum Director until his death February 17, 1937. He started and served as editor of *The Rhode Island School of Design Bulletin* beginning in 1913 (Banks 1937; Chase 1937; Gilman 1937; Who's Who 1942: 1062).

**Charles Sprague Sargent** (1841–1927) was born in Boston, Massachusetts, and graduated from Harvard University in 1862. Following graduation, he entered the Civil War as a second lieutenant, serving as an aide-de-camp in the Department of the Gulf. He left the military in August 1865 as a brevet major. Following his service he toured Europe for three years and then returned to Harvard University, becoming first the director of the Harvard Botanical Garden and then in 1873 director of the newly established Arnold Arboretum. In 1879, he became the Arnold Professor of Arboriculture, in which position he remained until shortly before his death in 1927. Among his major scientific contributions were Sargent (1894), Sargent and Faxon (1891–1902), and Sargent, Faxon, and Gill (1905). Sargent was elected as a member of the National Academy of Sciences and a fellow of the American Academy of Arts and Sciences (Smocovitis 1999).

**Henry Scadding** (1813–1901) was born in Dunkeswell, Devon, England, and immigrated to Canada with his parents in 1821 (Firth and Fahey 2000). He was educated at Upper Canada College in York and St. John's College, Cambridge University, England, graduating in 1837. Subsequently he received a M.A. (1840) and a D.D. (1852) from Cambridge and a D.D. (1867) from Oxford University. He was ordained as a priest of the Church of England, and in 1847 he was appointed rector of the Church of the Holy Trinity in Toronto, a position that he held until 1875. He was founding member of the Canadian Institute in 1849 and served as president from 1870 to 1878. He edited the *Canadian Journal of Science, Literature, and History* from 1868 to 1878. Scadding also served as president of the York Pioneer and Historical Society from 1880 to 1898. He wrote many pamphlets on literary, archeological, and antiquarian subjects, but his most important contribution was the book *Toronto of Old* (1873).

**Laura Woolsey Lord Scales** (1879–1990) of Hanover, New Hampshire, graduated from Smith College in 1901. She married Robert L. Scales, but the marriage lasted only four years, when he unexpectedly died, which forced Mrs. Scales to find employment. For seven years she worked as an instructor at the Museum of Fine Arts, Boston. She was hired as the dean of women for the Carnegie Institute of Technology in Pittsburgh, where she worked for two years. At this point, she wrote a children's book (Scales 1922). Mrs. Scales then was hired in 1922 as dean of students at Smith College, a position that she held until her retirement in 1944. One of her innovations during this time was to require all students to live on campus. Mrs. Scales received honorary degrees from Smith College in 1931 and from Dartmouth College in 1939. She was further honored by Smith College when one of the new dormitories was named the Laura

Scales House in 1936. Mrs. Scales was 110 years old when she died in Northampton on June 12, 1990 (Smith College Archives, RG 42).

**Frederick Starr** (1858–1933) was born in Auburn, New York. He graduated from Lafayette University in 1882 and received his Ph.D. from University of Rochester in 1884. He served as professor of biology at Coe College until 1889 and then served as head of ethnology at the American Museum of Natural History for three years. He was hired to organize anthropological teaching at the University of Chicago, where he remained until his retirement in 1923, serving as associate professor and curator of the Walker Museum. Starr's field studies took him to Mexico, Japan, Philippines, and Africa. In recognition of his research and work to bring better understanding among peoples of the world, he was awarded medals from Italy, Japan, France, Holland, Belgium, and Liberia (Cole 1934; Who's Who 1942:1172). Among his most important written works were Starr (1908, 1918, 1922) and Quatrefages de Bréau and Starr (1895).

**Strabo of Amaseia** (63 B.C.E.–23 C.E.) was a Greek geographer and historian best known for his work *Geography* (Clarke 1997; Richards 1941; Sihler 1923).

**Reuben Gold Thwaites** (1853–1913) was born in Dorchester, Massachusetts, and moved to Oshkosh, Wisconsin, in 1866. He read a college equivalency and did graduate study at Yale University in 1874 and 1875. Thwaites's early work history was with newspapers in Wisconsin, ending at the *Wisconsin State Journal* in Madison. While working at the latter newspaper, he also worked as an assistant to the executive of the State Historical Society of Wisconsin. When the executive position opened, he was elected effective January 1887 and held the position until his death. Under his leadership, the society's collections were greatly increased, he encouraged women to join his staff, and he worked for the construction of a joint library facility that was built on the campus of the University of Wisconsin. Thwaites was a prolific writer and editor. His edited volumes included *Proceedings of the State Historical Society of Wisconsin* (vols. 35–60), *The Jesuit Relations and Allied Documents* (73 vols.), *Early Western Travels, 1748–1846* (32 vols.), and *Original Journals of Lewis and Clark* (8 vols.). Among his original writings were Thwaites (1902, 1905, 1908). Thwaites served as president of the American Library Association in 1900 and the Mississippi Valley Historical Society in 1912 and 1913 (Gale 1999; Wisconsin Historical Society 2007). Museum historian Edward Alexander (1997) listed Thwaites among his museum "Innovators and Pioneers."

**Charles Haskins Townsend** (1859–1944) was born in Parnassus, Pennsylvania. He gained his knowledge of zoology with work at Philadelphia Academy of Natural Sciences and Ward's Natural Science Establishment in Rochester, New York. In 1883, he went to work for the U. S. Fish Commission, participating in expeditions in both the Atlantic and the Pacific oceans, including serving as the naturalist on the steamer *Albatross*. From 1902 until his retirement in 1937, Townsend was the director of the New York Aquarium ("C. M. B." 1938). Townsend was president of the American Fisheries Society in 1912 and 1913, and he was a tireless worker for conservation of a wide variety of marine organisms throughout his career (Who's Who 1950: 536). He wrote on a wide range of zoological topics with some of his most important work being on whales (1935), Galapagos tortoises (1925), and public aquariums (1928).

**William Trelease** (1857–1945) was born in Mount Vernon, New York, and received his undergraduate education at Cornell University, graduating in 1880. He received a D.Sc. from Harvard University in 1884, where he studied botany under Asa Gray. He took a position at the University of Wisconsin in 1881 and was professor and head of the botany department when he left in 1885 to take up the positions of Engelmann Professor of Botany at Washington University in St. Louis and chief administrator of the Missouri Botanical Gardens. In 1889, Trelease was officially appointed the first director of the Missouri Botanical Gardens. He remained in this position until 1912, overseeing the transformation of the private garden of founder Henry Shaw into a major public garden and center for botanical research. In 1913, he went to the University of Illinois to become head of the Department of Botany, a position in which he served until 1926, when he became a professor emeritus. He described over 2,500 taxa of plants, with particular reference to agaves, yuccas, and American oaks. Among his important publications were Trelease (1913, 1917, 1924). Trelease was elected to the National Academy of Sciences in 1902 and served as president of the Botanical Society of America (1894–1895, 1918) and American Society of Naturalists in 1903 (Buchholz 1945; Erickson 1999; Who's Who 1950: 538).

**Mariana Alley Griswold Van Rensselaer**, (published under Mrs. Schuyler Van Rensselaer) (1851–1934), of New York, married Schuyler Van Rensselaer in 1873, but he died young in 1884. Widowed, she began a career in writing and became a well-known art, architecture, and landscape critic and a writer of poetry and nonfiction. Her first book was published in 1886. In 1884, she had started a series of articles of architectural criticism in the *Century Magazine*, ending in her next major book (1888).

Major books among her other works were Van Rensselaer (1893, 1909). Mrs. Van Rensselaer served as president of the Public Education Association of New York City from 1899 to 1906 (Berrol 1970). Mrs. Van Rennselaer was honored for her many contributions, including becoming an honorary member of the American Institute of Architects (1890) and receiving an honorary doctoral degree from Columbia University (1910) and the gold medal from the American Academy of Arts and Letters (1923) (James, James, and Boyer 1971; Who's Who 1942: 1272).

**Marcus Terentius Varro** (116 B.C.E.–27 C.E.) was one of Rome's greatest scholars and prolific writers. He was a republican who sided with Pompey, but he was pardoned by Julius Caesar and appointed a librarian by him. Although Varro wrote about seventy-four works, his only complete work to survive is *Res rustica*, or "Farm topics" (Encyclopedia Britannica 2007).

**Alfred Russel Wallace** (1823–1913) was born in Monmouthshire, England. He was trained in a number of the technical trades, including surveying, mapmaking, mechanics, construction, watchmaking, and agricultural chemistry, but he also had an amateur's interest in natural history. In 1843, his brother helped him obtain the position of master at a collegiate school in Leicester. Wallace and his friend Henry Bates departed England in 1848, traveling to Para in Brazil. Wallace spent the next four years collecting and exploring in the central Amazon and Rîo Negro. With a solid reputation as a collector and eighteen months in England, he left for the Malay archipelago in 1854, with support from the Royal Geographical Society. Wallace spent nearly eight successful years collecting and exploring throughout Malaya and Indonesia. It was during this period that he began to formulate his ideas on evolution and the geographic distribution of animals. He is considered to be the father of modern zoogeography because of his extensive writing on the topic, and he along with Charles Darwin published the first essays on natural selection in 1858. Wallace's interests were broad, and he published on such topics as human evolution, defense of Darwinian evolution, museums, spiritualism, continental glaciation, physical anthropology, vaccination, women's suffrage, and social criticism (Smith 2004). Among his more important scientific books were Wallace (1869, 1876, 1889, 1905).

**Henry Levi Ward** (1863–1943) was born in York, New York, being the son of Henry Augustus Ward, later the proprietor of Ward's Natural Science Establishment in Rochester, New York. He attended the University of Rochester in 1883 and 1884 and worked for his father's museum supply establishment from 1884 to 1886. He served as a member of the

Geographic and Exploring Commission of the Mexican Government from 1887 to 1891. He returned to Ward's Natural Science Establishment in 1891 as director and manager and as vice president in 1901 and 1902. Ward then held a series of museum directorships at the Milwaukee Public Museum (1902–1920), Kent Scientific Museum in Grand Rapids, Michigan (1922–1932), and Neville Public Museum (1933–1941). He served as president of the Wisconsin Academy of Sciences, Arts, and Letters from 1916 to 1918. Ward was a charter member of the American Association of Museums and served as president of the organization in 1912 and 1913 (Who's Who 1950: 556).

**Elizabeth Manning [Gardiner] Whitmore** received an A.B. from Radcliffe College in 1901 and an A.M. from Wellesley in 1905 (Radcliffe College Alumnae Association 1931: 239), then attended the American School of Classical Studies at Athens from 1907 to 1908 (Meritt 1984: 346). On her return to the United States, she became librarian at the Worcester Museum of Art and was soon after promoted to assistant to the director, but Gardiner warned readers in her brief essay "Museum Work for Women" (1910) that the only positions normally open to women in museums were as clerical workers, librarians, or docents (Perkins 1910). She married the literary critic Charles Edward Whitmore in 1913 and joined him on the faculty of Smith College in 1918 (Harvard College 1957: 686). She later organized the docent program at the Museum of Fine Arts, Boston, and was a strong advocate of the use of photographs in art museums with small collections and prints and etchings in the home and the classroom. In 1924, she opened her own lithograph dealership, called the Print Corner, in Hingham, Massachusetts (American Federation of Arts 1952: 815), and she also published two instructional booklets (Whitmore 1925, 1927).

**Newton Horace Winchell** (1839–1914) was born in Northeast, New York, and educated in New York and Connecticut. He alternately taught in local schools and attended the University of Michigan, where he graduated in 1866 and took an A.M. in 1869, studying geology. He held brief positions with the Michigan State Geological Survey, studying copper and silver deposits in New Mexico, and the Ohio survey before being named the head of Minnesota Geological and Natural History Survey in 1872, a position that he held until 1900. He served as chair of geology and mineralogy at the university from 1872 to 1881 and curator of the survey collection from 1889 to 1900. Under his direction, the survey published twenty-four *Reports*, ten *Bulletins*, and six *Final Reports*. He was a founding member of the Geological Society of America and served as its president in 1902. In 1900, he turned his interests to the archeology and history of Minnesota, being placed in charge of the Department of Archeology of the Minnesota Historical Society in 1906. The University of Minnesota has honored Winchell by naming the Newton Horace Winchell School of Earth Sciences (Clarke 1914; Kohlstedt 1999b; Schwartz 2004). His important scientific contributions include Winchell (1875), Winchell and associates (1884–1901), Winchell and Winchell (1909), and Brower and associates (1911).

**Anthony Wood** (1632–1695) was born in Oxford, England, and devoted his life to collecting and publishing the history of Oxford and Oxford University. He graduated from Oxford in 1652. He possessed sufficient private funds to provide for his needs, and he held no official position at the university or elsewhere. Wood's history of the university was published in 1674, and in 1691–1692 his biographical dictionary of the writers and ecclesiastics educated at Oxford appeared as *Athenae Oxonienses* (Parry 2004).

**John George Wood** (1827–1889) was born in London, but his family moved to Oxford in 1830. He received a B.A. in 1848 and a M.A. in 1851 from Merton College, Oxford University. He worked for short time in an anatomical museum, but in 1852 he was ordained in the Church of England. Over the next twenty-five years he held a number of positions in several churches and parishes. Wood also was developing a career as a natural historian over this period with his first book, *The Illustrated Natural History*, published in 1851. In 1879, he decided to take up a career as a lecturer, giving "sketch-lectures" over the winter months at the Crystal Palace until 1888. Wood was a prolific writer, authoring more than seventy books, primarily on popular natural history topics (Woodward 2004).

# INDEX

Made in the USA
Middletown, DE
16 September 2022

10642807R00195